PRAGMATICS

Praise for the first edition:

'This is an ideal book for anyone ᴜᴇgɪɴɴɪɴg ᴛʜᴇ ꜱᴛᴜᴅʏ ᴏꜰ ᴅɪꜱᴄᴏᴜʀꜱᴇ and pragmatics; it is transparently written without being simplistic or patronising, and is thorough and detailed without being obscure or mystifying'.
Michael McCarthy, University of Nottingham

'Joan Cutting's book provides an excellent introduction to one of the most intensively researched areas in linguistics and communication studies – pragmatics and discourse analysis. It offers the novice in the field exciting, creative and accessible ways in which to gain an understanding of the most important issues, and it also gives us old hands stimulating new food for thought.'
Richard Watts, University of Berne, Switzerland

Routledge English Language Introductions cover core areas of language study and are one-stop resources for students.

Assuming no prior knowledge, books in the series offer an accessible overview of the subject, with activities, study questions, sample analyses, commentaries and key readings – all in the same volume. The innovative and flexible 'two-dimensional' structure is built around four sections – introduction, development, exploration and extension – which offer self-contained stages for study. Each topic can also be read across these sections, enabling the reader to build gradually on the knowledge gained.

Pragmatics and Discourse:

❑ has been revised and reorganised with the aim to place more emphasis on pragmatics
❑ covers the core areas of the subject: context, co-text, speech acts, conversation structure, the Cooperative Principle, politeness, corpora and communities, and culture and language learning
❑ draws on a wealth of texts: from *Bend it Like Beckham* and *The Motorcycle Diaries* to political speeches and newspaper extracts
❑ blogs provide classic readings from the key names in the discipline, such as Sperber and Wilson to Fairclough, Wodak and Gumperz
❑ is accompanied by a supporting website.

Key features of the new edition include two completely new strands: 'Corpora and communities' which incorporates corpus linguistics and communities of practice; and 'Culture and language learning' which analyses intercultural pragmatics and language learning theory and practice. The two strands of 'Context' and 'Co-text' have been merged and new material has been introduced from speaker-based cognitive linguistics. References have been updated and fresh examples and exercises have been included.

Written by an experienced teacher and author, this accessible textbook is an essential resource for all students of English language and linguistics.

Joan Cutting is a Senior Lecturer at the University of Edinburgh, UK. Her interests include in-group code, vague language and Chinese learners. She is author of *The Grammar of Spoken English and EAP Teaching* (2000), *Analysing the Language of Discourse Communities* (2000) and *Vague Language Explored* (2007).

ROUTLEDGE ENGLISH LANGUAGE INTRODUCTIONS

SERIES EDITOR: PETER STOCKWELL

Peter Stockwell is Senior Lecturer in the School of English Studies at the University of Nottingham, UK, where his interests include sociolinguistics, stylistics and cognitive poetics. His recent publications include *Cognitive Poetics: An Introduction* (Routledge, 2002), *The Poetics of Science Fiction, Investigating English Language* (with Howard Jackson), and *Contextualized Stylistics* (edited with Tony Bex and Michael Burke).

SERIES CONSULTANT: RONALD CARTER

Ronald Carter is Professor of Modern English Language in the School of English Studies at the University of Nottingham, UK. He is the co-series editor of the forthcoming *Routledge Applied Linguistics* series, series editor of *Interface*, and was co-founder of the Routledge *Intertext* series.

OTHER TITLES IN THE SERIES:

Sociolinguistics
Peter Stockwell

Grammar and Vocabulary
Howard Jackson

Psycholinguistics
John Field

World Englishes
Jennifer Jenkins

Practical Phonetics and Phonology
Beverley Collins & Inger Mees

Stylistics
Paul Simpson

Language in Theory
Mark Robson & Peter Stockwell

Child Language
Jean Stilwell Peccei

Sociolinguistics 2nd Edition
Peter Stockwell

Pragmatics and Discourse 2nd Edition
Joan Cutting

PRAGMATICS AND DISCOURSE

A resource book for students

JOAN CUTTING

Second edition

Routledge
Taylor & Francis Group

LONDON AND NEW YORK

First published 2002 by Routledge
Reprinted 2003, 2005, 2006, 2009

Second edition published 2008
by Routledge
2 Park Square, Milton Park, Abingdon, Oxon OX14 4RN

Simultaneously published in the USA and Canada
by Routledge
270 Madison Ave, New York, NY 10016

Routledge is an imprint of the Taylor & Francis Group, an informa business

© 2008 Joan Cutting

Typeset in Minion by
Graphicraft Limited, Hong Kong
Printed and bound in Great Britain by
CPI Antony Rowe, Chippenham, Wiltshire

British Library Cataloguing in Publication Data
A catalogue record for this book is available from the British Library

Library of Congress Cataloging in Publication Data
A catalog record for this book has been requested

ISBN10: 0–415–44667–8 (pbk)
ISBN10: 0–415–44668–6 (hbk)

ISBN13: 978–0–415–44667–9 (pbk)
ISBN13: 978–0–415–44668–6 (hbk)

HOW TO USE THIS BOOK

The Routledge English Language Introductions are 'flexi-texts' that you can use to suit your own style of study. The books are divided into four sections:

A Introduction – sets out the key concepts for the area of study. The units of this section take you step-by-step through the foundational terms and ideas, carefully providing you with an initial toolkit for your own study. By the end of the section, you will have a good overview of the whole field.

B Development – adds to your knowledge and builds on the key ideas already introduced. Units in this section might also draw together several areas of interest. By the end of this section, you will already have a good and fairly detailed grasp of the field, and will be ready to undertake your own exploration and thinking.

C Exploration – provides examples of language data and guides you through your own investigation of the field. The units in this section will be more open-ended and exploratory, and you will be encouraged to try out your ideas and think for yourself, using your newly acquired knowledge.

D Extension – offers you the chance to compare your expertise with key readings in the area. These are taken from the work of important writers, and are provided with guidance and questions for your further thought.

You can read this book like a traditional textbook, 'vertically' straight through from beginning to end. This will take you comprehensively through the broad field of study. However, the Routledge English Language Introductions have been carefully designed so that you can read them in another dimension, 'horizontally' across the numbered units. For example, Units A1, A2, A3 and so on correspond with Units B1, B2, B3, and with Units C1, C2, C3 and D1, D2, D3, and so on. Reading A5, B5, C5, D5 will take you rapidly from the key concepts of a specific area, to a level of expertise in that precise area, all with a very close focus. You can match your way of reading with the best way that you work.

The glossarial index at the end, together with the suggestions for further reading, will help to keep you orientated. Each textbook has a supporting website with extra commentary, suggestions, additional material and support for teachers and students.

PRAGMATICS AND DISCOURSE

In this book, six numbered sub-sections in Section A introduce you to the key concepts in pragmatics and discourse study. Terms and ideas are introduced quickly and clearly, so that if you read this section as a whole, you can rapidly start to link together the different approaches to the study of language. Then you can use the numbers for each area to follow a theme through the book. For example, Unit A4 sets out key ideas in the study of the structure of conversation. In Section B, you will find that Unit 4 presents a real conversation, together with my commentary. The idea behind this is to show you in as practical a way as possible that you can develop an understanding of the approach and the skills needed to undertake a study of language using pragmatics and discourse analysis in a fairly short space of time.

The best way to learn about language in use is to investigate the area for yourself and think about your own place in it. Section C gives you a chance to do this, and following on from A4 and B4, for example, Unit C4 provides you with some genuine data of conversations and some questions to consider. Finally, in Section D, Unit 4 offers some published reading and suggestions for further study, to complete your thorough understanding of the strand.

The same pattern applies for every numbered section throughout the book. In general, I have tried to increase the cumulative difficulty through each section, and giving you guidance at the beginning and then helping you to work more independently as the book advances. My hope is that you will become enthused by the study of language in use. If, by the end, I have encouraged you to discover more about pragmatics and discourse, and if you are encouraged to take issue critically with existing studies in the area, and want to continue to explore more, then this book will have served its purpose. I hope you will find your study stimulating, enlightening, and enjoyable.

Transcription conventions:

=	Interruption
//	Overlap
/.../	Lines from original omitted to make example quoted simpler
(0.5)	Pause (number of seconds in brackets)

CONTENTS

CONTENTS **CROSS-REFERENCED**

CONTENTS **CROSS-REFERENCED**

LIST OF TABLES

ACKNOWLEDGEMENTS

Bardovi-Harlig, Kathleen (2001) 'Evaluating the empirical evidence: grounds for instruction in pragmatics?', in Kenneth R. Rose and Gabriele Kasper (eds), *Pragmatics in Language Teaching*, Cambridge: Cambridge University Press, 2001, 13–32. Reproduced by kind permission of Cambridge University Press and the author.

Hunston, Susan (2002) *Corpora in Applied Linguistics*, Cambridge: Cambridge University Press, 2002, 170–97. Reproduced by kind permission of Cambridge University Press and the author.

Wardhaugh, Ronald (1985) *How Conversation Works*, Oxford: Blackwell, 16–20. Reproduced by permission of Blackwell Publishing.

Hoey, Michael (1991) *Patterns of Lexis in Text*, Oxford: Oxford University Press, 242–5. Reproduced by permission of Oxford University Press. © Oxford University Press 1991.

Wodak, Ruth (1996) *Disorders of Discourse*, London: Longman, 100–102. © Pearson, reprinted by permission of Pearson Education Ltd.

Fairclough, Norman (1989) *Language and Power*, Harlow: Longman, 9–11, 54–5 and 155–7. © Pearson, reprinted by permission of Pearson Education Ltd.

Gumperz, John J. (1982) *Discourse Strategies*, Cambridge: Cambridge University Press, 133–4 and 173–4. Reproduced by kind permission of Cambridge University Press and the author.

Sperber, Dan and Wilson, Deidre (1995) *Relevance*, Oxford: Blackwell, 36–64. Reproduced by kind permission of the authors.

Tannen, Deborah (1994) *Gender and Discourse*, Oxford: Oxford University Press, 32–4. Reproduced by permission of Oxford University Press and Deborah Tannen.

Nelson, Gayle L., Al-Batal, M. and Echols, E. (1996) 'Arabic and English compliment responses: potential for pragmatic failure', *Applied Linguistics* 18 (3), 411–33. Reprinted by permission of Oxford University Press and the authors.

Delia Smith (2000) *How to Cook*. Reproduced courtesy of Deborah Owen Ltd and the BBC.

Excerpt by Joe Plomin from Major and Plomin, *The Guardian*: 14 April 2001. Reprinted by kind permission of the author.

From the song 'Little Boxes'. Words and music by Malvina Reynolds. Copyright 1962 Schroder Music Co. (ASCAP). Renewed 1990. Used by permission. All rights reserved.

Excerpt from the British Academic Spoken English (BASE) corpus featuring a lecture on European imperialism delivered by Dr Iain Smith (ahlct019). [Lecture ahlct019 comes from the British Academic Spoken English (BASE) corpus http://www2.warwick.ac.uk/fac/soc/celte/research/base/. The corpus was developed at the Universities of Warwick and Reading under the directorship of Hilary Nesi (Warwick) and Paul Thompson (Reading). Corpus development was assisted by funding from the Universities of Warwick and Reading, BALEAP, EURALEX, the British Academy and the Arts and Humanities Research Council (Award Number: RE/AN6806/APN13545).]

Associated Press football news flash on the Internet, dated 9 October 2000, 12.27 p.m., and written by Dave Goldberg. Used with permission of The Associated Press, Copyright © 2007. All rights reserved.

Excerpt from *The Sydney Morning Herald* (7 November 2000) and 'Playing it straight: Australian Bach Ensemble' from *The Sydney Morning Herald*, 19 March 2000. Reproduced by kind permission of the author, Harriet Cunningham.

Excerpts from Michael Parkinson's interview with Tamzin Outhwaite, 31 March 2001. Reproduced by kind permission of the BBC and Conway van Gelder Grant Ltd.

AOL News (14 January 2007) 'Flying mice spark panic'; the AOL Travel page, 'The ten most dangerous animals in the world' (http://travel.aol.co.uk); AOL Chat 18 to 21 UK3 (6 November 2006); and AOL News article 'Here's a heads up: office jargon doesn't work' (6 November 2006). All reprinted by permission of AOL UK. http://tygerland.net/2007/01/24/a-polite-request/. Reprinted with permission.

Excerpts from BNC concordances, examples of usage taken from the British National Corpus (BNC) were obtained under the terms of the BNC End User Licence. Copyright in the individual texts cited resides with the original IPR holders. For information and licensing conditions relating to the BNC, please see the website at http://www.natcorp.ox.ac.uk.

Carter, R. and McCarthy, M. (2006) *Cambridge Grammar of English: A Comprehensive Guide to Spoken and Written Grammar and Usage*, Cambridge: Cambridge University Press. Reproduced by kind permission of the authors and publisher.

Bailey, B. (1997) 'Communication in respect of interethnic service encounters', *Language in Society*, 26: 327–56. Reproduced by kind permission of Cambridge University Press.

Excerpt from the Wellington Corpus of Spoken New Zealand English. Reproduced with permission.

Excerpt from the Hong Kong Corpus of Spoken English. Reproduced with permission.

Excerpt from the Michigan Corpus of Academic Spoken English. Reproduced with permission.

Excerpt from http://www.tes.co.uk/section/story/?section=Archive&sub_section= News+%26+opinion&story_id=376361. Reproduced by permission of *Times Education Supplement*.

Excerpt from http://www.srcf.ucam.org/cuchin/home/home_index.php. Reproduced by kind permission of Cambridge University Chinese Society.

Excerpt from Gerry Ryan show. Reproduced with permission.

Excerpt from http://www.shef.ac.uk/ssid/international/living/culture.htm. Reproduced with permission of the author, Scott Castle.

Excerpt from http://www.lingualearn.co.uk/managers/businessculture.htm. Reproduced courtesy of http://www.lingualearn.co.uk/.

Excerpt from *Bend it Like Beckham*, © 2003. Courtesy of Twentieth Century Fox. Written by Gurinder Chadha, Guljit Bindra and Paul Mayeda Berges. All rights reserved.

'United Nations' scientists join climate change chorus', *New Scientist*, 28 February 2007. Reprinted by permission of *New Scientist*.

'Road pricing' interview by Richard Hammond with Prime Minister Tony Blair on 1 March 2007, available online at http://www.number-10.gov.uk/output/Page11123.asp. Reproduced under the terms of the Click-Use Licence C2006010948.

Excerpt from *The Motorcycle Diaries*. Reproduced by permission of Channel 4.

Excerpt from *Father Ted*. Reproduced by kind permission of Hat Trick Productions Ltd and the estate of Dermot Morgan.

Section A

INTRODUCTION:
CONCEPTS IN PRAGMATICS AND DISCOURSE

A1 CONTEXT AND CO-TEXT

A1.1 Understanding concepts

❑ Introduction to pragmatics and discourse
❑ Context
  ○ situational
  ○ background knowledge
  ○ co-textual
❑ Language and the context
  ○ deixis
  ○ exophora
  ○ cohesion

A1.2 Introduction to pragmatics and discourse

Some of the approaches to language description that are described in this book involve both pragmatics and discourse analysis, others involve either one or the other. The first section of this unit defines them, and should serve as a reference guide to all the units of this book.

Pragmatics and **discourse analysis** are approaches to studying language's relation to contextual background features. In Queen Victoria's famous words 'We are not amused', they would take into account the fact that Victoria had been in a prolonged depression, caused by the death of her husband, Albert, and her courtiers knew this, and that her words were a response to a joke which they had just made. Analysts would infer that the Queen's intention was to stop them trying to make her laugh and lift her out of the depression, and that her statement implies a reminder that she has to be respected as Queen. Pragmatics and discourse analysis have much in common: they both study context, text and function.

First, let us look at **context**. Both pragmatics and discourse analysis study the meaning of words in context, analysing the parts of meaning that can be explained by knowledge of the physical and social world, and the socio-psychological factors influencing communication, as well as the knowledge of the time and place in which the words are uttered or written. (Stilwell Peccei 1999; Yule 1996). Both approaches focus on the meaning of words in interaction and how interactors communicate more information than the words they use. The speaker's meaning is dependent on assumptions of knowledge that are shared by both speaker and hearer: the speaker constructs the linguistic message and intends or implies a meaning, and the hearer interprets the message and infers the meaning (Brown and Yule 1983; Thomas 1995). This aspect is first explored in this book in this unit.

The second feature that pragmatics and discourse analysis have in common is that they both look at **discourse**, or the use of language, and **text**, or pieces of spoken or written discourse, concentrating on how stretches of language become meaningful and unified for their users (Cook 1989). Discourse analysis calls the quality of being 'meaningful and unified' **coherence**; pragmatics calls it **relevance**. Both approaches would take into account the fact that Victoria's words were intended to be seen as relevant to the courtiers' joke and to anything that they should say afterwards. Units A1–D1, concerned more with the discourse analysis, focus on **cohesion**, how words relate to each other within the text, referring backwards or forwards to other words in the text. Units A4–D4, dealing with the Cooperative Principle, an area of pragmatics, also examine **Relevance Theory**, which is the study of how the assumption of relevance holds texts together meaningfully.

Finally, pragmatics and discourse analysis have in common the fact that they are both concerned with **function**: the speakers' short-term purposes in speaking, and long-term goals in interacting verbally. In the example, the Queen's purpose was to stop the courtiers trying to make her laugh and to make them respect her. Units covering function are A2–D2, Speech acts. **Speech Act Theory** describes what utterances are intended to do, such as promise, apologise and threaten. These units also introduce **critical discourse analysis**, an ideological approach that examines the purpose of language in the social context and reveals how discourse reflects and determines power structures.

Where discourse analysis differs from pragmatics is in its emphasis on the **structure** of text. Discourse analysis studies how large chunks of language beyond the sentence level are organised, how the social transaction imposes a framework on discourse (Coulthard 1985). It has traditionally covered the topics of **exchange structure**, or how certain situations have fixed sequences in the overall framework of the exchange, and conversation structure or how what one speaker says can influence the next speaker's response. **Conversation analysis**, which examines conversation structure, would show that Victoria's response to the joke was not the preferred response: someone telling a joke expects a response containing laughter. Similarly, it would show that her reprimand predicts an apology in response: something like 'I'm sorry Your Majesty'. The units concerned with these two ways of approaching the structure of discourse are A3–D3, Conversation. They also discuss **interactional sociolinguistics**, which combines the conversation analysis approach, in that it studies the structural patterns of conversation, with a pragmatics approach, studying social interaction, and giving importance to context, function, and social norms, conventions and principles.

Pragmatics differs from discourse analysis in the importance given to the **social principles** of discourse. Pragmatics can explain the example thus: the Queen complied with the social maxims of the **Cooperative Principle**, being relevant, precise, clear and sincere, and her courtiers expected her to do so, and she obeyed the social principles of the **Politeness Principle** in that her request for the courtiers to stop is indirect, which aims to avoid offence. Pragmatics takes a socio-cultural perspective on language usage, examining the way that the principles of social behaviour are expressed is determined by the social distance between speakers. It describes the unwritten maxims of conversation that speakers follow in order to cooperate and be socially acceptable with each other. In this book, units dealing with these issues of pragmatics are: A2–D2, Speech acts, A4–D4, Cooperative Principle, and A5–D5, Politeness.

Studies with a discourse analysis or pragmatics focus can be carried out using **corpus linguistics**. Linguists analyse very large electronic databases of spoken and written text, as it occurs naturally in real life, to find the most frequent usages and grammar of words. Corpus linguistics provides a data-driven approach analysis of language dictated by context (social variables, social groups, domains of discourse), and related to function, structure and social rules. Units A6–D6 deals with corpus linguistics combined with other approaches.

Just as this book begins on the topic of context, it ends by bringing all the threads together through context, this time the global one, taking the **intercultural approach**. Studies using discourse analysis and pragmatics approaches examine how language varies according to whether speakers are talking in their first language to speakers of the same language, or whether they are using a lingua franca to be understood by speakers of another language. Units A7–D7 take an intercultural approach to context, function, structure and social rules, and explore the applications of findings to **language learning and teaching**.

The following table summarises how all these approaches and dimensions fit with discourse analysis and pragmatics, indicating which units in this book where they feature:

		Unit
Context: Discourse Analysis/Pragmatics	situation & background	1
	cohesion/coherence, relevance	1
	corpus/community	*6*
	culture/language learning	*7*
Function: Discourse Analysis/Pragmatics	Speech Act Theory	2
	corpus/community	*6*
	culture/language learning	*7*
Structure: Discourse Analysis	Conversation Analysis	3
	Exchange Structure	3
	corpus/community	*6*
	culture/language learning	*7*
Social principles: Pragmatics	Cooperative Principle	4
	Politeness Principle	5
	corpus/community	*6*
	culture/language learning	*7*

A1.3

Context

We said that Units A1 to D1 deal with the meaning of words in context (the physical and social world) and assumptions of knowledge that speaker and hearer share. Take a look at this excerpt from a conversation between MSc students in the common room of the Applied Linguistics department of the University of Edinburgh. DM, an English man, had planned to go to Spain for Easter but could not afford the tickets; he tells AF, a Scottish woman, that he ended up going hill walking in Arran, an island off the west coast of Scotland. What knowledge do they assume that they share?

AF   (2) So you went to Arran. A bit of a come-down isn't it! (laughing)
DM   It was nice actually. Have you been to Arran?
AF   No I've not. (1) Like to go.
DM   Did a lot of climbing.

AF   // (heh)

DM   // I went with Francesca (0.5) and David.

AF   Uhuh?

DM   Francesca's room-mate. (2) And Alice's, a friend of Alice's from London (1). There were six of us. Yeah we did a lot of hill walking. (0.5) We got back (1) er (2) Michelle and I got home she looked at her knees. (0.5) They were like this. Swollen up like this. Cos we did this enormous eight-hour stretch.

AF   Uhm.

(Students on hill walking 1996)

Typically, there are three sorts of context to observe here:

- ❏ the **situational context**, what speakers know about what they can see around them;
- ❏ the **background knowledge context**, what they know about each other and the world;
- ❏ the **co-textual context**, what they know about what they have been saying.

Outside the text: situational context   A1.4

In the excerpt about hill walking in Arran, there is an example of words taking on meaning in the situational context: 'They were like this. Swollen up like this'. DM must be holding his hands open and rounded to show what Michelle's knees looked like. The situational context is the immediate physical co-presence, the situation where the interaction is taking place at the moment of speaking. It is not by chance that DM uses the words 'like this'. 'This' is a demonstrative pronoun, used for pointing to something that speaker and hearer can see. An overhearer who cannot see DM's hands would not know how bad his wife's knees were.

Let us take an example from written language. You may be familiar with *The English Struwwelpeter*, a book from the beginning of the twentieth century that contains moralistic, humorous tales about naughty children who are punished for their bad behaviour. There is one such tale called 'The Story of Augustus Who Would not Have any Soup'. The tale begins with Augustus as 'a chubby lad who ate and drank as he was told, and never let his soup grow cold'. Then one day he screams, 'I won't have any soup today.' Here is verse two:

> *Next day, now look, the picture shows*
> *How lank and lean Augustus grows!*
> *Yet, though he feels so weak and ill,*
> *The naughty fellow cries out still –*
> *'Not any soup for me, I say:*
> *O take the nasty soup away!*
> *I won't have any soup today.'*

Needless to say, by the fifth day, he was dead. The poem is meant to be read to a child who can look at the book in front of them: the words 'the picture' refer to the one in the book, and the name 'Augustus' refers to the boy in the picture. The child who does not look at the picture will not know exactly 'how lank and lean' the boy is. The picture adds a visible situational context.

Outside the text: background knowledge context

The second type of context is that of assumed background knowledge. This can be either **cultural** (general knowledge that most people carry with them in their minds, about areas of life) or **interpersonal** (specific and possibly private knowledge about the history of the speakers themselves).

Cultural

In the hill-walking-in-Arran excerpt, AF and DM share cultural background knowledge about the low mountains on the island: AF does not appear surprised that DM and his friends went 'hill walking', that they could walk for eight hours there, or that the walk was strenuous enough to make somebody's knees swell. If interlocutors establish that they are part of the same group, they can assume mutual knowledge of everything normally known by group members (Sperber and Wilson 1995). Here, the community of people who could be assumed to know about the mountains are British people, or people who have visited or studied the British Isles.

Groups with mutual knowledge vary in size. Let us take the music world as an example. People with an interest in and knowledge of African music could constitute a community of millions. Within that community there are smaller groups of people who know all about a particular sort of African music, its singers and bands, its history and geography. Within that community, there will be an even smaller group of people who know every song that a particular African group has recorded, as well as the life histories of each of the band members. These social groups are known as **communities of practice**, if they have the broadly agreed common public goals, special mechanisms for communication and a special lexis or vocabulary (see Units A7–D7).

Interpersonal

In the hill-walking excerpt, we see that AF and DM know who 'Michelle' is. This is the interpersonal context. DM will have told AF in a previous conversation that his wife's name is 'Michelle'; he might also have told her where 'home' is – AF might have actually been to DM's home and learned quite a lot about Michelle. Shared interpersonal knowledge is knowledge acquired through previous verbal interactions or joint activities and experiences, and it includes privileged personal knowledge about the interlocutor.

There was a US television advertisement that featured a telephone dialogue like this:

Her: How are you?
Him: OK.
Her: Did you have friends in and get a video last night?
Him: Oh, I had friends in, but we just watched a little TV.
Her: Ah right.
Him: That was great. How do you feel?
Her: OK

It is only when she says 'OK' at the end that there is a flash-back and we see that she won a gold medal in an Olympics event. At this point, we understand that 'Oh, I had friends in, but we just watched a little TV' means 'I had friends in to watch you playing on TV and I know you won'. The interpersonal knowledge shared by a husband and wife is obviously enormous: this is why reference to any part of it can be so vague, implicit and minimal.

Inside the text: co-textual context

A1.6

The **co-textual context** is the context of the text itself, known as the **co-text**. If we go back to the hill-walking excerpt,

> DM // I went with Francesca (0.5) and David.
> AF Uhuh?
> DM Francesca's room-mate. (2) And Alice's – a friend of Alice's from London (1). There were six of **us**. Yeah **we** did a lot of hill walking.
> /.../ AF Uhm.

We can see that the personal pronouns 'us' and the 'we' refer back to Francesca, David, the room-mate and the friend, who are all mentioned elsewhere in the text. The inter-locutors assume that everyone in the conversation has enough knowledge of what they have been saying, to be able to infer who the 'us' and the 'we' include.

Language and the context

A1.7

The act of using language to refer to entities in the context is known as **reference**: an act in which a speaker uses linguistic forms to enable the hearer to identify something. The speaker uses linguistic forms, known as **referring expressions**, to enable the hearer to identify the entity being referred to, which is in turn known as the **referent**. For example, in the words '<u>I</u> went with <u>Francesca</u> (0.5) and <u>David</u>', the first-person singular personal pronoun 'I' is a referring expression which refers to the person speaking, who is the referent. Similarly, the proper nouns 'Francesca' and 'David' are the referring expressions that refer to the two people whose names are Francesca and David, the latter being the referents.

There are words actually **point to** the entity that they refer to. This is known as **deixis**. Deixis can take its meaning from the context outside or inside the text. There are three types: person, place and time. When we talk of **person deixis** we mean the use of expressions to point to a person, with the personal pronouns 'I', 'you', 'he', 'she', 'it', 'we' and 'they':

– **We** are not amused.
– So **you** went to Arran.
– **We** got back (1) er (2) Michelle and **I** got home **she** looked at her knees. (0.5)
– **They** were like this.
– Yet, though **he** feels so weak and ill.

Spatial or **place deixis** is words used to point to a location, the place where an entity is in the context, as in the demonstrative adverbs 'there', 'here', the demonstrative adjectives and pronouns 'this', 'that', 'these', 'those':

– They were like **this**.
– **That** was great.

- Cos there's another one **here**.
- Right, we've got forty-nine **there**, haven't we?

Time deixis is expressions used to point to a time, as in 'next day', 'then' and 'now':

- **Next day**, now look, the picture shows.

A1.8

Referring to the context outside: exophora

When the referring expression is the first mention of the referent, in the sense that there is no previous mention of the reference in the preceding text, we call it **exophoric** reference. Exophora is dependent on the context outside the text, either in the situation or in the background knowledge. Thus, in 'I went with Francesca (0.5) and David', 'I' is exophoric because the referent is the person speaking. The nouns 'Francesca' and 'David' are used as exophoric reference because they point to people who are in the cultural context and are not referred to previously in the text.

When a referring item refers to entities in the background knowledge, whether cultural or interpersonal, that have obviously been mentioned in a previous conversation or text, or have occurred in a previously shared situation or activity, we call this **intertextuality** (de Beaugrande and Dressler 1981). In the telephone call about the Olympic medal, the 'that' of 'That was great' is an example of intertextuality because it refers back to the wife's performance in the Olympic event. The previous text becomes part of background knowledge. Since 'That was great' refers to an event that millions of viewers around the world would have seen, it is in the cultural context. If the husband had been referring to a romantic evening with his wife, the intertextuality would have been interpersonal. Intertextuality is more often interpersonal than cultural, since it usually refers to knowledge gained in previous conversations between the people who are speaking. Common ground is a result of the interpenetrating biographies of the participants, of which the conversation of the moment is only a part (Coulthard 1986).

A1.9

Language of the context inside: cohesion

Grammatical cohesion

We can look at how the co-text hangs together from the point of view of reference. In the excerpt above, the pronouns 'us' and 'we' refer to items within the same text; this is **endophoric reference**. They refer back to DM, Francesca, David, Francesca's room-mate, the friend of Alice's and Michelle, who are all mentioned elsewhere in the text. When a referring expression links with another referring expression within the co-text, we say that it is **cohesive with** the previous mention of the referent in the text. This is part of what is known as **grammatical cohesion**; it is what meshes the text together. Let us take another example:

> We have been established by an Act of Parliament as an independent body to elimin-
> ate discrimination against disabled people and to secure equal opportunities for
> them. To achieve this, we have set ourselves the goal of: 'A society where all disabled
> people can participate fully as equal citizens'.
>
> (The Disability Rights Commission leaflet 2000)

Here, the personal pronoun 'them' refers to the same referent as the noun 'disabled people' did. There is also grammatical cohesion through the phrase 'To achieve this', in which the demonstrative pronoun 'this' is cohesive with the aim of eliminating 'discrimination against disabled people' and 'securing equal opportunities for them'. Endophora avoids unnecessary repetition. This is how the example would have sounded without it:

> We have been established by an Act of Parliament as an independent body to elim-inate discrimination against disabled people and to secure equal opportunities for disabled people. To achieve the aim of eliminating discrimination against disabled people and securing equal opportunities for disabled people, we have set ourselves the goal of: 'A society where all disabled people can participate fully as equal citizens'.

Notice how the repetition makes the text now seem over-explicit; it sounds as if the writer is assuming that readers will not understand unless it is all spelled out. It gives more information than is needed, as all readers would be able to make the connection between the pronoun and the phrase that it links with, if their short-term memory is functioning normally.

There are two types of endophora. In the example above, the pronouns 'them' and 'this' link back to something that went before in the preceding text. This is called **anaphora**, and it is the most frequent of the two types. The other, **cataphora**, is the opposite – pronouns link forward to a referent in the text that follows. This is in evidence in the next example:

> An actor with whom she was rehearsing caught Coral Browne's fancy. Informed by a colleague that she was *most* unlikely to get anywhere with that particular man, she bet the colleague a pound that she would. Next morning, the colleague who had accepted her bet asked her, loudly and meaningfully, in the presence of the actor, 'Well, dear, do you owe me anything?' Browne replied, disappointedly: 'Seven and six'.
>
> (Rees 1999: 30)

Here, the 'she' links cataphorically with 'Coral Browne'. Since seven shillings and six pence was much less than half a pound, we must suppose that she was not very suc-cessful. We can summarise reference with a diagram to make it easier to grasp:

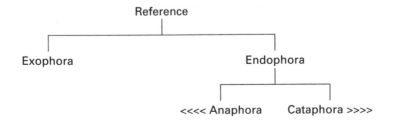

There are occasions when the noun phrases (these can be nouns or pronouns) are not linked explicitly to each other, but one noun phrase is linked to entities simply associated with the other noun phrase. This is called **associative endophora**. Here is an example from a Wikipedia article about YouTube (16 May 2007):

> **YouTube** is a popular <u>video sharing</u> website where users can upload, view, and share <u>video clips</u>. Videos can be rated, and the average rating and the number of times a video has been watched are both published.
>
> (http://en.wikipedia.org/wiki/Youtube)

Here, readers can infer, by drawing from their knowledge of the **presuppositional pool** of 'website', that the 'video sharing' being talked about is public viewing online rather than physically passing DVDs to friends. Similarly, if readers understand 'website' and 'YouTube', they will know that 'clips' in video clips are not the same as 'clips' in 'paper clips', and the 'users' are people that use the site (not exploitative people). Associative endophora is half way between endophora and exophora, because it depends partly on knowledge of what went before or after within the same text, and partly on background knowledge of the cultural or interpersonal context, in this case what is associated with 'website' and 'video'.

Endophoric reference is only one form of grammatical cohesion. There are two other forms that are **not part of reference**: substitution and ellipsis. Let us start with **substitution**. Many of you will be familiar with the song about the characterless little houses of the pretentious lower middle class:

> Little boxes on the hillside,
> Little boxes made of ticky-tacky,
> Little boxes, little boxes,
> Little boxes, all the same.
> There's a green one and a pink one
> And a blue one and a yellow one
> And they're all made out of ticky-tacky
> And they all look just the same.
>
> (Reynolds 1962)

The lines 'There's a green one and a pink one / And a blue one and a yellow one' contain the substitute 'one'. As with endophoric reference, substitution holds the text together and avoids repetition, the 'one' 'substituting' the 'box'. The plural substitute is 'ones'. We could have substituted 'boxes' in line two of the song with 'ones', and said 'Little ones made of ticky-tacky', but then the song would have lost some of its cynicism. Substitution tends to be endophoric: the noun phrase being substituted is usually in the text. In the next example, the substitute 'so' coheres with an adjectival phrase. It is from a *Guardian* Women's page article entitled 'Does length matter?'

> Self-confidence should not be a gender issue. Boys are not born more confident than girls. Society makes them so because it traditionally values their skills and aptitudes above those of women.
>
> (*Guardian* Women, 14 April 2001)

We understand 'makes them so' to mean 'makes them more confident than girls'.

The other form of grammatical cohesion is **ellipsis**. Take a look at this snatch from *Catch 22*, the famous World War II novel:

'He's afraid of you,' Yossarian said. 'He's afraid you're going to die of pneumonia.'
'He'd better be afraid,' Chief White Halfoat said. A deep low laugh rumbled through
his massive chest. 'I will, too, the first chance I get. You just wait and see.'

(Heller 1962)

'I will, too' is an example of ellipsis: Chief White Halfoat misses out a piece of text.
He means 'I will die of pneumonia' but he omits 'die of pneumonia' because it is not
necessary. Just like substitution, ellipsis avoids repetition and depends on the hearer
or reader's being able to retrieve the missing words from the context. The same
happens in the next snippet of a conversation between two sixteen-year-old female
students:

Catriona: What was he doing? Tell me, make me cringe.

Jess: Oh nothing to make you cringe or anything. He was just, he was just like . . .
              saying you know just stuff that was really pretty well sick.

Catriona: Oh last night, last night he was as well with Romeo and Juliet.

(British National Corpus (BNC): kp6 Catriona, 1993)

Catriona uses ellipsis in her 'he was as well', and thus avoids saying 'he was saying
stuff that was really pretty well sick as well' Ellipsis occurs more often in conversation
than in written text because conversation tends to be less explicit.

Lexical cohesion

Grammatical cohesion (reference, substitution and ellipsis) holds texts together, but
so does lexical cohesion. The following diagram above summarises what both types
of cohesion consist of, and points to what the rest of this unit will discuss, in terms
of lexical cohesion.

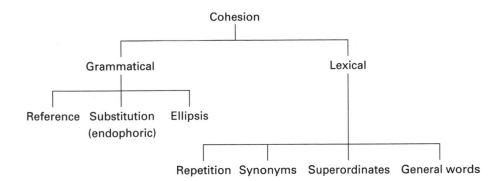

Of all the lexical cohesion devices, the most common form is **repetition**, which
is simply repeated words or word-phrases, threading through the text. Take this
example from D. H. Lawrence's short story 'Odour of Chrysanthemums':

The child put the pale chrysanthemums to her lips, murmuring:
    'Don't they smell beautiful!'
    Her mother gave a short laugh.

'No,' she said, 'not to me. It was chrysanthemums when I married him, and chrysanthemums when you were born, and the first time they ever brought him home drunk,
he'd got brown chrysanthemums in his button-hole.'

(Lawrence 1981)

Here, the repeated 'chrysanthemums' have the effect of pounding through the text and
showing how they have been a repeated and unwelcome feature of the mother's life.
Substitution and ellipsis avoid repetition; lexical repetition exploits it for stylistic effect.

Instead of repeating the exact same word, a speaker or writer can use another word
that means the same or almost the same. This is a **synonym**. Again, it avoids repetition. Take this little excerpt from the *AOL News* (14 January 2007) entitled 'Flying
mice spark panic':

When 80 mice escaped on a Saudi domestic flight the squeaks of panic drowned out
the roar of the engines. The rodents had escaped from a bag on the overhead luggage
rack. Screams were heard when they began dropping into the laps of the 100 panic-
stricken passengers. Authorities detained the owner of the bag after the aircraft
landed in Tabuk, in the north west of the country.

Here, 'mice' and 'rodents' are two ways of referring to the same animal 'rodent' being
a superordinate (see below). 'Flight' and 'aircraft' are synonyms. As the saying goes,
'variety is the spice of life': using different ways of referring to an entity makes for
more interesting prose or conversation.

In order to observe the lexical cohesion device of **superordinates**, let us go back
to 'Odour of Chrysanthemums' and continue with the story:

The candle-light glittered on the lustre-glasses, on the two vases that held some of the
pink chrysanthemums, and on the dark mahogany. There was a cold, deathly smell
of chrysanthemums in the room. Elizabeth stood looking at the flowers.

(Lawrence 1981)

Here again there is repetition of 'chrysanthemums', but then they are referred to
with the words 'the flowers'. This not a synonym of 'chrysanthemums'; it is a more
general term is known as a superordinate, an umbrella term that includes 'pansies',
'tulips', 'roses', etc. This is another way of avoiding repetition and still referring to
the referent with a noun. Lawrence could have used an endophoric 'them' instead,
and said 'Elizabeth stood looking at them', but this might have given them less pro-
minence; he does want them at the centre of his story.

The last form of lexical cohesion that we cover here is the **general word**. These
can be general nouns, as in 'thing', 'stuff', 'place', 'person', 'woman' and 'man', or
general verbs, as in 'do' and 'happen'. In a way, the general word is a higher level superordinate: it is the umbrella term that can cover almost everything. In the following,
Peter, a 49-year-old chemist, uses the general noun 'place' to refer back either to the
'Poly' or to the city:

and so he went off to Wolverhampton Poly which he selected for, you know, all the
usual reasons, reasonable place, reasonable course, a reasonable this a reasonable that
t-t erm to do computer science which of course all the kids want to do now erm

twentieth centu- no it isn't it's a sort of nineteen eighties version of wanting to be an engine driver.

(BNC: kc3 Frederick, 1992)

General nouns and verbs do not carry much information; they depend on the co-text for their meaning, so are used when hearers and readers can identify what is being referred to from the rest of the text.

SPEECH ACTS

Understanding concepts

- ❑ Direct speech acts
- ❑ Felicity conditions
- ❑ Indirect speech acts
- ❑ Interactional / transactional function

Introduction

> To a hostess who had sent an invitation stating that on a certain day she would be 'At home', George Bernard Shaw succinctly replied: 'So will G. Bernard Shaw'.
>
> (Rees 1999)

At the risk of killing a funny tale, we can explain what happened here in terms of speech acts. The hostess's invitation will have read something like 'Mrs Eleanor Higgins will be at home 10th April 7–9 p.m.', which are words usually taken as performing the speech act of 'inviting'. Shaw pretended to read it literally as a statement of where she would be and responded in kind; his answer consisted of words to be taken as performing the speech act of 'declining'.

Speech acts

Austin (1962) defined speech acts as the actions performed in saying something. **Speech Act Theory** said that the action performed when an utterance is produced can be analysed on three different levels. Let us look at the action in the conversation below. Three students are sitting together at the 'bun lunch', the social occasion at which the university lays on filled rolls and fruit juice on the first day of the course, to welcome the students and help them to get to know each other.

MM   I think I might go and have another bun.
AM   I was going to get another one.
BM   Could you get me a tuna and sweetcorn one please?
AM   Me as well?

(Students at bun lunch 1996)

The first level of analysis is the words themselves: 'I think I might go and have another bun', 'I was going to get another one', and so on. This is the **locution**, 'what is said', the form of the words uttered; the act of saying something is known as the **locutionary act**. The second level is what the speakers are doing with their words: AM and MM are 'asserting' and 'expressing intentions about their own action', and BM and AM are 'requesting action on the part of the hearer'. This is the **illocutionary force**, 'what is done in uttering the words', the function of the words, the specific purpose that the speakers have in mind. Other examples are the speech acts 'inviting', 'advising', 'promising', 'ordering', 'excusing' and 'apologising'. The last level of analysis is the result of the words: MM gets up and brings AM and BM a tuna and sweetcorn bun each. This is known as the **perlocutionary effect**, 'what is done by uttering the words'; it is the effect on the hearer, the hearer's reaction.

Austin developed, but soon abandoned, the **performative hypothesis** that behind every utterance there is a **performative verb**, such as 'to order', 'to warn', 'to admit' and 'to promise', that make the illocutionary force explicit. The example above could be reformulated:

MM   I express my intention to go and have another bun.
AM   I inform you that I was going to get another one.
BM   I request you to get me a tuna and sweet corn one.
AM   I request you to get me one as well.

Austin realised that often the implicit performatives, ones without the performative verbs, as in the original version of this dialogue, sound more natural. He also realised that implicit performatives do not always have an obvious explicit performative understood. Take the expression, 'I'll be back!' It can mean either '*I promise* that I'll be back' or '*I warn you* that I'll be back'. Searle's (1976) solution to classifying speech acts was to group them in the following macro-classes:

Declarations

These are words and expressions that change the world by their very utterance, such as 'I bet', 'I declare', 'I resign'. Others can be seen in: 'I baptise this boy John Smith', which changes a nameless baby into one with a name, 'I hereby pronounce you man and wife', which turns two singles into a married couple, and 'This court sentences you to ten years' imprisonment', which puts the person into prison.

Representatives

These are acts in which the words state what the speaker believes to be the case, such as 'describing', 'claiming', 'hypothesising', 'insisting' and 'predicting'.

'I think girls work harder than boys. Maybe not doing your work is a sign of being cool', said Jack Niveson, a 14-year-old student at Winslow Middle School.

(Boston.com News, 26 March 2006)

I came; I saw; I conquered.

(Julius Caesar)

Macbeth shall never vanquished be until / Great Birnam wood to high Dunsinane hill / Shall come against him.'

(Shakespeare, *Macbeth*)

Commissives
This includes acts in which the words commit the speaker to future action, such as 'promising', 'offering', 'threatening', 'refusing', 'vowing' and 'volunteering'.

Ready when you are.
I'll make him an offer he can't refuse.   (Mario Puzo, *The Godfather*)

I'll love you, dear, I'll love you / Till China and Africa meet, / And the river jumps over the mountain / And the salmon sing in the street.
                                        (W. H. Auden, 'As I Walked Out One Evening')

Directives
This category covers acts in which the words are aimed at making the hearer do something, such as 'commanding', 'requesting', 'inviting', 'forbidding', 'suggesting', etc.

From ghoulies and ghosties and long-leggety beasties / And things that go bump in the night, / Good Lord, deliver us.   (Scottish prayer)

Better remain silent and be thought a fool, than open your mouth and remove all possible doubt.   (Ancient Chinese proverb)

Do not do unto others as you would they should do unto you. Their tastes may not be the same.   (G. B. Shaw, *Man and Superman*)

Expressives
This last group includes acts in which the words state what the speaker feels, such as 'apologising', 'praising', 'congratulating', 'deploring' and 'regretting'.

A woman without a man is like a fish without a bicycle.   (Gloria Steinem)

I've been poor and I've been rich – rich is better.   (Sophie Tucker)

If I'd known I was gonna live this long, I'd have taken better care of myself.   (Eubie Blake)

Felicity conditions

A2.4

In order for speech acts to be appropriately and successfully performed, certain **felicity conditions** have to be met. For Austin, the felicity conditions are that the context and roles of participants must be recognised by all parties, the action must be carried out completely, and the persons must have the right intentions. For Searle, there is a general condition for all speech acts, that the hearer must hear and understand the language, and that the speaker must not be pretending or play-acting. For declarations and directives, the rules are that the speaker must believe that it is possible to carry out the action, they are performing the act in the hearer's best interests, they are sincere about wanting to do it, and the words count as the act.

To understand the need for felicity conditions, let us return to the students in their bun lunch:

MM   I think I might go and have another bun.
AM   I was going to get another one.
BM   Could you get me a tuna and sweetcorn one please?
AM   Me as well?

Here, we have a directive speech act of 'requesting' ('Could you get me a tuna and sweetcorn one please?') which can be explained using Austin's model. The context of the bun lunch is recognised by all parties: it is an appropriate place to talk about the buns and about wanting another one. The roles of participants are recognised: the students are equals, and it is not a great imposition, therefore, for one to ask another to get a bun. The persons have the right intentions: BM and AM must trust that MM is indeed going to get a bun and they presumably intend to eat the buns that they ask for.

The situation can also be explained using Searle's model. AM and BM seem to believe that it is possible for MM to get them buns: he has functioning legs, and the buns are not too far away. They genuinely want the buns to eat; they are sincere. Their words count as a request. It cannot be said that BM and AM are performing the act in MM's best interests, however, as they are performing it in their own interests. On the other hand they are not asking for the buns in order to burden MM and make it difficult for him to bring all the buns back, and if MM wants to appear sociable and obliging, he is being offered an occasion to demonstrate it.

Let us look at an example of a declarative speech act. There was a situation reported, in the local press, of a man and woman who discovered, a month before their wedding, that they had not completed all the necessary paperwork and that it would not be ready in time. They decided to go ahead with the wedding ceremony as if nothing were wrong and sign the papers later, because all the preparations had been made and they wanted to save face. Thus, the priest's words 'I now pronounce you man and wife' did not marry them, legally because the papers were missing, and pragmatically because not all the felicity conditions were met. Although the context and roles of participants were recognised by all parties, and the priest was saying the words in the couple's best interests, the speech act was not successfully performed since they were 'putting on a show' for the benefit of the guests: the action was not carried out completely, and the priest did not believe that it was possible to carry out the action, did not have the intention to carry it out and was not sincere about wanting to do it.

A2.5   Indirect speech acts

Much of the time, what we mean is actually not in the words themselves but in the meaning implied. In the bun-lunch example, we said that AM's words 'I was going to get another one' had illocutionary force of 'expressing intentions about his own action'. It should noted, however, that he says this straight after MM's 'I think I might go and have another bun'. It is possible that in fact he was implying that he would like MM to get him one while he was there and save him the bother of getting up. If this is so, he is expressing a directive, 'requesting' indirectly, with the force of the imperative 'Get me one'; this is what we call an indirect speech act.

Searle said that a speaker using a **direct speech act** wants to communicate the literal meaning that the words conventionally express; there is a direct relationship between the form and the function. Thus, a declarative form (not to be confused with declaration speech acts) such as 'I was going to get another one' has the function of a statement or assertion; an interrogative form such as 'Do you like the tuna and sweetcorn ones?' has the function of a question; and an imperative form such as 'Get me one' has the function of a request or order.

On the other hand, Searle explained that someone using an **indirect speech act** wants to communicate a different meaning from the apparent surface meaning; the form and function are not directly related. There is an underlying pragmatic meaning, and one speech act is performed through another speech act. Thus, a declarative form such as 'I was going to get another one', or 'You could get me a tuna and sweetcorn one' might have the function of a request or order, meaning 'Get me one'. Similarly, an interrogative form such as 'Could you get me a tuna and sweetcorn one please?' or 'Would you mind getting me one?' has the function of a request or order, and 'Can I get you one while I'm there?' can be taken as an offer. Finally, an imperative form such as 'Enjoy your bun' functions as an statement meaning 'I hope you enjoy your bun', 'Here, take this one' can have the function of an offer, and 'Come on a walk with me after the lunch' serves as an invitation.

Indirect speech acts are part of everyday life. The classification of utterances in categories of direct and direct speech acts is not an easy task, because much of what we say operates on both levels, and utterances often have more than one of the macro-functions ('representative', 'commissive', 'directive', 'expressive', etc.). A few examples will illustrate this.

The following excerpt from the novel *Regeneration* demonstrates that, in indirect speech acts, it is the underlying meaning that the speaker intends the hearer to understand. Graves arrives after Sassoon at the convalescent home and asks:

'I don't suppose you've seen anybody yet?'
    'I've seen Rivers. Which reminds me, he wants to see *you*, but I imagine it'll be all right if you dump your bag first.'

(Barker 1991)

On the surface, Sassoon's reply 'he wants to see you' is a declarative with the function of a statement and a direct representative describing River's wishes. However, it appears to be intended as an order or a suggestion to Graves, meaning the same as the imperative 'Go and see him', and therefore an indirect directive, and the suggestion is reinforced by the 'but I imagine it'll be all right if you dump your bag first', which is uttered as if he had actually said 'Go and see him'.

Let us take another example, this time from the thriller *Tooth and Nail*. Inspector Rebus and Inspector Flight come out of an autopsy:

'Come on,' he said, 'I'll give you a lift.'
    In his fragile state, Rebus felt this to be the nicest kindest thing anyone had said to him in weeks. 'Are you sure you have room?' he said, 'I mean, with the teddy bear and all?'

Flight paused. 'Or if you'd prefer to walk, Inspector?'

Rebus threw up his hands in surrender, then, when the door unlocked, slipped into the passenger seat of Flight's red Sierra. The seat seemed to wrap itself around him.

'Here', said Flight, handing a hip flask to Rebus. Rebus unscrewed the top of the flask and sniffed. 'It won't kill you,' Flight called. This was probably true. The aroma was of whisky.

(Rankin 1992)

Here again, there is a declarative that is more than a statement: 'I'll give you a lift' is a direct commissive offering a lift to the inspector, and committing himself to future action, although is could be classed as an indirect directive, carrying the meaning of an imperative such as 'Get in the car'. More complex is 'Or if you'd prefer to walk'. It is not a declarative, and yet it is not just a direct directive suggesting alternative action either, since it implies 'If you're going to be cheeky, I won't give you a lift', which is an indirect commissive making a threat. Similarly, 'It won't kill you' looks, on the surface, like a representative, describing the contents of the flask, but in fact the implication is 'Drink it', an indirect directive commanding.

Film lovers will be familiar with the film star Mae West, who once said to an admirer, 'Why don't you come up and see me some time?'. She did not actually say 'Come up and see me some time'. The hearer will, however, have understood the indirect directive inviting, and ignored the direct representative asking why.

A2.6 Speech acts and society

Social dimensions

Indirect speech acts in many languages and cultures constitute one of many forms of politeness, and we will look at this in more detail in Units A5–D5 when we look at all the linguistic features of politeness. In most Englishes, indirectness is so much associated with politeness that directives are more often expressed as interrogatives than imperatives. This is especially the case with people with whom one is not familiar. An interesting case here is the sign to the general public in many British restaurants, bookshops and petrol stations that says, 'Thank you for not smoking'. The expressive 'thanking' speech act is presumably used because it sounds more polite and friendly to all the strangers who read the sign, than the impersonal directive 'prohibiting' 'No Smoking'.

Other factors that can make speakers use indirect directives, in addition to lack of familiarity, are the reasonableness of the task, the formality of the context and social distance (differences of status, roles, age, gender, education, class, occupation and ethnicity). Social distance can give speakers power and authority, and it is generally those of the less dominant role, etc., who tend to use indirectness. Thus, in the short story 'Dealer's Choice', a young woman walks into the office of a private detective, older, male and in a position of authority:

She got to her feet. Perched on top of her boxy four-inch heels she just about cleared my armpit.

'I've been hoping to see you, Mr Marlowe. Hoping to interest you in taking a case for me. If you have time, that is.'

She made it sound as though her problem, whatever it was, was just a bit on the dull side, and that if I didn't have time for it the two of us could forget it and move onto something more interesting.

(Paretsky 1995)

She expresses her request indirectly, 'hidden' under a representative describing herself: 'I've been hoping to see you, Mr Marlowe. Hoping to interest you in taking a case for me'.

Cultural dimension

Speech acts, their linguistic realisations (how people express them) and their relationship to the social dimensions mentioned above are very much culture bound. The ways of expressing speech acts vary from social group to social group, country to country, from culture to culture. This is a major point to get to grips with in Speech Act Theory, and it is one of the main issues that we explore in depth in Units A7–D7, Culture and language learning.

Let us take a few examples for the moment. In India, the expressive speech act of 'praising' and 'congratulating' a person on their appearance can be realised by the words 'How fat you are!', because weight is an indicator of prosperity and health, in a country where there is malnutrition. In Britain, these words express a speech act of 'deploring' or 'criticising', since the fashion and diet foods industries, and possibly health education, have conditioned many into thinking that 'slim is beautiful'.

Differences in speech act conventions can cause communication difficulties interculturally. The following example comes from Cuba: person A, a British woman, telephoned the work-centre of Mr Perez. B, a Cuban who worked with Mr Perez, picked up the phone:

A   Is Mr Perez there?
B   Yes, he is.
A   Em . . . can I speak to him, please?
B   Yes, wait a minute.

A's question, 'Is Mr Perez there?', is intended as an indirect request for the hearer to bring Mr Perez to the phone. B only hears an interrogative with the function of direct representative checking whether Mr Perez is in his place of work.

Spencer-Oatey (2000: 1) tells an anecdote about her being accosted at a Hong Kong bus-stop by her students, who asked 'Where are you going?' As a British person, she found this question intrusive and disrespectful. She later learned that, in Chinese, it is a friendly greeting with no expectation of an explicit answer. She also learned that whereas a British English greeting mentions the weather, as in 'Hi, bit colder today', a Chinese greeting mentions meals, as in 'Hello, have you had your lunch?', which is not a preliminary to an invitation, but a question about welfare.

A2.7
Limitations of Speech Act Theory

When we try to categorise utterances in terms of speech acts, we often find that there is an **overlap**, that one utterance can fall into more than one macro-class. Take the following example from the novel *Lord of the Flies*:

> 'They're all dead,' said Piggy, 'an' this is an island. Nobody don't know we're here. Your dad don't know, nobody don't know –'
>
> His lips quivered and the spectacles were dimmed with mist. 'We may stay here till we die.'

(Golding 1954)

On the face of it, this is a representative, a description of the present state of affairs, when the boy realises that they are all alone on the island, and yet it is a very emotive little outburst – the boy is obviously crying, so it could also be classified as an expressive.

Another problem with the speech act model is that it has no provision for the **'messiness'** of everyday spoken language. Utterances such as 'So there you go' and 'You know' amount to **fillers** that say very little; this lack of semantic content makes it difficult to put in any of the classifications, as they are neither representatives nor expressives. This type of utterance has an interactional, socially cohesive function of avoiding silence, so that all speakers feel comfortable, and it intensifies the relevance of surrounding utterances. There is not a neat speech act category for it, however. Likewise, **backchannels** and feedback, the responses that show that the hearer is listening and encourage a speaker to continue taking, such as 'Was it?' and 'Oh really?', do not fit neatly into the speech act model either. They too have a social function, but do not constitute a speech act. The same goes for **incomplete sentences**, as in: 'But she didn't do the – er – no'; this type of sentence does not fit neatly into any category. A lot of what we say in everyday speech is left unfinished either because we have no need to complete the sentence or because we are interrupted.

The following excerpt, from a law seminar on the topic of accomplice liability, taken from the British Academic Spoken English (BASE) corpus (see References), has instances of fillers, backchannels and incomplete sentences. The lecturer is L, and the students S1 and S2:

S2: // isn't that implied, surely that /.../ implied, that you're driving a car, you haveduties that are implied, not necessarily don't have to only be statutory um possibility they also have to be implied sort of . . .

L: well umm, that's an argument although it is slightly odd isn't to base criminal liability on a duty that's merely implied //

S1:   // yeh

S2: when I say impli . . .

L: you may not realise you have outset

(Listening to lectures, BASE 2000)

S2 has difficulty formulating his thoughts and on two occasions leaves his sentences incomplete: 'to be implied sort of . . .' and 'when I say impli . . .' The Lecturer opens his comment with a filler, 'well umm'. S1 just contributes a 'yeh' backchannel. All of this is perfectly normal in real-life spontaneous talk, yet it is difficult to categorise each utterance in terms of speech acts. Units A4–D4 take another approach to the analysis of real-life spontaneous talk, this one designed to take into account speech acts and also handle casual conversations.

Macro-functions

A2.8

Finally, it should be noted that, over and above speech acts, there are two main macro-functions of talk. Brown and Yule (1983) describe them as the **transactional** and **interactional** functions. The transactional is the function which language serves in the expression of content and the transmission of factual information. Here is a purely transactional excerpt from the AOL Travel page about the ten most dangerous animals in the world (http://travel.aol.co.uk), which says that the mosquito is number one:

> What we Brits regard as an annoying pest is actually the most dangerous creature on the planet, thanks to its ability to spread disease with alarming efficiency. Best known for spreading deadly malaria, mossies also spread elephantiasis, yellow fever, dengue fever and West Nile virus, which was recently introduced to the US and is now prevalent in all states.

The interactional is that function involved in expressing social relations and personal attitudes, showing solidarity and maintaining social cohesion. Speakers establishing common ground, sharing a common point of view and negotiating role-relationships are speaking with an interactional purpose. For example, emails tend to start with words with an interactional function:

Espero que al recibo de esta te encuentres bien al igual que la chiquitica. Nosotros bien en lo que cabe.
(I hope this finds you well, and also the wee one. We're as well as can be expected.)

In fact, most talk has a mixture of the two functions: there seems to be a cline from the purely transactional to the purely interactional. At the extreme end of the transactional is the language used when a policeman is giving directions to a traveller, and a doctor is telling a nurse how to administer medicine to a patient. At the extreme end of the interactional is what is known as **phatic communion**, language with no information content used purely to keep channels of communication open. Brown and Yule give the following example:

> When two strangers are standing shivering at a bus-stop in an icy wind and one turns to the other and says 'My goodness, it's cold', it is difficult to suppose that the primary intention of the speaker is to convey information. It seems much more reasonable to suggest that the speaker is indicating a readiness to be friendly and to talk.

> (Brown and Yule 1983: 3)

Brown and Yule point out that much of everyday human interaction is characterised by the primarily interpersonal rather than the primarily transactional use of language.

A3 CONVERSATION

A3.1 Understanding concepts

❏ Exchange moves and IRF Felicity conditions
❏ Conversation analysis
❏ Interactional sociolinguistics

A3.2 Introduction

So far, we have described language as if it existed in isolated sentences and speech acts, first one speaker talking and then another in an unrelated manner. Although we studied the way that words are grammatically and lexically cohesive with each other, we did not focus on the fact that complete utterances are linked to other complete utterances through their function, and indeed that whole chunks of conversation are related to the surrounding chunks by the structure of conversation.

Look at how the following excerpt hangs together. BM and DM, have finished their core courses, which all students did together, and moved on to options (e.g. Second Language Acquisition). They are in different classes and have not seen each other as much as before.

BM   You do you do Language Planning don't you?
DM   Yeah. I've stopped doing that though. I did stop doing that last week. SLA?
BM   I'm not doing that.
DM   Ah. We haven't got many things in common then.
BM   Wow. We've parted ways.
DM   That's right. That's right. Yes. (2)
BM   We'll have to go out sometime.
DM   Yeah.
BM   Before we forget each other's faces. // (heh heh) It's true.
DM   // (heh heh heh)

(Students on parting ways 1996)

BM and DM are not just talking: they are talking *to each other*. Each speaker is affected by what the previous speaker said, and what each speaker says affects what the next speaker will say. Thus, BM asks a question, 'You do you do Language Planning don't you?', and DM gives him an answer, 'Yeah. I've stopped doing that though'. DM expresses regret with his 'We haven't got many things in common then', and BM agrees with him: 'We've parted ways'. BM makes a suggestion, 'We'll have to go out sometime', and DM takes him up on it with 'Yeah'. Conversations tend to occur in strings of related and combined utterances.

In this unit, we examine two approaches to looking at the structure of discourse. One analyses the **exchange structure** or the conventional overall patterns that occur when people are talking. The other is **conversation analysis**, studying the way that what speakers say dictates the type of answer expected, and that speakers take turns when they interact. The two approaches are radically different in that exchange structure starts with a model and sees how real data fits it, whereas conversation analysis starts by observing real data and describes what patterns emerge. Let us begin with exchange structure.

Exchange structure

A3.3

This is the approach taken by Sinclair and Coulthard (1975) and the Birmingham School of Discourse Analysis. They studied primary school lessons and found a regular structure. Take a look at the excerpt below (from the Scottish Council for Research in Education database), from a secondary school lesson. The teacher is guiding a pupil in colouring in a map on the computer, using information from an atlas:

---

1 T: The mountain ranges brown. How will you know the mountain ranges?
2 C: They are brown.
3 T: How can you spot the mountain ranges? What's the clue from the key?
4 C: The mountain ranges are brown.
5 T: Only brown? Any other colours?
6 C: Purple.
7 T: Why do you think some are purple?
8 C: Because some are smaller than the others.
9 T: And the purple ones are what?
10 C: Inaudible.
11 T: Are they going to be the taller mountains or the shorter mountains?
12 C: Shorter.
13 T: They're actually (inaudible). The purple ones are the taller ones. These are very tall ones called the Alps, and they're purple. You've got to put them on this map. Now, are you sure you know what to do here? I'll leave you to get on with it.

(McPake/SCRE 2000)

This is not a real conversation, in the sense of people having a casual chat. There is an unequal power balance: the teacher does all the asking and Christine does all the answering, and it is the teacher who expresses the directive (see Unit A2), ordering with 'You've got to put them on this map', and the commissive, expressing intention with 'I'll leave you to get on with it'. It is quite typical of the structure of a lesson, however, according to the Birmingham School. They said that the lesson can be broken down into five levels of structure, or ranks.

The **act** is the lowest rank. Sinclair and Coulthard build on Austin and Searle's speech act categories (see Unit A2), but their acts are more general and they are defined by their interactive function. They cover the 'messiness' of spoken discourse such as fillers, as in 'you know' and 'I mean', and backchannels, as in 'Was it?' and 'Oh really?' Their categories include, for example, 'Marker', as in 'Well', 'OK' and 'Right', which mark a boundary between ideas or topics, and 'Acknowledge', which is what we have called 'backchannel'. Importantly, their categories also include acts such as 'Cue', as in 'Hands up' and 'Don't call out', which encourage a hearer to contribute, and 'Evaluate', as in 'Good' and 'Interesting', evaluating a hearer's answer. As you will appreciate, these are acts that occur more typically in a classroom than anywhere else.

Sinclair and Coulthard say that these acts tend to be carried out a fixed order of **moves**, as they call the next rank up. They find that there are three basic moves: the **initiation** from the teacher, the **response** from the student, and the **follow-up**, which is the teacher's comment on the pupil's answer, the three moves being abbreviated to **IRF**. Lines 1–12 in the geography lesson above come in pairs of 'interrogative representative' and 'statement representative'; they would say that the structure is I–R–I–R–I–R with, in this case, no follow-up.

Each part of the IRF has characteristic acts that occur in it. What follows below is just a sample of the sort of acts:

Move Acts	Function	Example
Initiation		
Inform	gives information	'The purple ones are the taller ones'
Direct	gives orders	'You've got to put them on this map'
Elicit	requests response	'Any other colours?
Cue	encourages hearer to contribute	'Hands up', 'Don't call out'
Nominate	names responder	'Christine?', 'Johnny'
Check	checks progress	'Finished?', 'Ready?'
Prompt	reinforces directives and elicitation	'Go on', 'Hurry up'
Response		
React	non-linguistic reply to a directive	[nod], [raise hand]
Reply	to an elicitation	'Purple'
Follow-up		
Accept	shows heard correct information	'Yes', 'Good', 'Fine'
Evaluate	evaluates hearer's answer	'Good', 'Interesting'

The combination of moves in the IRF structure is known as the **exchange**. The exchange is the series or chain of moves in the interaction. In the geography lesson, we have one exchange in lines 1–2, another in lines 3–4, another in lines 5–6, and so on. Exchanges then combine to make the **transaction**, the next rank up. Thus lines 1–2, 3–4, 5–6 combine to make the whole transaction, which is lines 1–16. The **lesson** is the highest rank; it is the speech event that consists of combinations of transactions.

The diagram below shows the rank structure for classroom interaction. Obviously a lesson contains many transactions, not just two as the diagram appears to suggest.

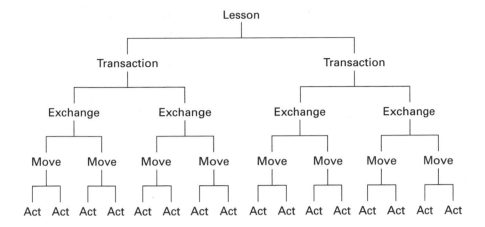

Limitations of IRF

The IRF model has certain limitations as a model of classroom transactions. It does not accommodate easily to the real-life pressures and unruliness of the classroom, such as a pupil not responding to the teacher but asking a friend to respond, or a pupil returning the question with another question.

Another limitation of the model is that it reflects the traditional teacher-centred classroom, in which the teacher is permitted long turns and the students can have short turns in response but cannot interrupt. In the 2007 Western learner-centred classroom, pupils work in pairs and groups, carrying out tasks and solving problems, and the exchanges with the teacher are generally more interactive, with the learner initiating talk.

The IRF approach as described here is rarely used today. It was explicitly restricted to classroom discourse, and there have been adaptations of this framework (Stenström, 1994). Although the structure of classroom transactions is not typical of everyday talk, it is typical of transactions of a formal and ritualistic nature with one person in a position of power over the other(s), controlling the discourse and planning it to a certain extent: interviews and trials are examples. The doctor–patient exchange in the medical surgery or accident and emergency ward context is another example. The following excerpt is taken from the British TV series *Casualty*, which takes place in the Accident and Emergency ward of a hospital. D is the doctor, N the nurse, and P the patient:

D: So how long have you been having these symptoms?
P: This morning.
D: What did you eat yesterday?
P: What did I eat?
D: Uhuh.
P: Er. I don't really remember.
N: Er his temperature's 38.5. Pulse 1/10
D: Well have a think, because you may be suffering from food poisoning.
S: Food poisoning?

(*Casualty*, BBC1, 16 December 2000)

Notice that the doctor has all the initiations and the patient all the responses. We could begin to analyse this excerpt like this: I (elicit with question), R (reply with answer), I (elicit with question), but this is where the pattern alters. The patient wants to avoid answering what he ate, because he stole it, and so he replies with a question, 'checking': 'What did I eat?'. The doctor implies a repetition of his question with his 'Well have a think, because you may be suffering from food poisoning'.

Another speech event that the IRF model has been applied to is the TV quiz show. The following excerpt is taken from the British TV programme *Who Wants to be a Millionaire?*, in which individual contestants are given a series of multiple-choice questions and, on getting each question right are offered larger sums of money. The quizmaster is Chris Tarrant, and, on this occasion, the aspirant millionaire is Gary.

CT: Which of these countries is not a member of the Commonwealth: Ghana, Malaysia, India, Philippines?

G: It's the Philippines.

CT: Sure?

G: Yeah.

CT: Final answer?

G: Final answer.

CT: It's the right answer. You've got eight thousand pounds.

(*Who Wants to be a Millionaire?*, ITV, 14 December 2000)

This transaction has such a formulaic structure that the moves used are all predictable: I (elicit with a question with four optional answers), R (reply with one of the options), I (check), R (reply reaffirming), I (check), R (reply reaffirming), F (accept/reject and reward/consolation).

A3.4   **Conversation analysis**

The exchange structure approach looked at discourse as a predetermined sequence. It started with the theory of a patterning of units and showed how what people say fits the model, thus viewing conversation as a product. Conversation analysis (CA), on the other hand, takes a 'bottom-up' approach: starting with the conversation itself, it lets the data dictate its own structure. CA looks at conversation as a linear, ongoing event that unfolds little by little and implies the negotiation of cooperation between speakers along the way, thus viewing conversation as a process. CA differs, too, in its methodology from discourse analysis. Whereas discourse analysis takes the concepts and terms of linguistics and then examines their role in real data, conversation analysis takes real data and then examines the language and demonstrates that conversation is systematically structured. Unlike exchange structure, both CA and discourse analysis are approaches that have evolved over the last decades and are very much alive today.

Let us start by defining conversation. Conversation is discourse mutually constructed and negotiated in time between speakers; it is usually informal and unplanned. Cook (1989: 51) says that talk may be classed as conversation when:

1. It is not primarily necessitated by a practical task;
2. Any unequal power of participants is partially suspended;

3. The number of the participants is small;
4. Turns are quite short;
5. Talk is primarily for the participants not for an outside audience.

This is why classroom transactions, doctor–patient interviews and TV quiz shows are not conversations: they do not have all the properties listed here. Remember that we said, in analysing the geography lesson teacher–pupil exchange above, that it was not a conversation, because of the unequal power balance. We can add now that it was necessitated by a practical task and that it might have been partly 'for an outside audience', if the instructions were intended to be overheard by the children nearby. The doctor–patient interview was primarily necessitated by the practical task of diagnosing and prescribing, and there is unequal power in that the doctor is in control of the event. The quiz show is primarily for an outside audience.

On the other hand, the dialogue about option courses on Language Planning/ SLA, with which we started this unit, can be classified as a conversation, following Cook's list of properties. It is informal (note the 'Yeah', 'Wow') and unplanned (note the two-second pause, the sentence emerging in separate clauses as in 'Before we forget each other's faces', and the spontaneous laughter). It is neither for an outside audience (the topic is interpersonal) nor necessitated by a practical task (they are just socialising, not doing serious planning). In addition, neither BM nor DM is asserting power, they are the only two participants, and their average length of turn is just six words.

Many linguists would contend Cook's property of 'not primarily necessitated by a practical task', and say that most of what we say is outcome oriented. Even the most casual of conversations have an interactional function. Casual conversations in parties can have the practical task of ascertaining whether future social cohesion is possible and desirable and, for some, whether establishing an intimate relationship is going to be feasible. Chats between old friends over coffee can have the goal of establishing norms and priorities in a particular situation and determining the course of action that one participant should take. Other linguists, such as Fairclough (1989: 12), would contend the property 'Any unequal power of participants is partially suspended', pointing out that, in all exchanges, there is unequal power, in varying degrees, and that conversation *can* occur when there are significant power differentials between participants.

Let us now turn to the patterns that CA linguists find emerge as interaction unfolds. Typically, these are unwritten conventions about taking turns, and observable pairs of utterances.

Turn-taking

Cooperation in conversation is managed by all participants through turn-taking. In most cultures, generally speaking, only one person speaks at a time: speakers take turns, first one talking and then another. All cultures have their own preferences as to how long a speaker should hold the floor, how they indicate that they have finished and another speaker can take the floor, when a new speaker can start, whether the new speaker can overlap and interrupt, when speakers can pause and for how long. For example, Latin Americans have pauses of a fraction of a second, and it is socially acceptable to overlap and interrupt, whereas North American Indians expect a two-second pause between turns, and for the Japanese it is unacceptable to interrupt.

A point in a conversation where a change of turn is possible is called a **Transition Relevance Place** or TRP. Next speakers cannot be sure that the current speaker's turn is complete, but they will usually take the end of a sentence to indicate that the turn is possibly complete. When speakers do not want to wait until the TRP, this is called an interruption. In the following example, adapted from Gumperz (1982: 175), the moment when the interruption begins is indicated with a //.

B: yes. Tell, tell me what it // is you want
A: // umm. Um, may I first of all request the introduction please?

When hearers predict that the turn is about to be completed and they come in before it is, this is an overlap. In the following example, adapted from Schiffrin (1994: 240), the overlap is indicated with a =.

Interviewee   But not no more. Yeah =
Interviewer   = What happened to them?

Note that in the orderly classroom, doctor–patient exchange and quiz show, there are neither overlaps nor interruptions. This is partly because of the power structure and the conventions: students are not supposed to interrupt the teacher but to wait till the turn is handed to them, and quiz contestants do not usually challenge the quizmaster but wait until they are asked to speak. The lack of overlaps and interruptions in the serials and shows can also be explained by the fact that they are scripted or semi-scripted: the language is more 'tidy' than real-life discourse, and the turns are pre-planned.

Each culture seems to have an unwritten agreement about the acceptable length of a pause between two turns. In any culture, if the pause is intended to carry meaning, analysts call it an **attributable silence**. In the following sort of exchange:

A: Did you have a good time last night?
B: (3) Yeah.
A: So he asked you out then?
B: He did.

B pauses for three seconds before her 'Yeah', and A attributes to this silence an affirmative answer and very positive sentiments. In the cultures in which there is a low level of tolerance of silence between turns, if there is a lull in the conversation extending past about ten seconds, speakers tend to utter something like 'um' or 'So there you go', in order to break the silence. For those who do not know each other well, a long, non-attributable silence can feel awkward.

Adjacency pairs
CA analysts say that there is a relation between acts, and that conversation contains frequently occurring patterns, in pairs of utterances known as 'adjacency pairs'. They say that the utterance of one speaker makes a certain response of the next speaker very likely. The acts are ordered with a first part and a second part and categorised as

question-answer, offer-accept, blame-deny, and so on, with each first part creating an expectation of a particular second part. This is known as **preference structure**: each first part has a **preferred** and a **dispreferred** response. The pairs are endless; here are a few examples.

a question	has the preferred response of an answer
an offer	an acceptance
an invitation	an acceptance
an assessment	an agreement
a proposal	an agreement
a greeting	a greeting
a complaint	an apology
a blame	a denial

The dispreferred responses tend to be the refusals and disagreements. These are the more unusual responses, and they can be taken as meaningful or rude. An absence of response can be taken as the hearer not having heard, not paying attention, or simply refusing to cooperate.

We can express what is going on in the Language Planning/SLA dialogue above, in terms of CA. Their adjacency pairs are mainly 'assess' and 'agree': they want to show solidarity. Even when BM's assumption in the question 'You do you do Language Planning don't you?' is wrong, DM agrees first before putting him right: 'Yeah. I've stopped doing that though' (this is known as a pseudo-agreement). DM's 'We haven't got many things in common then' gets the preferred response of agreement in BM's 'We've parted ways' which almost echoes his sentiment. This is followed by a strong agreement: 'That's right. That's right. Yes'. Finally BM suggests an outing, and DM gives the preferred response of an acceptance.

It can happen that the second part does not follow on from the first, and this is a dispreferred response. Let us imagine this scene in which a husband and wife are reading in the kitchen, while their dinner is cooking:

Wife: Do you want to test the potatoes?
Husband: Can I just finish this sentence?
Wife: Of course.

The question is not met with something that looks like an answer. Here the second question is presumably intended to mean that the husband will check the potatoes once he has finished his sentence. It implies a positive answer to the question.

Sequences
Conversation analysts claim that as speakers are mutually constructing and negotiating their conversation in time, certain sequences, which are stretches of utterances or turns, emerge. These can be pre-sequences, insertion sequences and opening and closing sequences.

Pre-sequences prepare the ground for a further sequence and signal the type of utterance to follow. There are pre-invitations ('I've got two tickets for the rugby match . . .'), pre-requests ('Are you busy right now?') and pre-announcements

('You'll never guess!'). You will have heard conversations like the following, in which A uses a pre-invitation sequence:

A: You know that new film that's on in the Odeon?
B: Yes?
A: Do you want to go and see it tonight?
B: Yeah, why not?

In the case of an **insertion sequence**, the pairs occur embedded within other adjacency pairs which act as macro-sequences. The example above could have run like this:

A: You know that new film that's on in the Odeon?
B: Yes?
A: Do you want to go and see it tonight?
B: What time does it start?
A: Eight thirty-five
B: Yeah, why not?

Here, the 'What time does it start?' and 'Eight thirty-five' constitute the insertion sequence: the rest of the conversation could in theory stand without it, except that the timing seems to be important for B. Likewise:

Wife: Do you want to test the potatoes?
Husband: This is a really interesting article about racism in the police force. They're saying there's got to be a massive education campaign to change the way people think.
Wife: There certainly has.
Husband: Yeah.
Wife: Potatoes.
Husband: Fork.

The second part, about racism, is not a response to the first, unless the irrelevance of his answer can be interpreted as implying that he is refusing to check the potatoes. The dispreferred response turns into an insertion sequence, because A repeats her request with 'Potatoes' and this time gets something that constitutes an acceptance ('Fork') even though it serves a double purpose of also making a request for a fork.

Finally, there are conventional **opening** structures and **closing** structures. Openings tend to contain a greeting, an enquiry after health and a past reference (as in 'How did it go last night?'). In the following example, Brenda, a 34-year-old house-wife, greets Lee, a fifteen-year-old student, with a formulaic health enquiry:

Brenda: Hi, Lee.
Lee: Hi. Hi, Jean.
Jean: Hi, hi.
Brenda: How are you?
Lee: Not bad. I'll be in, in a minute.

(BNC: kbf Brenda, 1991)

The British and North Americans tend to have a pre-closing-sequence rather than just ending with a farewell. This sequence can be long and drawn out on occasions. In the following exchange, we can see an insertion sequence within the 'saying goodbyes':

A: Anyway, I'm gonna have to go.
B: Yeah. See you.
A: See you tomorrow.
C: What time is it?
D: Oh. I've left my lights on.
E: Half three.
C: Three.
E: Tarrah.

(BNC: kb1 'Albert, 1992')

Since CA was born before the advent of electronic discourse, it needs to adapt to new varieties of structure and language conventions of conversations in Computer Mediated Communication (CMC). Witness this chatroom, AOL Chat 18 to 21 UK3 (6 November 2006):

Babyblue07135160: owz u
Manville1984: hi how is everyone
BluEydBoy87: im ok babe u>?
Mhodder103939930: ne girls on wanna chat on msn
Babyblue07135160: am gr8 ta
BluEydBoy87: gd gd asl plz?
V Jamesosaurus V: BabyBlue, asl?
Babyblue07135160: 19 f Scotland
BluEydBoy87: kool
Babyblue07135160: u
Adiy gangster 4l: ne girls on wanna chat on msn
BluEydBoy87: 19 m Manchester

In chatrooms, openings and closings can occur simultaneously. Studies of structural conventions of written conversations on email, message boards and blogs are under way.

Limitations of CA

One problem with CA is that there is a lack of systematicity in the sense that there is not an exhaustive list of all adjacency pairs, or a precise description of how adjacency pairs or TRPs might be recognised (Eggins and Slade 1997). In addition, researchers and students of language cannot and should not choose this form of analysis in the hope that it will lead to quantifiable results. CA sets out to be a qualitative not a quantitative approach. CA analysts do not count up instances of types of pairs, the most typical response or grammatical or lexical features, in order to find densities and distributions, or give empirical validity to claims about conversation organisation.

Another criticism levelled at CA is that it does not take into account pragmatic or sociolinguistic aspects of interaction, the background context of why and how people say what they say, the components of situation and the features of the social world and social identity such as occupation and gender of participants. For CA analysts, text is context; they focus on the sequential progression of interaction, and the way that each utterance is shaped by the previous text and shapes the following text. CA sees context as something created in talk, rather than talk as something created by context. Although some background knowledge context is relevant to text, it is only in as much as it can be seen and understood in text. The drawback is, as Fairclough (1989: 12) says, that conversation does not exist within a social vacuum. Conversation structures are connected to structures of social institutions and societies, and conventions of everyday action is determined by wider social structures. There is an approach to discourse analysis that takes into account both the structure of discourse and the social aspects of interaction: it is interactional sociolinguistics.

Interactional sociolinguistics

This approach takes into account the pragmatic and sociolinguistics aspects of interaction, as well as adjacency pairs, turn-taking and sequences, giving importance to the way that language is situated in particular circumstances in social life. It brings to the forefront the situational context and the context of shared knowledge about speakers, their histories and their purpose in speaking. It looks at grammar, social structure and cultural patterns.

Interactional sociolinguistics focuses on the fact that social groups have their own ways of expressing meaning with their language. Gumperz (1982) says that language relates to context through 'contextualisation cues'. These are the linguistic features that indicate the aspects of the context relevant to what the speaker means and that only take on their full meaning when the hearer is familiar with the rest of the context, as he or she is a member of the social group.

Let us return to the dialogue about Language Planning/SLA from the beginning of this unit. In this conversation, the speakers' adjacency pairs of agreement, echoing and acceptance, relaxed two-second pause and overlapped laughter suggest that they want to show solidarity with each other and claim in-group membership of the student academic discourse community (Swales 1990).

Their language relates to the socio-cultural context of the course. They speak the in-group code of Edinburgh MSc Applied Linguistics students, described by Cutting (2000: 142) as containing vague and implicit grammatical and lexical features, heavily dependent on the context for their meaning. They use the general noun 'things', as in 'We haven't got many *things* in common then', referring in this context to 'option courses'. They use general 'do' verbs, as in 'You do you *do* Language Planning don't you?' and 'I've stopped *doing* that though. I did stop *doing* that last week', to mean specifically 'take the course'. They use in-group proper nouns, such as *Language Planning* and *SLA*, normally referring to fields and applications of language study, but referring here to courses.

Although the main goal of interactional sociolinguistics is not to describe the structure of discourse, and that is the main goal of conversation analysis, the two approaches have come together now (Ochs, Schegloff and Thompson 1996), with analysts looking at the relationship between grammar and social interaction, within the larger schemes of human conduct and the organisation of social life.

Cultural approaches

Cross-cultural and intercultural approaches to CA expand the notion of social group out to whole nations of people who share a common first language. Studies have also looked CA in bilinguals. Here is an example of adjacency pairs in a dialogue between two Cantonese-English bilinguals, in which the mother switches to Cantonese to get a preferred response to her question (Li 2002):

Mother speaking to a 12-year-old boy who is playing with the computer.
A: Finished homework?
B: (2.0)
A: Steven, *yiu mo wan sue?*
      want NEG. PERF. review book
      'Do you want to do your homework?'
B: (1.5) I've finished.

Studies that compare the conversation structure of speakers with different cultures and analyse how conversation can break down when people of different cultures interact are discussed in Units A7–D7.

THE COOPERATIVE PRINCIPLE

A4

Understanding concepts

A4.1

❑ Observing maxims
❑ Flouting and violating
❑ Relevance Theory

Introduction

A4.2

The excerpt that opens this unit comes from a sociological survey of the living conditions of senior citizens in Scotland, and factors affecting their housing satisfaction. X is the interviewer and Y is a lady living in sheltered housing (apartments for retired people with a warden living on site, responsible keeping an eye on them and alerting public services if help is needed):

> X Do you find the place is warm enough?
> Y Yes, oh yes. Very comfortable I think. It's all that you need really, you don't need any more.
> X And you say that the warden is a nice person.
> Y Oh yes, you will get other opinions, but that's my opinion.

> **X** Well you can't please everybody can you?
> **Y** She's been very good to me.
> **X** What would the other people say?
> **Y** Ah well I don't know. I wouldn't like to repeat it because I don't really believe half of what they are saying. They just get a fixed thing into their mind. But it's always been, I mean, we had another one – this is our second one. But if she's off ill and that it's, oh off ill again and I mean she's got certificates to prove it. But they just seem, what irks them really is we can't get a warden that will be overnight you see.
> **X** Right, sort of 24 hours, 7 days a week.
>
> (Wilson and Murie 1995)

Verbal exchanges, whether interviews, conversations or service encounters, tend to run more smoothly and successfully when the participants follow certain social conventions. This interview is no exception. The interviewer asks questions, and the lady gives answers that give just the right amount of information and are relevant to the question, truthful and clear. When asked if the place is warm enough, for example, her answer, 'Yes, oh yes. Very comfortable I think', says all that is needed; she is presumably being honest; she is keeping to the topic established by the interviewer; and she is not saying anything that is ambiguous. She is following the conversational maxims of the **Cooperative Principle** (Grice 1975). Let us look at the four maxims of the principle, by seeing how they are observed.

A4.3

Observing the maxims

The first maxim of the Cooperative Principle is the maxim of **quantity**, which says that speakers should be as informative as is required, and that they should give neither too little information nor too much. Some speakers like to point to the fact that they know how much information the hearer requires or can be bothered with and say something like 'Well, **to cut a long story short**, she didn't get home till two'. People who give too little information risk their hearer not being able to identify what they are talking about because they are not explicit enough; those who give more information than the hearer needs risk boring them.

The second maxim is that of **quality**, which says that speakers are expected to be sincere, to be saying something that they believe corresponds to reality. They are assumed not to say anything that they believe to be false or anything for which they lack evidence. Some speakers like to draw their hearers' attention to the fact that they are only saying what they believe to be true and that they lack adequate evidence. In

> **A:** I'll ring you tomorrow afternoon then.
> **B:** Erm, I shall be there **as far as I know**, and in the meantime have a word with Mum and Dad if they're free. Right, bye-bye then sweetheart.
> **A:** Bye-bye, bye.
>
> (BNC: kc8 Gillian, 1991)

B says 'as far as I know', meaning 'I can't be totally sure if this is true', so that if A rings up and finds that B is not there, B is protected from accusations of lying by the fact that she did make it clear that she was uncertain. Most hearers assume that speakers are not lying, and most speakers know that.

The third is the maxim of **relation**, which says that speakers are assumed to be saying something that is relevant to what has been said before. Some speakers like to indicate how their comment has relevance to the conversation, as in the following from a market research meeting:

A: I mean, **just going back to your point**, I mean to me an order form is a contract.
     If we are going to put something in then let's keep it as general as possible.
B: Yes.

(BNC: j97 British Market Research Monthly Meeting, 1994)

The last is the maxim of **manner**, which says that we should be brief and orderly, and avoid obscurity and ambiguity. In this exchange from a committee meeting, the speaker points to the fact that he is observing the maxim:

A: Thank you Chairman. Jus – **just to clarify one point**. There is a meeting of the
     Police Committee on Monday and there is an item on their budget for the provision
     of their camera.

(BNC, j44 West Sussex Council Highways Committee Meeting, 1994)

Grice said that hearers assume that speakers observe the Cooperative Principle, and that it is the knowledge of the four maxims that allows hearers to draw inferences about the speakers' intentions and implied meaning. The meaning conveyed by speakers and recovered as a result of the hearers' inferences is known as **conversational implicature**.

Flouting the maxims

A4.4

Let us look at an example, now, of maxims *not* being observed:

> When Sir Maurice Bowra was Warden of Wadham College, Oxford, he was interviewing a young man for a place at the college. He eventually came to the conclusion that the young man would not do. Helpfully, however, he let him down gently by advising the young man, 'I think you would be happier in a larger – or a smaller – college'.
>
> (Rees 1999: 5)

Here, Sir Bowra was not adhering to the maxim of quality, since he was not really saying what he thought. Nor was he following the maxim of manner, since he was being ambiguous and contradictory. The question is, was Sir Bowra lying to the young man in order to deceive him, or was he telling a white lie, or was he just finding a nice way of letting the young man down gently? The answer hinges on whether he thought that the young man knew the painful truth and could infer what he was trying to communicate.

It is more likely that the young man did know that Sir Bowra was trying to tell him that he had failed the interview. Obviously, if Sir Bowra had said, 'You won't do', or even 'Unfortunately you're not quite good enough for this college', he might have hurt him. If the young man knew that his 'I think you would be happier in a larger – or a smaller – college' meant 'You won't do', then it is no longer a question of lying. It is a question of face saving (see Unit A5). The young man can answer, 'OK, thanks for the advice. I'll look somewhere else', and save Sir Bowra's face in his turn.

When speakers appear not to follow the maxims but expect hearers to appreciate the meaning implied, we say that they are **flouting** the maxims. Just as with an indirect speech act, the speaker implies a function different the literal meaning of form, when flouting a maxim, the speaker assumes that the hearer knows that their words should not be taken at face value and that they can infer the implicit meaning.

Flouting quantity

The speaker who flouts the maxim of quantity seems to give too little or too much information. If Peter asks, 'Well, how do I look?' and Mary replies 'Your *shoes* are nice', Peter knows that Mary is not impressed with the rest of what he is wearing. If we look again at the old lady in the sheltered home, in the example that started this unit, we see that she flouts the maxim of quantity when she says, 'Oh yes, you will get other opinions, but that's my opinion'. The interviewer knows that she is not giving all the information that he needs in order to fully appreciate what is being said. This will be why he later asks 'What would the other people say?' The old lady knew that the interviewer would know that she had more information, but maybe she wanted to be pressured for it. It is similar to 'I had an amazing time last night', which invites 'Go on – tell me what happened then!'

Flouting quality

The speaker flouting the maxim of quality may do it in several ways. Firstly, they may quite simply say something that obviously does not represent what they think. We saw an incidence of this in Sir Bowra's 'I think you would be happier in a larger – or a smaller – college', which flouts the maxim if he knew that the student would understand what he was getting at and hear the message behind his words.

Speakers may flout the maxim by exaggerating as in the **hyperbole** 'I could eat a horse', or 'I'm starving', which are well-established exaggerating expressions. No speaker would expect their hearer to say, 'What, you could eat a whole horse?' or 'I don't think you are dying of hunger – you don't even look thin'. Hearers would be expected to know that the speaker simply meant that they were very hungry. Hyperbole is often at the basis of humour. Take this example from *Social Studies*:

> Remember that as a teenager you are at the last stage in your life when you will be happy to hear that the phone is for you.
>
> (Leobowitz, 1985, quoted in Sherrin 1995)

It is an exaggeration to say that adults are *never* happy to hear that the phone is for them, even though this may often be the case. Anybody reading this humorous line would know not to take it at its face value.

Similarly, a speaker can flout the maxim of quality by using a **metaphor**, as in 'My house is a refrigerator in January' or 'Don't be such a wet blanket – we just want to have fun'. Here again, hearers would understand that the house was very cold indeed, and the other person is trying to reduce other people's enjoyment. Similarly, we all know how to interpret the meaning behind the words 'Love's a disease. But curable' from *Crewe Train* (Macaulay 1926) and 'Religion . . . is the opium of the people' (Marx 1844). Conventional euphemisms can also be put into this category too. When people say 'I'm going to wash my hands' meaning 'I'm going to urinate', and when they say 'She's got a bun in the oven' meaning 'She's pregnant', or 'He kicked the bucket' meaning 'He died', the implied sense of the words is so well-established that the expressions can only mean one thing.

The last two main ways of flouting the maxim of quality are **irony** and **banter**, and they form a pair. As Leech (1983: 144) says, 'While irony is an apparently friendly way of being offensive (mock-politeness), the type of verbal behaviour known as 'banter' is an offensive way of being friendly (mock impoliteness).'

Thus, in the case of irony, the speaker expresses a positive sentiment and implies a negative one. If a student comes down to breakfast one morning and says, 'If only you knew how much I love being woken up at 4 a.m. by a fire alarm', she is being ironic and expecting her friends to know that she means the opposite. **Sarcasm** is a form of irony that is not so friendly; in fact it is usually intended to hurt, as in 'This is a lovely undercooked egg you've given me here, as usual. Yum!' or 'Why don't you leave *all* your dirty clothes on the lounge floor and then you only need wash them when someone breaks a leg trying to get to the sofa?'

Banter, on the contrary, expresses a negative sentiment and implies a positive one. It sounds like a mild aggression, as in 'You're nasty, mean and stingy. How can you only give me one kiss?', but it is intended to be an expression of friendship or intimacy. Banter can sometimes be a tease and sometimes a flirtatious comment. The following example contains a slightly different example of banter: BM has just told AF that his wife has got a job teaching English as a Foreign Language, and AF, herself a teacher of EFL pretends to be angry:

AF   I'm beginning to realise why em why jobs in language schools run out so sharply in the autumn and in the spring. It's all these damn MSc students and their wives, // (heh heh)

BM   // (heh heh heh heh)

AF   Now I know why I was never wanted after October.

BF   Yeah that's right. (heh)

(Students on EFL schools 1996)

This example shows that hyperbole and banter can coexist – she is both exaggerating and mock-attacking. The danger with banter is that it can offend if the hearers do not recover the conversational implicature, or if they suspect that there is an element of truth in the words.

Flouting relation

If speakers flout the maxim of relation, they expect that the hearers will be able to imagine what the utterance did *not* say and make the connection between their utterance and the preceding one(s). Thus, if we hear 'The baby cried. The mommy picked it up' (Garfinkel 1967), we assume that the 'mommy' was the mother of the crying baby and that she picked the baby up because it was crying. Similarly, in the following exchange:

A: There's somebody at the door.
B: I'm in the bath.

B expects A to understand that his present location is relevant to her comment that there is someone at the door, and that he cannot go and see who it is because he is in the bath.

Flouting manner

Those who flout the maxim of manner, appearing to be obscure, are often trying to exclude a third party. Thus if a husband says to a wife: 'I was thinking of going out to get some of that funny white stuff for somebody', he speaks in an ambiguous way, because he is avoiding saying 'ice-cream' and 'Michelle', so that his little daughter does not become excited and ask for the ice-cream before her meal.

A4.5

Violating the maxims

A speaker can be said to **violate** a maxims when they know that the hearer will *not* know the truth and will only understand the surface meaning of the words. They intentionally generate a misleading implicature (Thomas 1995: 73); maxim violation is unostentatiously, quietly deceiving. The speaker deliberately supplies insufficient information, says something that is insincere, irrelevant or ambiguous, and the hearer wrongly assumes that they are cooperating.

If a speaker violates the maxim of **quantity**, they do not give the hearer enough information to know what is being talked about, because they do not want the hearer to know the full picture. The speaker is not implying anything; they are 'being economical with the truth'. You may know the Peter Sellers film in which Inspector Clouseau asks a hotel receptionist about a little dog beside the desk:

Clouseau: Does your dog bite?
Receptionist: No.
Clouseau: [Bends down to stroke it and gets bitten] Ow! You said your dog
                          doesn't bite!
Receptionist: That isn't my dog.

The receptionist knew that he was talking about the dog in front of her and not her dog at home, yet she intentionally did not give him enough information, for reasons best known to herself. If a husband asks 'How much did that new dress cost, darling?', and the wife replies 'Less than the last one', she ambiguously covers up the price of the dress by not saying *how much* less than her last dress.

The same wife could have answered by violating the maxim of **quality** and not been sincere, giving him the wrong information: 'Thirty-five pounds'. If Mr Bowra, in the example above, knew that the young man did not realise that he had failed the interview because of his performance, and if he knew that the young man would believe that it was the size of the college that was wrong for him, then he could be said to be telling a lie, because he was violating the maxim of quality.

Not all violations of the maxim of quality are blameworthy. In many cultures it is acceptable to say to a child of five, 'Mummy's gone on a little holiday because she needs a rest', rather than 'Mummy's gone away to decide whether she wants a divorce or not'. A lie that protects is a lie with good intentions, what we call a **white lie**. If Sir Bowra knew that the young man did not realise that he had failed the interview, and that he would be devastated to be told that, then he is telling a white lie and covering up the truth to be kind.

In many cultures, it is acceptable to violate the maxim of quality if one does not know the hearer very well, and it may in fact be part of polite behaviour to (see the Politeness Principle in Unit A5). Thus, we might prefer not to say to a shop assistant, as we hand back a dress, 'This looks awful on; I don't want it after all', but rather 'I'll go away and think about it and maybe come back later'. This is a conventional lie, but the shop assistant might hope that it is true. The following advice comes from *Teach Yourself Beginners Chinese*:

> Even if your Chinese is very poor you will usually be told how good it is! The correct response to such compliments is **Guojiang, guojiang** (*you praise me too much*), or **Nali, nali** (lit. *where, where?*) (meaning that you don't see it the way they do).
>
> (Scurfield and Song 1996: 92)

In answer to 'How much did that new dress cost, darling?' the wife could have answered violating the maxim of **relation**, in order to distract him and change the topic: 'I know, let's go out tonight. Now, where would you like to go?' She could have violated the maxim of **manner** and said, 'A tiny fraction of my salary, though probably a bigger fraction of the salary of the woman that sold it to me', in the hopes that that could be taken as an answer and the matter could be dropped. In the sheltered home example, the old lady answers the interviewer's question in a way that could be said to be violating the maxim of manner, in that she says everything except what the interviewer wants to know:

X   What would the other people say?
Y   Ah well I don't know. I wouldn't like to repeat it because I don't really believe half of what they are saying. They just get a fixed thing into their mind.

Her 'half of what they are saying' is an obscure reference to the other people's opinion, and 'a fixed thing' contains a general noun containing vague reference. She may be using these expressions to avoid giving a brief and orderly answer, for the moment.

Other forms of non-observance of maxims   A4.6

Grice listed two other ways to fail to fulfil a maxim: to infringe it and to opt out. A speaker infringing a maxim or opting out of a maxim is not implying something different from the words or being intentionally misleading.

A speaker **infringing** a maxim fails to observe a maxim because of their imperfect linguistic performance. This can happen if the speaker has an imperfect command of the language (a child or a foreign learner), if their performance is impaired (nervousness, drunkenness, excitement), if they have a cognitive impairment, or if they are simply incapable of speaking clearly (Thomas 1995: 74). President Bush is a master at infringing the maxim of manner:

> Our enemies are innovative and resourceful, and so are we. They never stop thinking about new ways to harm our country and our people, and neither do we.
>
> George W. Bush, Washington, DC, 5 August 2004

> You never know what your history is going to be like until long after you're gone.
>
> George W. Bush, Washington, DC, 5 May 2006

A speaker **opting out** of a maxim indicates an unwillingness to cooperate, although they do not want to appear uncooperative. They cannot reply in the way expected, sometimes for legal or ethical reasons, and they say so (e.g. 'I'm afraid I can't give you that information'). Examples are a priest or counsellor refusing to repeat information given in confidence, and a police officer refusing to release the name of an accident victim until the relatives have been informed (Thomas 1995: 74–5).

<table><tr><td>A4.7</td></tr></table>

Limitations of the Cooperative Principle

A major objection that one may have to Grice's model is that different cultures, countries and communities have their own ways of observing and expressing maxims for particular situations. This we revisit in Units A7–D7, Culture and language learning. Let us examine this with some cross-cultural examples of maxim observance. In Britain it is not acceptable to say, 'We'll call you in about two weeks' and then not call, as this would be considered a violation of the maxim of quality, whereas in some countries this is quite a normal way of flouting the maxim and saying 'We're not interested'.

The maxim of quantity is another that separates cultures. In Britain, to talk of a family member always giving them the label of the relationship, as in 'My nephew Paul came round last night', is thought to be unnecessary and an opting out of the maxim. In other cultures this is a routine form of reference. In the United States, the question 'How are you?' expects the answer 'Fine'; any interlocutor that launches into a full description of their state of health would again be thought to be violating the maxim of quantity. On the other hand, in other cultures, 'How are you?' is a genuine request after the state of health and expects a full report.

The whole matter of conversational implicature in requests and suggestions may just be a very British thing. In the United States, instead of saying 'Do you find it's getting a bit chilly in here?' as the British do, people tend to come straight to the point and say, 'I'm cold. Is it OK if I put the fire on?' This is related to the matter of politeness and cultural conventions.

The second problem with the Cooperative Principle is that there is often an overlap between the four maxims. It can be difficult to say which one is operating, and it would be more precise to say that there are two or more operating at once. In the following example, the meaning lies in a flouting of the maxims of both quantity and manner. A woman (we will call her Pat) telephoned a female friend (Melanie), whose boyfriend (Phil) was staying for the weekend, and part of the conversation ran like this:

Pat: How's it going with Phil?
Melanie: One of us thinks it's OK.

Melanie intended Pat to infer that Phil was satisfied but that she herself was not. The expression 'One of us' carried little explicit information and it was ambiguous, but Pat assumed that it was relevant to her question and understood that Melanie was flouting maxims so that Phil, who must have been within earshot, would not know that he was the topic of conversation.

Sperber and Wilson (1995) say that all maxims can be reduced to the maxim of relation, since relevance is a natural feature of all exchanges in which speakers have the aim of achieving successful communication. The maxim of quantity can be expressed as 'give the right amount of relevant information', the maxim of quality can be stated as 'give sincere relevant information', and the maxim of manner 'give unambiguous relevant information'. We assume that everything we read and hear contains utterances that make sense, and that they are relevant to each other and form a coherent whole. Sperber and Wilson say that the principle of relevance applies without exceptions, so that it is not a question of communicators following, violating or flouting the principle.

Relevance Theory

A4.8

Sperber and Wilson propose Relevance Theory and say that conversational implicature is understood by hearers simply by selecting the relevant features of context and recognising whatever speakers say as relevant to the conversation. When hearers and readers make sense of a text, they interpret the connections between utterances as meaningful, making inferences by drawing on their own background knowledge of the world. They say that the purpose of communication is not to 'duplicate thoughts' but to 'enlarge mutual cognitive environments' (1995: 193).

The degree of relevance is governed by **contextual effects** and **processing effort**. Contextual effects include such things as adding new information, strengthening or contradicting an existing assumption, or weakening old information. The more contextual effects, the greater the relevance of a particular fact. A new fact unconnected to anything already known is not worth processing, whereas a new fact taken with something already known is worth processing.

As far as the processing effort is concerned, the theory says that the less effort it takes to recover a fact, the greater the relevance. The speaker assumes which facts are accessible for the hearer and speaks in such a way that the hearer can make the correct inferences without too much effort. The context for the interpretation of an utterance is chosen by the hearer, and the speaker assumes that the facts are relatively accessible for the hearer. The hearer interprets what is said by finding an accessible context that produces 'the maximum amount of new information with the minimum amount of processing effort' (Trask 1999: 58).

To understand an utterance is to prove its relevance, and proving relevance is determined by the **accessibility** of its relevance to the addressee. Take a look at the next example, adapted from Grundy's (2000) data:

A: Well there's a shuttle service sixty pounds one way. When do you want to go?
B: At the weekend.
A: What weekend?
B: Next weekend. How does that work? You just turn up for the shuttle service?
A: That might be cheaper. Then that's fifty.

(Grundy 2000)

Here, B assumes that A will know that 'At the weekend' means 'Next weekend'. A may know that that is what he means, but she needs to be sure, since she is about to sell an air-ticket. A's answer, 'That might be cheaper. Then that's fifty', is not a full answer; a more explicit answer would have been: 'If you buy the shuttle now, you have a seat booked, and it's £60. If you just turn up on the day to buy the ticket, it's £50'. A assumes that B can infer all of this and fill in the missing words.

This filling in the missing words, elaborating or 'enriching the propositional form' is what Sperber and Wilson call **explicature** and they say that this is a necessary stage before implicature. They say that the explicature of an utterance consists of the propositions that are explicitly communicated by the speaker, and that some of this has to be inferred by relevance-driven processes. It is usually the context, or cognitive environment, that stops what we say being ambiguous and that helps the hearer fill in any incomplete parts of the utterance or understand the connection between utterances and thus infer the meaning implied. Sperber and Wilson say that nothing is ambiguous, taken in its proper cognitive environment.

A4.9

Limitations of Relevance Theory

Relevance Theory too has its limitations, however. As Mey (1993: 81) says, the fact that Sperber and Wilson feel that their principle accounts for all Grice's maxims, and that it is without exception and irrefutable means that the notion of relevance is so encompassing that it loses its explanatory force. In fact, it could be said that everything implies something that is not said, since every utterance depends on associations and background knowledge, even 'What's the time?' which may mean 'Don't you think we should be getting ready to go now?', 'You're boring me' or anything at all according to the context.

Another limitation of Relevance Theory is that it says nothing about interaction and does not include cultural or social dimensions, such as age, gender, status and nationality. An objection that one may have to Sperber and Wilson's model, as with Grice's Cooperative Principle model, is that different cultures, countries and communities have their own ways of observing and expressing maxims.

POLITENESS

Understanding concepts

❏ Negative politeness
❏ Positive politeness
❏ Maxims of politeness

Introduction

In pragmatics, when we talk of 'politeness', we do *not* refer to the social rules of behaviour such as letting people go first through a door, or wiping your mouth on the serviette rather than on the back of your hand. The following anecdote is an example of the politeness that we are talking about:

> During her successful General Election campaign in 1979, Margaret Thatcher undertook various photo opportunities to emphasise how in touch she was with ordinary people. On one occasion, she was photographed standing on the back of a platform bus.* As this was taking some time, she said, 'I'm beginning to feel like a clippie** . . .' And then, observers recall, you see the realisation in her eyes that she might have said something patronising, so she added, '. . . who are all doing a *wonderful* job.'
>
> (Graeme Greene, BBC Radio *Quote . . . Unquote*, 1979)
> * a double-decker bus which has an open entrance at the back.
> ** a bus conductor, who sells and clips tickets.

We refer to the choices that are made in language use, the linguistic expressions that give people space and show a friendly attitude to them. This anecdote shows how important it is to be seen to show a friendly attitude, if one wants to save face and be appreciated in return.

Politeness and face

Brown and Levinson (1987) analysed politeness and said that in order to enter into social relationships, we have to acknowledge and show an awareness of the **face**, the public self-image, the sense of self, of the people that we address. They said that it is a universal characteristic across cultures that speakers should respect each others' expectations regarding self-image, take account of their feelings and avoid Face Threatening Acts (FTAs). When FTAs are unavoidable, speakers can redress the threat with **negative politeness** (which does *not* mean being impolite!) that respects the hearer's **negative face**, the need to be independent, have freedom of action, and not be imposed on by others. Or they can redress the FTA with **positive politeness**, which attends the **positive face**, the need to be accepted and liked by others, treated as a member of the group, and to know one's wants are shared by others.

There are many ways of achieving one's goals and showing an awareness of face. Let us imagine that you are in a resource centre trying to find a particular website, but since you are having no luck, you would like one of your fellow students to help you. If you want to **avoid an FTA**, you can avoid saying anything at all. You can just show to those around you that you are having difficulty, by sighing loudly and shaking your head, and maybe someone will notice and ask if you need help.

Off record

On the other hand, you can say something. You are then faced with a choice: to **do the FTA** on record or off record. If you do it **off record**, you ask for help *indirectly* and say, in a voice loud enough for your neighbours to hear, something like 'I wonder where on earth that website is. I wish I could remember the address'. This particular off-record communicative act is an indirect speech act (see Unit A2, Speech acts) in which you are using a declarative representative functioning as a question 'to yourself' that also needs the hearers to interpret it as a directive, a request for help, as in 'Help me find where on earth that website is'. This off-record communicative act also constitutes a flouting of the maxim of quantity (see Unit A4, Cooperative Principle), if you consider that your not saying openly that you need help means that you are not appearing to make your contribution as informative as possible. It is off record because, if challenged to say that you were asking for help finding the website, you could in theory deny that you were.

Indirectness in the form of indirect speech acts and cooperative maxim flouting allows a speaker to make suggestions, requests, offers or invitations quite casually, without addressing them to anyone in particular, therefore. The illocutionary force will most likely be understood by hearers, but they can choose to ignore it.

Indirectness also enables speakers to address particular people but be polite by giving them options and retreating behind the literal meaning of the words. You may recall the example of a flouting of the maxim of quantity that we saw in Unit A4, in which B was threatening A's face and passing negative judgement on his clothes, answering his 'Well, how do I look?' with 'Your *shoes* are nice'.

A speaker can also be polite off record by flouting the cooperative maxim of relation and dropping a hint, as in 'Interesting book. Pity I don't have $30 on me', or flouting the maxim of quality and pretending to ask a question, as in 'Why does no one ever throw out the rubbish in this house?', or flouting the maxim of manner by being obscure and ambiguous, as in 'Looks like someone had a good time last night'. Hearers usually know what is implied, but they have the freedom to respond to it or ignore it, without losing face. In this sense, the speaker is showing a great awareness of face and not imposing much at all.

On record – baldly

Back in the resource centre with your computer, you could turn to your neighbour and say, 'Mary, tell me the address for that website they were talking about this morning', and then she has to tell you, unless she wants to be rude or actually does not know the address. If a speaker makes a suggestion, request, offer or invitation in an open and direct way, we say that they are doing an FTA **bald on record**. These are direct speech acts; such utterances tend to contain the imperative with no mitigating devices, as in 'This door-handle's falling off. Fix it' or 'Give that note to me', which leave the hearers little option but do as they are told or be seen as uncooperative. For this reason, this is the most face-threatening mode of action.

On the other hand, sometimes bald-on-record events can actually be oriented to saving the hearer's face. In 'Have some more curry' or 'Marry me', the risk that the hearer may not wish to be imposed upon is small, and the FTA is quite pleasant. The directness also makes the hearer less reluctant to threaten the speaker's face by impinging through accepting: they are unlikely to say 'No, I can't possibly deprive you of any more curry' or 'No, I really shouldn't occupy your life like that'. For this reason, the firmer the invitation, the more polite it is (Brown and Levinson, 1987). Besides, directness often indicates a wish to be seen as socially close, as we shall see later in this unit.

Most of the time, however, speakers do FTAs on record, taking account of face, with 'face-management'. They can do this on record, with redressive action, using negative politeness or positive politeness.

On record – with negative politeness

Negative politeness strategies pay attention to negative face, by demonstrating the distance between interlocutors, and avoiding intruding on each other's territory. Speakers use them to avoid imposing or presuming, and to give the hearer options.

Speakers can avoid imposing by emphasising the importance of the other's time and concerns, using apology and hesitation, or a question giving them the opportunity to say no. In your resource centre, you could have asked for help with the website by saying to Mary, 'I don't want to be nuisance, but could you possibly tell me the address for that website they were talking about this morning?' Note that the politeness can be quite formulaic, as in 'Sorry to bother you. I couldn't borrow $30, could I?', 'Feel free to come to the party if you have got the time'. Note that in the second example, the speaker gives the hearer the option to turn down the invitation to the party without losing face, by 'handing them an excuse on a plate': they did not have time.

The extent of the option-giving influences the degree of politeness. In many cases, the greater chance that the speaker offers the hearer to say 'no', the more polite it is. Thus 'I couldn't borrow $30, could I?' is more polite than 'Could I borrow $30?' The former, being a negative question, follows the negative politeness strategy that Brown and Levinson call 'be pessimistic'.

Speakers can minimise the imposition by making it seem smaller than it is, or by adding devices such as hedges that mitigate the imposition, such as 'if possible', 'in a way', 'I wonder'. Witness 'Would you mind moving just slightly? I can't see the screen very clearly' and 'Er, I think you may be late if you don't go now'.

They can also emphasise the distance between interlocutors by impersonalising, stating the imposition as a general rule ('People generally leave plenty of time, going from here, if they don't want to be late') or a nominalisation:

> The aim is not to – not to gain weight, and, the control has been lost when – when it's necessary to binge.
>
> (BNC: fl6 Eating Disorders: Television Discussion, date unknown)

Pre-sequences can also be used with a negative-face-saving function. As you may remember, in Unit A3, Conversation, there was this instance of a pre-invitation:

A: You know that new film that's on in the Odeon?
B: Yes?
A: Do you want to go and see it tonight?
B: Yeah, why not?

Here, A gives B space, in that she gives him time to predict what speech act is coming and stall it if he wishes.

On record – with positive politeness

Positive politeness strategies aim to save positive face, by demonstrating closeness and solidarity, appealing to friendship, making other people feel good and emphasising that both speakers have a common goal. Asking about the website, in the resource centre, with on record with positive politeness would mean emphasising the strengthening of friendship and closeness: 'Mary sweetie – I'd really appreciate it if you'd tell me the address for that website they were talking about this morning'.

Brown and Levinson (1987) say that one of the main types of positive politeness strategy is claiming common ground. Speakers can do this by attending to the hearer's interests, wants and needs. The invitation to the party that we saw in the discussion above on negative politeness can be rephrased to show positive politeness thus: 'I know you hate parties, Jen, but come anyway. We'll all be there, and it'll be cool seeing if Ally is with Andrea! Come on – get a life!' This example contains many solidarity strategies – knowledge of personal information, nicknames, shared dialect and slang, and gossip. The inviter claims common ground by including her in a common activity, by exaggerating the interest, predicting that the party will be 'cool', and by using in-group identity markers: her familiar nickname 'Jen' and young people's in-group slang 'cool' and 'get a life'. The gossip about Ally and Andrea asserts common ground: the inviter is saying, 'I know that you know about them, just like we do'. In addition, the speaker here is optimistic that the hearer will accept the invitation.

A common positive politeness strategy is that of seeking agreement and avoiding disagreement. One way of avoiding disagreement is to use a pseudo-agreement as in:

Jean: Don't wash them and put them on the rack.
Raymond: But all //
Jean: // Get the dryer, dry them, do the tops, and then it's all done.
Raymond: Yes – yes but if you do that, your – your – your tea-towel's soaking, and at the end of the night, nothing's getting dried.

The speaker can also show that hearer and speaker are 'cooperators', by offering and promising, and assuming reciprocity, as in: 'If I let you lend you my Artic Monkeys CD, will you lend me your Killers one?'

Relationship with the Cooperative Principle

The politeness strategies sometimes conflict with the Cooperative Principle. Speakers can violate cooperative maxims if they want to show positive politeness. If you were to answer the question 'Well, how do I look?' with 'Good!', even though you thought the person looked awful, you would be choosing to violate the maxim of quality, rather than offend A with the truth. Speakers may also choose to opt out of cooperative maxims to show negative politeness. Speakers can opt out of the maxim of quantity (giving more information than is required), when making a polite request to strangers: 'I'm terribly sorry to bother you but I couldn't help noticing you've got a copy of the new Artic Monkeys CD, and I wondered whether you wouldn't mind me just having a quick look at it'.

Politeness maxims

A5.4

According to Leech (1983), there is a Politeness Principle with conversational maxims. He lists six maxims: tact, generosity, approbation, modesty, agreement and sympathy. The first and second form a pair, as do the third and fourth.

Let us start with the maxims of tact and generosity. The **tact** maxim ('perhaps the most important kind of politeness in English-speaking society', Leech 1983: 107) focuses on the hearer, and says 'minimise cost to other' and 'maximise benefit to other'. The first part of this maxim fits in with Brown and Levinson's negative politeness strategy of minimising the imposition, and the second part reflects the positive politeness strategy of attending to the hearer's interests, wants and needs. Examples are 'Could you I interrupt you for half a second – what was that website address?' and 'If I could just clarify this then'. The maxim of **generosity**, the flip-side of the tact maxim since it focuses on the speaker, says 'minimise benefit to self' and 'maximise cost to self'. This is present in 'Could I copy down the website address?', and this online advertisement (http://boston.craigslist.org/bmw/hss/292190956.html):

Let Me Clean While You Relax

Let us move on to the second pair: approbation (other) and modesty (self). The maxim of **approbation** says 'minimise dispraise of other' and 'maximise praise of other'. The first part of the maxim is somewhat similar to the politeness strategy of avoiding disagreement. The second part fits in with the positive politeness strategy of making other people feel good by showing solidarity. Examples are 'Mary, you're very efficient and make notes of everything – you must have a copy of that website address we were given today' and 'I heard you singing at the karaoke last night. It was, um . . . different'. You may remember Sir Bowra's comment to the young man applying to his college (see Unit A4, Cooperative Principle); he avoided telling him that he was no good by reducing his dispraise to an absolute minimum, with 'I think you would be happier in a larger – or a smaller – college'.

The **modesty** maxim, on the other hand, says 'minimise praise of self' and 'maximise dispraise of self'. The website example would be 'Oh, I'm so stupid – I didn't make a note of that website address! Did you?' Witness also

> I don't dislike going to the dentist, but, but I'm terrible with dentists, hairdressers, and all these things, though, I work quite hard, I never really sort of . . .
> (BNC: kcb Graeme, 1992)

Modesty is possibly a more complex maxim than the others, since the maxim of quality can sometimes be violated in observing it. Cutting (1998) found that in conferences, members of the audience preface their questions to the speaker with self-deprecating expressions such as:

A very obvious question from a non-specialist . . .
There is an idiot question I want to ask you . . .
Um, I don't know much about this area but I think that . . .

Although on the surface, the questioners seem to be saving their own face, they are also saving the face of the speaker by reducing the threat of their question. The following story illustrates well how exaggerated modesty can be a counterbalance to exaggerated praise.

> In the 1930's, a critic described the actor Robert Donat as a 'half-Greek god who had winged his way from Olympus'. Donat's response was to sigh, 'Actually, I'm a half-Pole who's winged his way from Withington, Manchester.'
>
> (Williams 1973)

The last two maxims do not form a pair, and Leech gives them less importance than the others. The maxim of **agreement** – 'minimise disagreement between self and other' and 'maximise agreement between self and other' – is in line with Brown and Levinson's positive politeness strategies of 'seek agreement' and 'avoid disagreement', to which *they* attach great importance. We saw an example of this above in:

Raymond: Yes – yes but if you do that, your – your – your tea-towel's soaking, and at
           the end of the night, nothing's getting dried.

The **sympathy** maxim – 'minimise antipathy between self and other' and 'maximise sympathy between self and other' – includes such polite speech acts as congratulate, commiserate and express condolences, as in, 'I was sorry to hear about your father'. This small group of speech acts is already taken care of in Brown and Levinson's positive politeness strategy of attending to the hearer's interests, wants and needs. Note that the speaker does not say, 'I was sorry to hear about your father's *death*'. Speakers often soften the distress and embarrassment with euphemisms. We saw a polite euphemism when we discussed metaphors flouting the maxim of quality (see Unit A4, Cooperative Principle): 'I'm going to wash my hands' meaning 'I'm going to urinate'.

Very close to this is a maxim proposed by Cruse (2000: 366): **consideration**, which is 'minimise discomfort/displeasure of other' and 'maximise comfort/pleasure of other'. Cruse points out that this is Leech's Pollyanna Principle – 'always look on the bright side of life', by softening painful, distressing, embarrassing, shocking events. We are back to Brown and Levinson's positive politeness strategy of making other people feel good. An amusing tale told by Billy Connolly, the Scottish actor and stand-up comedian, will serve as an example:

Seeking to cheer up a patient in hospital, the visitor told her: 'You're lucky to be in here. It's pelting outside.'

(Rees 1999: 108)

Overlaps and gaps

A5.5

Brown and Levinson differ from Leech, in that they are social psychologists who start from data, and he takes a philosophical approach starting from principles. This unit has shown, however, that there is considerable overlap between the categories of Brown and Levinson's model and the categories of Leech's model. There is also overlap within both Brown and Levinson's model and Leech's: the categories themselves are not mutually exclusive.

One utterance can contain both positive and negative politeness. The speaker in the following example mixes the two quite successfully: 'Could you be a pal and give me a lift home? Don't bother if you're not going my way'. Similarly, one utterance can obey two or more maxims. In the following, the speaker observes both tact and generosity: 'Have as many cakes as you want'.

Another criticism that could be levelled at Leech's model is that a new maxim could be added for every new situation that occurs. Remember that we saw that Cruse wanted to add a consideration maxim. There should also possibly be a **patience** maxim, which says 'minimise the urgency for other' and 'maximise the lack of urgency for other'. To give an example: 'Could I take a quick look at your paper? No hurry – whenever you're finished with it'. There may be endless gaps not covered by the maxims; no model can describe all human interactions.

Politeness and context

A5.6

Form and function

Politeness is a pragmatic phenomenon. Politeness lies not in the form and the words themselves, but in their function and intended social meaning. In the following, the form is polite but the intention is not:

Do me a favour – piss off.   (*The Older Woman*. BBC Radio 4, 1994)

So, if you'd be as kind as to shut up, I'd appreciate it.   (Leonard 1989)

Interestingly, if you type 'polite request' into Google, the majority of the first hits are anything but polite: writers say something quite negative in a forceful ironic way. Here is an example from a blog site at http://tygerland.net/2007/01/24/a-polite-request/:

A polite request

Please don't bother commenting on this site if you're bereft of a sense of humour.
I don't pay for this bandwidth for humourless individuals to miss the point completely.

If speakers use more polite forms than the context requires, hearers might suspect that there is an intention other than that of redressing an FTA, as in the playwright Richard Brinsley's invitation to a young lady (attributed in *The Perfect Hostess*, 1980),

'Won't you come into my garden? I would like my roses to see you', which is aimed to flatter.

Politeness is not the same as **deference**, which is a polite form expressing distance from and respect for people of a higher status, and does not usually include an element of choice. Deference is built into languages such as Korean and Japanese and can be seen in the pronouns of many European languages (tu/vous, tu/Usted, du/Sie). It is rare to find it grammatically signalled in English, although it is present in honorifics such as 'Sir' and 'Madam'.

Situational context

Since politeness is a pragmatic phenomenon, it is influenced by elements of the context. There are two situational context factors that influence the way that we make a request. One is the size of imposition, the routiness and reasonableness of task, and the rule seems to be 'the greater the imposition, the more indirect the language is'. For example, to borrow a large sum of money, one might employ a series of hedges and other negative politeness phenomena, as in, 'I couldn't borrow thirty dollars, could I? I know it's a bit much to spring this on you', and to borrow a small sum, one's request could be bald on record, as in 'Give me five cents'.

The other factor is the formality of the context, and here the tendency is 'the greater the formality, the more indirect the language is'. Whereas a student, sitting informally in the common room over a coffee, might stop a colleague from interrupting her with a direct directive bald on record, 'Hang on – I haven't finished!', she would say to the same colleague, in the formal context of a seminar, 'I wonder if I might just finish what I'm trying to say', an indirect directive redressing the FTA with negative politeness.

Social Context

The choice of the politeness formulation depends on the social distance and the power relation between speakers. When there is social distance, politeness is encoded, and there is more indirectness; where there is less social distance, there is less negative politeness and indirectness. The variables that determine social distance are degree of familiarity and differences of status, roles, age, gender, education, class, occupation and ethnicity.

The degree of familiarity between speakers is one of the most obvious social variables that affect how politeness is expressed. Speakers who know each other well do not need to use formulas encoding politeness strategies, and when they do use them, it can imply quite the opposite of politeness. Basil Fawlty, in the British TV comedy series *Fawlty Towers*, over-applies Leech's generosity maxim to his wife with his 'Have another vat of wine, dear'. He flouts the maxim of quality since he is not offering her a vat of wine, but using a directive to imply an expressive, to deplore the amount that she drinks.

Differences of status, roles, age, gender, education, class, occupation and ethnicity can give speakers power and authority. It is those of the lower status, the less dominant role, etc., who use more indirectness and more negative politeness features such as hedges and mitigation, than those with higher status, etc., do. Expressions that are bald on record are used by people who assume that they have got power. Thus is it that a lecturer, because of their role and status, is expected to give generalised orders when addressing a class of students, directly and bald on record, as in the following, taken from the transcription of a seminar entitled 'Using Video Clips in ELT':

> Now. What we're going to do is um a quick game of twenty questions: you'll get some points up here. Now these people can only answer Yes or No, so you must ask Yes/No questions. So you can't ask a question like: 'What happened?'
>
> (BASE 2000)

Conversely, a participant in a COHSE/NALGO/NUPE meeting has to address the chair using the negative politeness devices of hedges and requests for permission to speak: 'Erm chairman could I ask a question in relation to that?' (BNC: f7j business meeting, 1992).

This is a big area of study. To take an example, Mills (2003) examined the relationship between gender, communities of practice and politeness, looking at the way that speakers negotiate with what they see as gendered stereotypes within their particular group. She says that only participants within communities can 'judge whether a language item or phrase is polite for them or not', although 'community members do not necessarily agree on which forms of behaviour are the dominant ones': they are negotiated and changed by the community.

Cultural Context

The relationship between indirectness and social variables is not so simple: the whole issue of politeness and language is exceedingly culture-bound, as you will see in Unit A7. Culture and language learning is a major variable in differentiating one culture from another along the lines of politeness and saving face. As interactional sociolinguist Tannen says, the use of indirectness 'can hardly be understood without the cross-cultural perspective' (1994: 32–4). In some cultures, for example, a lecturer making suggestions to a student would do so directly, bald on record, because of their status. This explains why some international students interpret the option-giving literally, when faced with British lecturers' indirect suggestions, negative politeness hedges and mitigation, as in, 'I think this part of your essay could possibly come a little bit nearer the beginning, if you like'.

Travellers may find that the British put more emphasis on negative politeness than other cultures do. In Cuba, for example, friends should not show any distance at all, and to say 'thank you' for a cup of coffee, 'maximising praise of other', can cause offence as it appears to put up barriers. Thomas (1995: 161) mentions that Chinese hosts will choose a guest's menu for them and put the 'choicest pieces' on their plate, to show positive politeness. Here it seems that the tact maxim 'maximise benefit to other' of positive politeness in the Chinese mind overrides the 'don't impose' and 'give others options' maxim of negative politeness.

The use of the maxims of tact and generosity varies greatly from country to country. Thomas (1995: 161) quotes a Japanese PhD student who, on drafts of her thesis, wrote notes such as 'This is a draft of chapter 4. Please read it and comment on it'. To Thomas, this message seemed over-explicit and actually imposing in its directives; in fact the student intended to acknowledge how much work she was asking her to do and was going on record with the degree of her indebtedness. She was not observing the tact maxim of 'minimise cost to other' but observing the sympathy maxim of 'maximise sympathy between self and other'.

The use of the maxims of approbation and modesty are also deeply rooted in culture. The British reject praise in the form of a personal compliment, 'minimising praise of self', whereas the Japanese accept a compliment graciously. Cubans respond to a personal compliment about an article of clothing or an accessory with 'Es tuyo' ('It's yours whenever you want it'), a formula which appears to observe the tact maxim 'maximise benefit to other'. Similarly, in some Western cultures, refusals demand a specific excuse, if speakers are to avoid threatening positive face and 'minimise dispraise of other', whereas in other cultures, this is not necessary. Approbation in the form of positive feedback from a teacher to a student in a British lecture, 'maximising praise of other', is quite an acceptable teaching technique in Britain, but a study carried out on Chinese students in the University of Dundee (Catterick 2001) showed that they felt that their face was threatened by being praised by the teacher in front of everyone. On the other hand, British lecturers are unused to being praised by their students, whereas for the Chinese, this is a standard politeness routine. As Scurfield and Song (1996: 93) say, Chinese 'keqi hua' (polite talk) includes not just modesty but self-deprecation:

> You are invited to somebody's house and the table is groaning with delicious food and you are told that it is only **bianfan** (*simple/convenience food*). The cook asks you to forgive his/her poor cooking when you can see that the opposite is the case.

Of course, self-deprecation vis-à-vis food offered to a guest is, in varying degrees, widespread in several cultures round the world.

In summary, politeness is related to the context, the language used, the speech acts, the structure of the conversation and the principle of cooperation. Politeness is a basic form of cooperation and it underlies all language in some way or another.

CORPORA AND COMMUNITIES

Understanding concepts

❑ Corpus linguistics
❑ Corpora, pragmatics and social factors
❑ Corpora, domains and communities

Corpus linguistics

Corpora

If we were to think of examples of how the verb 'mean' is most frequently used, our intuition might suggest to us that it is mostly used in sentences like 'Mandarin "Xie xie" means "thank you"', or like Tom Stoppard's definition of linguistic analysis:

> A lot of chaps pointing out that we don't always mean what we say, even when we manage to say what we mean.
>
> (*Professional Foul*, 1978)

But our intuition might be wrong. If we were to consult a **corpus**, on the other hand, we would find the most frequent usages of the word in a database of millions of words that have actually occurred in real life. Using corpus linguistics and pragmatics, we would then study in what context 'mean' is used and what its main functions are; ideally we would discover the most usual intention of speakers.

A corpus is a large collection of naturally occurring authentic texts, stored in an electronic database to be accessed on a computer. **Corpora** consist of both written texts (newspaper articles, advertisements, letters, emails, blogs) and spoken ones (casual conversations, telephone conversations, interviews, service encounters, speeches, lessons, podcasts).

Corpora from English-speaking countries have been collected mostly from the late 1980s or early 1990s onwards. The largest have hundreds of millions of words:

○ The Cambridge International Corpus (CIC): 700 million
○ The Bank of English: 500 million
○ The British National Corpus (BNC): 100 million
○ The Longman Written American Corpus: 100 million

There are many medium-sized ones, with 10 to 30 million words, for example:

○ The Longman/Lancaster Corpus: 30 million
○ The American National Corpus (ANC): 22 million
○ The International Corpus of English (ICE): 15 million

The ICE has corpora from fifteen countries, including East Africa, Hong Kong, India, Philippines and Singapore. There are even more in the one-to-four-million-word category, such as:

○ The Scottish Corpus of Texts and Speech (SCOTS): four million
○ The Australian Corpus of English (ACE): one million

○ The Hong Kong Corpus of Spoken English (HKCSE): one million
○ The Kolhapur Corpus of Indian English: one million

There are numerous large corpora in other languages: Danish, German, Greek, Hungarian, Italian and Spanish, to name a few. The list below names some, chosen randomly:

○ The Modern Chinese Language Corpus (MCLC): 900 million
○ The Czech National Corpus (CNC): 900 million
○ The Sejong Balanced Corpus (Korea): 140 million
○ The Corpus of Spontaneous Japanese: seven million

Learner corpora (mostly learners' essays and exam scripts) are developing too. Here are but a few examples, again chosen randomly:

○ The HKUST (Hong Kong University of Science and Technology) Corpus of Learner English: 25 million
○ The Corpus of English by Japanese Learners: one million
○ The Chinese Learner English Corpus: one million

Concordance and frequency lists

In order to find **all the occurrences** of words in a corpus, researchers use a computer software package known as a **concordance programme**; examples are WordSmith, Sara and MonoConc. Using these, they can display all the database lines containing the words that interest them and examine the co-text to see the most frequent lexical phrases and grammar within the same line.

Below is a sample of lines containing the verb 'mean', taken from the British National Corpus Sampler (two million words), using Sara-32 concordancer.

There are 2,352 lines with occurrences of 'mean' in the Sampler, but even these 55 lines give an indication of the usage. There are only 18 instances with the sense of signifying and implying (as in 'Mandarin "Xie xie" means "thank you"'), e.g. 'What do you mean by decent music?' The biggest function is the interactional (37 instances). 12 of these have 'I mean' as a hesitation phenomenon, filling silence and keeping the turn, e.g. 'Well, I, will, you know, I mean, will carry on as Chairman'. There are 19 with 'I mean' as a topic-shift indicator and emphasiser, e.g. 'I mean because your dad isn't gonna agree'. Many of these may mitigate disagreement, a positive politeness strategy, e.g. 'I mean, do something, you know!' There are five with 'I mean' as a filler and comprehension checker, e.g. 'see what I mean?'

Concordance programmes calculate the **number of occurrences** of words and list them in order of **frequency**. Carter and McCarthy (2006: 12) analysed the 20 most frequent words in five-million-word samples of written and spoken English in CIC and found that 'I' and 'you' are higher to the top of the spoken list than they are on the written, reflecting the interactivity of talk. Many of the spoken list words have an interactional function: 'know' is there partly because of the discourse marker 'you know'; 'yeah', 'mm' and 'er' are frequent because they are backchannels or silence-fillers. 'So' and 'but' have many social functions such as intensifying, as in 'In Teens' Web World, MySpace Is So Last Year' (*Washington Post*, 29 October 2006), or marking a

ccd(2404(2405))	fears a mischief has been done, do you mean?"
cel(0991)	repossessed homes to flog off does not mean the rest of us should be forced to
cn4(0961(0955))	ıst Museums Service, the extension will mean, says the director, Mary Gavagan
dch(0788)	holiday apartment in Cumbria and the, I mean the idea is you take a book and try
dch(0831)	Well, I, will, you know, I mean, will carry on as Chairman, but I, I'
f7g(0265)	mean.
f7g(0436)	some sort of definitions, guidelines of, I mean, effort's effort, I do , do you have t
f7g(0613)	well not saying tha , I mean I and again I, I think what I need to
f7j(0186)	ı but it's er we've still got members but I mean we well we're you know all about t
f7j(813(814))	I mean we could all spend all day discuss
f7j(827(828))	I mean can anybody answer that?
f7j(892(893))	ed recognition of the River Authorities, I mean erm the latest pay awards I mean
fls(0896(0897))	Is that not sort of I mean, I wasn't aware that anybody wasr
fmp(0132)	The character you By that you mean the character the boundary
fu6(0466(0462))	ROS: I mean, I've heard of — but I've never act
fuh(0564(0566))	ɔf put in here one one third what does it mean?
fx5(0146)	I mean, if if if the council
fx5(0708)	y and the people who, you know, I don't mean that all people, a lot of people who
fxr(0947)	I mean there's no huge hurry for those, is
fxr(1402)	I mean God Rest ye Merry is a very good
fy8(0147)	I thi I mean there were quite a number of peop
fyj(0376)	What do you mean by decent music?
g0a(2736(2730))	I mean, why milk?
g3n(068(062))	Informally this must mean that P " is essentially the same as
g3n(530(440))	ı; and &formula; are the same, does not mean that there is any uniform equivaler
g4n(0037)	t mean to be over the men, but what we mean is for you to come down the office
g4n(0207)	ome more on what I'd made, see what I mean.
g4n(0374)	an one way or another, you know what I mean and er I did job for the casters, sai
g4n(0452)	ɔ that, whether or not, you follow what I mean, that's how I've lived me life, Micha
h5d(0180)	Erm and I mean I've had a recent bereavement, I r
h5d(0287)	I mean servicing a school regardless of ho
h5d(0675(0673))	know whether we'd be able to get that I mean
h5d(0683(0681))	I mean if they did, fine.
h8w(447(446))	The new developments would mean other businesses relocating outsic
hm4(0181)	I mean, I only have one er, I would like tw
hm4(0200)	I mean the B B C er television and radio i:
hm4(0311)	you are going to be roving reporters will mean that you will have to, if you becom
hm4(0463)	ırrassing personal stories, and there's, I mean it just becomes a battleground, yo
hm4(0609)	I mean, if we take this as a game, as you
j24(0071)	It may mean operating with associate compani
j2h(185(164))	of interest because it can be derived by mean field methods, which otherwise pro
j44(0378)	I mean, what is the use of a if you're miles
j8g(0216)	lot about at all, er it's a very good idea I mean two, there's mainly two different ty
j97(516(515))	But, I mean that D P team do a lot of work on t
kb1(0960(4867))	I mean, actually lots of things her mother
kb2(0751)	e's George claim nowt, you know what I mean?
kb2(1110)	e go steady, don't you, you know what I mean?
kb9(0125(4017))	I mean, because your dad isn't gonna agr
kb9(0909(4801))	That's what I mean.
kb9(1276(5168))	ɔut there again if I get the enquiries fas I mean, that obviously is the enquiry came
kb9(1380(5272))	I gi him general things on their own, I mean, it's, it's really quiet.
kbg(0305)	Well I mean that should be
kbg(1039(1432))	From Wilby School you mean?
kbk(0419)	Yeah, I mean you're not particularly trad jazz inc
kbl(0554(3834))	I mean, do something, you know!

relevant transition to an end of topic as in 'And that's how I came to be here. So, there we are'.

Concordance programmes can also find the most frequent usage of **word clusters**. Here are the 20 most frequent five-word clusters from the same samples (ibid.: 830–1):

Spoken		Written	
1	you know what I mean	1	at the end of the
2	at the end of the	2	by the end of the
3	do you know what I	3	for the first time in
4	the end of the day	4	at the top of the
5	do you want me to	5	at the back of the
6	in the middle of the	6	on the other side of
7	I mean I don't know	7	in the centre of
8	this that and the other	8	the end of the day
9	I know what you mean	9	for the rest of the
10	and all the rest of it	10	the middle of the night
11	and all that sort of	11	the other end of the
12	I was going to say	12	at the bottom of the
13	and all the rest of	13	the rest of the world
14	and that sort of thing	14	for the first time since
15	I don't know what it	15	had nothing to do with
16	all that sort of thing	16	at the foot of the
17	do you want to go	17	in and out of the
18	to be honest with you	18	in the direction of the
19	an hour and a half	19	is one of the most
20	it's a bit of a	20	the end of the year

The spoken ones express interpersonal meanings. Expressions such as 'do you want me to' do negative politeness; ones like 'to be honest with you' are hedging mechanisms. Speakers use vagueness as in 'and all the rest of it', assuming that their hearers can understand the possible referents. They use expressions that facilitate turn-taking and elicit hearer response, e.g. 'do you know what I mean'.

'At the end of the day' is second only to 'do you know what I mean' in the six-word cluster list, despite what Plain English Campaigners may feel about it:

> The most irritating phrase in the English language, nominated by straight-talkers around the world, has been identified. 'At the end of the day' was a clear winner over 'at this moment in time' in a poll of 5,000 members of the Plain English Campaign.
>
> (http://www.writewords.org.uk/news/436.asp 24 March 2004)

Annotation

So that they can analyse systematically how words are used, researchers **annotate** corpora, with or without concordance packages. They **tag** or label words to indicate the **lexical** features (e.g. common/proper nouns), and the **grammatical** (e.g. parts of speech, cohesion), **phonetic** (e.g. stress, intonation), **turn-taking** (e.g. pauses, overlaps) and **paralinguistic** (e.g. laughter, coughing) features.

The excerpt below, adapted from The Wellington Corpus of Spoken New Zealand English, shows paralinguistic features, amongst others.

Key	<.> </.>	incomplete words	,> <,,> <,,> <&> 4 </&>	pauses
	<&> </&>	editorial comments	<O> </O>	paralinguistics
	<laughs>	features in speech	CAPITALS	stress

Z1>   the schools are perhaps <,> <drawls> more </drawls> disciplined and
       authoritarian than ours but singapore children don't seem wildly unhappy
       <laughs> to the casual eye </laughs>

HS>   so it's something that they have there as well

HS>   what can we learn from their success or is their success in a way irrelevant to
       OUR lifestyle and OUR attitudes

Z1>   no i think we can learn a great deal

Z1>   keep in mind that when i first went to singapore thirty years ago they had leprous
       beggars in the streets and most of the houses didn't have running water in old
       chinatown and so on and er <O> voc </O> there was wall to wall slums

Z1>   now <&> 3:00 </&> everybody's um housed properly they certainly have running
       water and so on er <O> voc </O> and <,> ONE of the reasons for that i think is
       er very CLEAR sighted government er and economic policy

Z1>   er WE debate the virtues or otherwise of intervention

Z1>   um the <?> p a p </?> government in singapore has certainly regarded one of
       their roles as being to direct the economy to encourage investment from outside
       to make er <,,> decisions about the TYPE of economy they want to encourage

Let us speculate on the function of the annotated features. In the utterance 'singapore children don't seem wildly unhappy <laughs> to the casual eye </laughs>', 'laughs' might be to imply a low degree of confidence in the truth of the utterance. The vocalisation in 'and er <O> voc </O> there was wall to wall slums' and the pause in 'to make er <,,> decisions about the TYPE of economy they want to encourage' might be hedges mitigating disturbing statements and apologising strategies.

The following excerpt from the Hong Kong Corpus of Spoken English shows phonological annotation for discourse intonation carrying pragmatic meaning.

Key	Tone unit:	{ . . . }	Prominence:	UPPER CASE LETTERS
	Tone:	fall rise - V, rise - /, fall - \, rise fall - Λ, level - =		
	Key:	high - [^], mid - [ ], low - [_]		
	Termination:	high - < ^ >, mid - < >, low - < _ >		

1   . . . { \ it's [RAIning] < outSIDE > } { \ i'll [BUY] you < LUNCH > } { \

2   [WHAT] would you < LIKE > } { = < HOTdog > } { \ or < HAMBURger > }

Here, the speaker limits the list of options for lunch to 'hotdog' and 'hamburger' by the fall tone on 'or hamburger' (Warren 2007). If they had used a rising tone on 'or hamburger', the hearer would have understood that there were other alternatives.

Some corpora provide background information for the data file, giving it **contextual headers**, which indicate **social variables** gender, age, class and region. The Michigan Corpus of Academic Spoken English (MICASE) allows the researcher to call up lines with two social variables from a list of headers of gender, age-range, academic role and first language. **Pragmatics dimensions** such as speech acts, politeness and cooperative maxims are as yet less frequently included in file contextual headers.

A6.3

Corpora, pragmatics and social factors

Studying corpora, pragmatists can discover how the most frequent language patterns relate to contexts, interpersonal meaning, relationships and genre, as well as personal social factors. Let us look at a few examples.

Pragmatics

If you wanted to use corpus linguistics to test hunches such as this:

> One thing talk can't accomplish, however, is communication. This is because everybody's talking too much to pay attention to what anyone else is saying.
>
> (O'Rourke 1984)

you would gain access to a database of spoken interactions and calculate the frequency of lines in which cooperative maxims are infringed.

The earliest **conversation analysis studies** were carried out on the London-Lund Corpus. An example of studies using CA is that of Stenström (1987), who looked at the interactional function of the pragmatic marker 'right' in various forms. She found that 'right' on its own was used as a response evaluating a previous response or terminating an exchange, 'all right' was used to mark a boundary between two stages in discourse, and 'that's right' was used as an emphasiser.

Corpus linguistics has been combined with **politeness studies**. Schauer and Adolphs (2006) analysed the use of formulaic sequences in expressions of gratitude such as 'cheers' and 'thank you', in the Cambridge and Nottingham Corpus of Discourse in English (CANCODE). They found that 'thank you' collocates with words expressing other speech acts. The following concordance lines show how it combines with compliments to the interlocutor:

<S1> Yes. <S2> **Thank you that's smashing.** <S1> <S2> And she n
le's home. <S1> **Thank you. That's very good of you.** <S5> And I'm sending
<S1> **Thank you. That's fine that's lovely.** Mhm. Mm. <S2> Is it all
That's brilliant. **Thank you very much. That's much appreciated.**

'Thank you' also combined frequently with 'a reason' ('Thank you very much for your time', 'Thanks for the help' and 'Thanks for coming') and very frequently with expressions politely rejecting an offer ('Ah, no, it's OK thanks' and 'No, honestly, that's fine. But thank you anyway').

Social factors

Studies into social factors cover language and **gender, age, class** and **geographical location**. You will have read about projects such as the one below that looks at the language of a particular generation:

> A Qualifications and Curriculum Authority pilot project is encouraging youngsters to analyse the way they speak, believing it will give them a better grasp of language. The academic co-ordinating the work believes pupils should not be discouraged from using vague terms such as 'like' or 'whatever', which he says can be quite sophistic-ated uses of language.
>
> (http://www.tes.co.uk/section/story/?section=Archive&sub_section
> =News+%26+opinion&story_id=376361)

You can be sure that, nowadays, such a project is using corpus linguistics.

Let us take an example of a study about the relationship between language and **gender**. Shalom (1997) surveyed the adjectives in a corpus of 776 Western personal advertisements in lonely hearts columns of magazines and newspapers. Here is one of the advertisements (p. 197):

> GAY WOMAN, 45. Young, attractive, feminine, caring, wants similar adventurous, funny, stable, lovely woman to explore life's opportunities. Friendship initially. Box 1718.

She noted that they contained a lot of vague meaning, and that the vagueness was interactive: the description had to fit and appeal to any reader, who was supposed to supply their own meaning and apply it to themselves.

Corpora, domains and communities

A6.4

Corpora have been used to study **domains of discourse**: interactions typical of specific settings, such as office settings, reception desks or shops, classrooms or hospitals. For example, the domain of a restaurant requires the discourse structure: waiter/waitress asks, customer answers, and the topic is usually the food on the menu, as in:

> Bush and Gore were sitting in a restaurant to discuss the craziness of the election. When the waitress came to take their orders, Gore said, 'I'll take the steak.' When she asked Bush, he said, 'I'll take the quicky.' Gore motioned for the waitress to come closer, and whispered into her ear, 'He means the quiche.'
>
> (http://www.villainsupply.com/jokes/political_jokes.asp)

Corpus linguistics helps researchers to discover the features of the language used in specific areas, situations and contexts, and find what is said and how.

Corpora have been used to understand pragmatics features of social group inter-actions and discover who says what to whom and why. Lawyers, cleaners, home-care volunteers, football team supporters, science fiction buffs or peace protesters are all examples of what we call **communities of practice** (Lave and Wenger 1991). These are groups of people brought together by a common interest and mutual engagement, sharing knowledge, values and beliefs, and maintaining membership through their linguistic and behavioural social practices. Communities of practice have their own conventions that are pragmatic (preferred speech acts, cooperative maxims and politeness rituals), linguistic (domains of discourse, codes and lexis) and behavioural (physical rituals and accepted habits).

There is a growing number of corpora of the language of **virtual communities of practice**. These maintain their membership through computer-mediated communication (CMC); they share an identity, social conventions and group-specific variety of Netspeak. Some communities exist both physically and virtually, for example offices, universities and societies. The following web home page description of the Cambridge University Chinese Society shows features of a community of practice:

> Welcome to the Cambridge University Chinese Society (CUCS or ChiSoc) official website! Here you can find out about the latest CUCS events and other updated news of the Society. You can also check out the CUCS sports sessions schedule and download photos which capture the most exciting moments of CUCS events; not to mention the chat box and the forum where you are most welcome to express your opinion.
>
> (http://www.srcf.ucam.org/cuchin/home/home_index.php)

Other communities exist only in cyberspace; these tend to be ones who belong to an interest group such as newsgroups, message boards and discussion lists with regular visitors, and blog and YouTube sites, to which the same visitors return and recognise each other. Some chatrooms have a migrant community. CMC must be treated with caution as far as communities of practice are concerned, however: as Crystal (2001: 59) says, 'The mere fact of having engaged in an Internet activity does not produce in a user the sort of sense of identity and belonging which accompanies the term *community*.'

Domains of discourse

Let us look at three studies that use corpus linguistics to examine domains of discourse: service encounters, media and the courtroom.

There has been a lot of work done on **service encounters**. Kuiper and Flindall (2000) examined a small New Zealand corpus (200 interactions) and found that small talk at the supermarket checkout begins the operator's formulaic greetings (e.g. 'Hello there. How are you today?'), following the firm's guidelines for conversing sociably with customers, and then sometimes moves into the individually designed conversation of genuine sociability ('Oh, what've you got there? Fattening foods?'). Here is a dialogue from their database (ibid: 194–5).

```
 1   O:   Hi, how are you?
 2        Lovely day today.
 3   C:   Yes . . . you should be busy today.
 4   O:   Yes.
 5   C:   There's no many other shops open, though.
 6   O:   We were, um, very busy during the week.
 7   C:   Yes – oh, I think you'll always be busy . . . people still
 8        eat, don't they?
 9   O:   Yes.
10   C:   No matter what . . . what they still . . . taste food.
11   O:   's twenty-eight dollars eighty-five thanks
12        Doing anything special for Easter?
13   C:   No, no . . .
14   O:   No
15   C:   . . . caravan. But . . . expensive
16   O:   Yeah, yeah. Twenty-eight, twenty-nine and one's thirty
17   C:   . . . Doing up . . . house, fixing up the garden and things, you
18        know.
19   O:   Okay, well have a good weekend.
20   C:   Thank you.
```

Note how the dialogue starts off with the operator's formula 'Hi, how are you?' and the semi-formulaic 'Lovely day today', and then the customer moves the topic onto a discussion of the day's business ('you should be busy today') and the fact that people have to eat ('people still eat, don't they?'). The operator reciprocates with the sociable topic of the Easter weekend ('Doing anything special for Easter?'), while she takes the money and gives the change with the required formulae (lines 11 and 16).

O'Keeffe (2006) has investigated **media discourse**. She uses a corpus (271,553 words, 92 interviews) of extracts from online transcripts from a variety of sources including the Australian Broadcasting Company, NBC, ABC, and BBC. She looks at the function of pragmatic markers that show the speakers' intentions and interpersonal knowledge: hedges, discourse markers and response tokens ('wow', 'umhmm'). She investigates how interactions are controlled by the presenter and how pseudo-intimate relationships are created and sustained are marked through language use. Here is part of a dialogue from *The Gerry Ryan Show*, an Irish radio talk show:

Gerry Ryan: Generally you wouldn't turn away a fella?
Caller: No absolutely no way.
Gerry Ryan: And do you get many of them coming over to you in these places that
              you go to?
Caller: They usually are married.
Gerry Ryan: Married men?
Caller: Yes.

Gerry Ryan:	And do they make it abundantly clear that they are only looking for the wild thing?
Caller:	Yes yes.
Gerry Ryan:	Umm.
Caller:	Yes.
Gerry Ryan:	And are you keen on the wild thing?
Caller:	Absol= of course as keen as anybody else.
Gerry Ryan:	Right but under the right circumstances says you.
Caller:	ᴸ* Under the right circumstances and certainly not on the first night.

(* ᴸ = overlap.)

Note how the level of intimacy, seen in the blatant self-disclosure, here is not what you would expect between strangers in an interaction; it comes about because of the pseudo-relationship due to the sense of common identity and co-presence.

Cotterill (2007) has examined the domain of **courtroom discourse**. In one of her studies, she draws on a one-million-word corpus of witness examinations and cross-examinations taken from trials held in the late 1990s in the UK, and studies the vague responses (e.g. 'this, that and the other', 'something like that') given by witnesses to lawyers' questions in the courtroom setting. She discovers that the law context is characterised by a search for precision, and that, in contrast, the language of witnesses and defendants at trial is typified by imprecision and doubt, because they are uncertain, have forgotten or are attempting to be evasive or deceptive. An example will demonstrate this:

Q. Mr S, can you help us at all as to which year this was?
A. 1996.
Q. In 1996?
A. Yes.
Q. Can you tell us, please, as to what month it might have been?
A. Roughly, to be honest, I can't know. At the time I was receiving treatment for depression.

Communities of practice

Let us look at a sample of studies of students, office workers, healthcare professionals, and virtual communities, to see the relevance of the research findings to pragmatics.

We start with an example of a study of a **student** community. Cutting (2000) ana-lysed the in-group code of Edinburgh University MSc Applied Linguistics students in a 26,000-word corpus of common-room conversations. The code contained elements of the global community of applied linguists: technical terms and proper nouns, as in 'That-that seems to umm to bear some relation to the <u>lexical syllabus</u> doesn't it?' It contained elements of the local community of Edinburgh University MSc Applied Linguistics: proper nouns used metonymically, as in 'I haven't done any <u>Chomsky</u>', and nouns relating to the programme, as in 'What about your <u>core project</u>?' The code also reflected membership of the particular group of students: non-anaphoric pro-nouns, as in 'Did <u>he</u> like the idea?', general words, as in 'I didn't pick my <u>thing</u> up' and 'What are you <u>doing</u>?', and vague noun clauses, as in 'Are you going to do <u>what</u> <u>you thought you'd do</u> about your project?' Pragmatics analysis showed that the in-group code was used mostly in exchanges with a socially cohesive function, to assert in-groupness. The code was used when showing a positive attitude to the interlocu-tor, using speech acts such as 'empathise' and 'encourage', and showing a negative attitude to the course (students complained that a lecturer was 'really fanatic' and a certain course was 'bloody tosh') and to themselves (one had 'totally uninformed sort of basically stupid ideas for a project'). Here is an example of them being negative about themselves and empathising with each other in an exchange imbued with vagueness:

BM <u>And I reached the stage where I'd no idea</u>.
BF Yeah. ((1))
BM And also when I- when I was looking back I realised I actually hadn't read the first part again which gave me a real big clue for one of the first.
BM <u>It was really stupid</u>.
BF Yeah.
BM But em (1.5) I didn't do any reading. (0.5)
BM I just had one book which wasn't on the list which was too- too long really to give // me any conclusions.
BF // <u>No I- I haven't read anything specific for it</u>.

Let us turn now to an example of a study on **office workers**. Holmes (2000) ana-lysed a relatively small corpus (121 hours of material, 330 interactions) of interactions in New Zealand government departments and found that small talk featured in both interactional and transactional talk, mostly showing sociability and social cohesion. Small talk was 'managed' by those with power: superiors controlled when and how it was used. An example (p. 32) that she cites is:

Context: Diana enters Sally's office at the beginning of the day to collect mail
1 D: good morning Sally lovely day
2 S: yes don't know what we're doing here we should be out in the sun
3 D: mm pity about the work really
4 S: how are your kids?
5 D: much better thank goodness <u>any mail</u>?

Next let us look at a corpus linguistics study about the community of **healthcare professionals**. Ragan (2000: 267–9), describing sociable talk in women's healthcare contexts (corpus of 118 interactions), asserts that small talk is central to achieving trans-actional goals, and that humour and self-disclosure reduce the unequal power rela-tion of the provider-patient encounter. She quotes Beck, Ragan and DuPré's (1997) example of an exchange just after a pelvic examination:

1 Provider All done (2.4) that's it (3.5)
2 Patient   hhh gee <u>that</u> wuz fun [(.1 heh heh heh heh] heh heh (1.2)
3 Provider [heh heh heh heh heh]
4   oh you wanna do it <u>again</u>? Heh heh heh heh=

A6.5   **Uses and limitations of corpus linguistics**

Uses

Corpus linguistics provides writers of **dictionaries** and **grammars** with a relatively objective evidence-based description of patterns and functions.

It also provides descriptions of real language use which **foreign language teachers** and **language-learning text-book writers** can use as a guide when choosing authentic texts and classroom tasks. Teachers and writers alike can use corpora to help learners acquire pragmatic communicative competence. To present a new point, teachers can bring to class some concordance lines (specially selected, so as to omit unusual usages), recontextualise them and guide the learners to recognise the most common uses of the words and the grammar round them. This data-driven learning approach (Hunston 2002) can also respond to learner needs: students make an error, the teacher brings relevant concordance lines, and the learners find the correct usage.

Corpora also serve **forensic linguistics**, in which linguists analyse police transcripts and tape-recordings of suspects' conversations, to determine whether they are real or fabricated, and what the intentions of the interlocutors are. Let us take the Derek Bentley case: Coulthard (2000) analysed the record of Bentley's statement to see whether it had been tampered with. He focused on the word 'then', and found that 'then' was the eighth most frequently occurring word in Bentley's text, whereas it was the 83rd most frequent word in the whole Bank of English corpus. He noted that 'I then' occurred seven times in Bentley's text, but that the Bank of English spoken corpus showed 'then I' to be ten times as frequent as 'I then'. When he found that 'I then' also occurred frequently in the corpus of police statements, he was able to say that Bentley's 'confession' was, in part, the work of police officers.

Limitations

Like all the theories in this book, corpus linguistics has its limitations. Fairclough (2003: 6) says that corpus findings on their own have little value, and that they need to be 'complemented by more intensive and detailed qualitative textual analysis'. To a certain extent this is true, given that not all corpora have contextual headers, and lines are rarely annotated for speech act or cooperative or politeness features. However, most of the studies described in this chapter have studied the context, function and speaker intention.

Grundy (2006) dismisses corpus linguistics as concentrating on 'superficial' patterns of use on a descriptive social level and not taking into account cognitive linguistics, which studies internal mental states, such as belief, desire and motivation. He also feels that those who compile concordances set the extent of co-text in the concordance lines in a mechanical way, without considering that for each case there will be an appropriate amount of co-text. He believes that corpus linguistics does not serve the needs of pragmatists, who are interested more in salient meaning, which is 'recovered at different levels on different occasions', than in frequency.

Finally, we should be aware that the use of electronic text may tempt the analyst to analyse only that which is readily available in electronic form, seek only that which is easy to find, and count only that which what is easy to count.

CULTURE AND LANGUAGE LEARNING

Understanding concepts

❑ Cross-cultural pragmatics
❑ Intercultural pragmatics
❑ Interlanguage pragmatics
❑ Teaching intercultural pragmatics

From English pragmatics to global pragmatics

Barron, an Irish learner of German as a foreign language, tells an anecdote about when she first arrived in Germany:

> Upon an offer of coffee, I, at that time, automatically said 'No, I'm fine' – not because I did not want the coffee – quite the contrary in fact! I said I was fine because that is what we conventionally do in my home country, Ireland. I, of course, fully expected to be asked a second time, was I sure I would not like a cup. Upon such a reoffer, I would, naturally, have graciously said, okay, so, just the one! On a later visit to Germany, I also distinctly remember often feeling very foolish and also annoyed at German native speakers' reactions to my innocent polite question, '*Bist du sicher?*' (Are you sure?), in response to their refusing an offer of coffee which I had just made. I was quickly told on several occasions that yes, they were sure – had they not just said no! They, on the other hand, probably felt insulted that I did not seem to believe that they had meant what they had said.
>
> (Barron 2002: 1)

UK Television viewers of the Channel 4 sit-com *Father Ted* (1995), about three Irish Catholic priests and a housekeeper, Mrs Doyle, will recall Mrs Doyle's offer of tea:

> 'You'll have some tea . . . are you sure you don't want any? Aw go on, you'll have some. Go on go on go on go on go on go on go on go on GO ON!'

The story illustrates the fact that there are cultural, pragmatic differences from society to society, culture being taken to mean:

> any of the customs, worldview, language, kinship system, social organisation, and other taken-for-granted day-to-day practices of a people which set that group apart as a distinctive group.
>
> (Scollon and Scollon 1995: 125–7)

Studies comparing cultures can have a **pragmalinguistic** focus (part of in linguistic competence, e.g. greeting with 'Where are you going?' as opposed to 'How are you?') and a **sociopragmatic** focus (sociological, related to customs and values, e.g. accepting an offer, as opposed to refusing on the assumption that there will be another offer).

The findings described in this chapter should be treated with great caution: they are based on personal experience, case studies and small experiments. The descriptions must be seen as possible tendencies (some referring to particular social groups in Time and Space) rather than generalisations, so that they do not amount to stereotyping.

Cross-cultural pragmatics

Cross-cultural pragmatics provides **synchronic** studies of **first language use**. It involves **contrastive** studies of the language of two or more social groups, using **comparative** data obtained independently from the different groups. It compares the manifestations of a particular pragmatic principle in two societies, for example, how Mandarin speakers apologise to each other in China, compared to how English speakers apologise to each other in Australia.

Cross-cultural pragmatics studies began in the 1980s. They cover mainly speech acts, politeness and cooperation, showing an overlap of these approaches.

Speech acts

Offers and invitations have been studied across cultures. According to Wierzbicka (1991: 30–2), whereas English offers can take the form of a question, as in 'Would you like another beer?' or 'Would you like to go to the cinema with me?', this form does not exist in Polish and Japanese invitations, as it is not good manners to ask what the addressee would like. Polish speakers tend to press a guest and make direct suggestions, as in 'Perhaps we would go to the cinema?', and Japanese hosts usually prefer to offer a little of all the dishes.

There have been many studies of requests and commands. In English, direct commands with imperatives can be interpreted as rude if used indiscriminately; other cultures use imperatives widely but soften them. Polish and Greek people often use particles, affixes and tone of voice, Cubans use a high fall-rise intonation, and Spaniards can use vocatives e.g. 'Carlos, ven aquí' ('Charles, come here' sometimes), pronouns e.g. 'Tú, callate!' ('You, be quiet!') and interjections e.g. 'Deja de llorar, anda!' ('Stop crying, eh?') (Haverkate 1979).

There have been some studies of apologies. Whereas the Anglo-American apology for an offence tends to contain an acknowledgement of fault, the Japanese one does not: studies have shown that they prefer an offer to do something to remedy it. Where an Anglo-American apology for refusing an invitation has a precise explanation (e.g. 'I have a business lunch that day'), the Japanese frequently has a vague one (e.g. 'I have something to do') (Barnlund and Yoshioka 1990; Beebe et al. 1990).

Politeness and cooperation

Positive politeness makes different cultures observe the cooperative maxim of quality differently. The Javanese culture is said to require dissimulation and pretence: people are expected to conceal their feelings, wants and thoughts, in order to achieve harmony and peaceful interpersonal relations (Geertz 1976). Anglo-Americans tend to sacrifice honesty and straightforwardness, preferring to tell a white lie in order to protect apparently their interactant from being offended. To Germans and Poles, on the other hand, honesty is a sign of friendship; lying to avoid telling someone an unwelcome truth is not highly valued (Barron 2002; Wierzbicka 1991). The same goes for Peninsula Spanish (Briz 1998):

A: Me ha dicho Pepa que se ha ligado al professor de literatura y que va a salir con él el jueves.

B: En serio. Mira que eres idiota! y tú te lo crees!?

(A: Pepa told me she pulled the literature teacher and she's going out with him this Thursday.

B: Really. You're so stupid! And you believe that!?)

The politeness maxim of modesty varies from culture to culture. Whereas a British person, asked what time the film starts, might answer, 'I don't know, nine-fifteen or something', possibly in order to avoiding displaying knowledge, to comply with the modesty maxim, an Anglo-American person is more likely to answer, 'Nine-fifteen', since displaying knowledge is not a problem (Carter and McCarthy 2006). Some young black Americans are said to indulge in uninhibitedly drawing attention to themselves: self-praise, boasting and theatrical self-aggrandisement is not viewed negatively (Spencer-Oatey 2000).

The politeness maxim of agreement is culturally variable too. At the one extreme, Japanese speakers are said to avoid direct confrontation, as in 'you're wrong' or 'that's not true'; they look for harmony. In the middle of the cline, there are Anglo-Americans, who will disagree directly with a 'no', and then add comments that soften the disagreement, so that the addressee does not feel bad. At the other extreme, it would seem, are Spanish speakers, who have a speech act category 'dissentives', defined as declaring and carrying out disagreement. In some contexts, speakers actually max-imise disagreement, as in:

A: No, es que los niños están mejor con la madre hasta los dos o tres años.

B: Pero tú qué vas a opinar de la educación familiar, tú que eres una cualquiera, que no sabes hacer la O con un canuto! Ten un poco de dignidad y vergüenza y cállate!

(A: No, the thing is children are better off with their mother until they're two or three.

B: How can *you* talk about bringing up families – you're a tramp that couldn't organise a piss-up in a brewery! Have a bit of pride and shame and shut up!)

(Herrero Moreno 2002)

Intercultural pragmatics

A7.4

Intercultural pragmatics provides **synchronic** studies of **second language (L2) use by non-native speakers with other non-native speakers or native speakers**. Using **interactional** data obtained when people from different societies or social groups communicate with each other using a lingua franca, it examines the effect of their different norms and values. It looks at how pragmatic principles manifest themselves in interactions between people from different groups, for example, how Mandarin speakers apologise in English to English speakers in Australia and how the English speakers react.

Studies often focus on miscommunication and misunderstandings when the cultures are juxtaposed. Pragmatic failure can be pragmalinguistic (e.g. the non-native speaker intends a request, but because of inappropriate directness or modification, the native speaker interprets it as a command) and sociopragmatic (e.g. the non-native speaker misunderstands the native speaker's social status and so acts impolitely) (Barron 2002: 28).

Intercultural pragmatics began in the 1980s but it burgeoned in the 1990s and 2000s, reflecting the era of globalisation and world-wide communication networks. It combines intercultural communication, linguistic anthropology and sociolinguistics, taking into account politeness theory, conversational implicature and conversation analysis.

Politeness and cooperation

Differences vis-à-vis the politeness maxim of modesty can cause misunderstanding. Žegarac and Pennington (2000: 170–4) give the example of the Korean student who went to help the Anglo-American tutor on the computer. When the student asked the tutor if he knew about scoring bowling on the computer, he said 'approximately', obeying the modesty maxim. The student thought he knew nothing.

Differences vis-à-vis the politeness maxim of agreement can cause culture clash. Günthner (2000: 218) describes a study of a first-time meeting between two Germans and two Chinese students. The Germans made their disagreements directly and even highlighted the dissent:

Yang: yes like this. When this problem is solved, then of course
          (0.3) It is easier to discuss (0.3) [the other problem]
Doris: [no. Eh no. Wait a minute]
Yang: eh to understand. To understand
Doris: no. Wait a minute. Eh:m eh eh for me it's no problem for me it's clear
Yang: yes
Doris: ehm women and men are naturally equal.
          this is not a problem

The Chinese interactants signalled consent before indicating a disagreement:

Doris: [well] do you believe there is a NATURAL LIMITATION?
          (0.7)
Yang: I belie:ve (-) NOT, but I (hi) I must say, there is. (1.0)
          a bit

When the Chinese finally conceded the argument to end the conflict, the Germans challenged their change of position; when the Chinese made a concession, the Germans provided a fresh disagreement. The Chinese found the Germans aggressive and offensive; the Germans in turn found the Chinese boring.

Forms of address, deference and hierarchy are dramatically different from culture to culture, and miscommunication can occur if a speaker does not know the face values of the other cultural group. There was the case of a learner of Spanish in Mexico who used 'tu' to address everyone, ignorant of the fact that Mexicans reserve 'tu' for intimates or people trying to pick a fight. Differences are evident in business negotiations: Anglo-American business people prefer close, friendly, egalitarian relationships, symmetrical solidarity, using first names from the beginning. Asians usually prefer symmetrical deference, and to keep to surnames. They invent Western first names to get round the Westerners insistence on first names, and often protect their own Chinese first name, which is reserved for intimates. (Scollon and Scollon 1995: 33–122).

Differences in the cooperative maxim of Quality can be misinterpreted. Žegarac and Pennington (2000: 180) refer to a study of Greek and British students, in which it emerged that the Greek students found the British people's thanks lacking in sincerity because, whereas the British say 'thank you' for everything, the Greeks only say 'thank you' when a large favour has been done. The British 'thank you' is so ubiquitous that the University of Sheffield feels the need to have a note on its website for international students:

a. **'Please' and 'thank you'**, are probably the three most important words in the British-English vocabulary.

b. **British people are easily offended** if the words are not used. In many languages and cultures such fundamental importance is not attached to these words; one can be perfectly polite without uttering them. In Britain almost the first words children are taught are 'please' and 'thank-you' (or 'thanks' or 'ta').

(http://www.shef.ac.uk/ssid/international/living/culture.html)

Again there can be East–West misunderstandings in business negotiations. If Westerners end a conversation with 'we must do lunch sometime', it is not a specific invitation but a conventional farewell formula. Scollon and Scollon (1995) say that if East Asians hear it, they expect it to be followed up soon by a concrete invitation with a statement of time and place; if it is not followed up, this gives negative impression of the other speaker.

Structure

There are also differences in terms of discourse structure. Because East Asian style is mostly inductive (they start with the topic or background and then move on to the main point) and Westerners have a deductive style (they give the main point and then explain the reasons), understanding between them can be slow or inhibited.

Misunderstandings can occur because of conversation structure differences. Raga Gimeno and Sánchez López (1999) found in conversations between Spaniards and low-Spanish-proficiency Chinese speakers that the Spaniards interpreted the Chinese speakers' long pauses as lack of comprehension and repeated their questions and contributions before the Chinese could answer. Differences can also be seen opening and closing sequences. In meetings, Westerners generally want to get down to business straight away, whereas the Asian business people usually want to do socialising first. Likewise, Asian people tend to prefer slow conclusions, whereas Westerners make quick negotiations. Each closing sequence has its own ritual: I recall an incident in my flat at the end of a party with my South-east Asian students. The goodbye sequence in the hallway seemed unending until finally one said to me, 'Look Joan, if you don't come and open this door for us, we're going to be here all night!' I was expecting them to open the door for themselves.

Interlanguage pragmatics

A7.5

Interlanguage pragmatics provides **synchronic or diachronic/developmental** studies of **second language learning**. The synchronic ones describe one level of language learner; the diachronic ones compare two levels or follow the development of one level. It looks at how people learn pragmatic principles, for example, how Mandarin speakers learn to apologise in English.

Interlanguage pragmatics began in the 1990s but is still coming into its own in the 2000s: there are fewer diachronic studies than synchronic. Research explores factors influencing second language learning, and uses methods from cross-cultural and Second Language Acquisition studies.

Synchronic studies

Some learners have difficulty with indirect speech acts. Carrell (1981) found that lower-proficiency EFL learners at university could interpret English requests expressed as statements ('You should color the circle blue') but had more difficulty interpreting them stated as questions ('Should you color the circle blue?') or negation ('You shouldn't color the circle blue').

Learning the L2 conversation structure (pre-sequences, opening and closing sequences) can cause problems for learners. Wolfson (1989) tells of learners who understood the illocutionary force but missed the conversational function. In the example

A: Your blouse is beautiful
B: Thanks
A: 'Did you bring it from China?'
B: Yeah

the learner heard the compliment but did not see it as a conversational opener or pre-sequence. Liddicoat and Crozet (2001) tried to teach French learners of English about opening sequence differences in Monday-morning greetings. For Australians, the greeting 'Did you have a good weekend?' is a formulaic question asked of everyone, expecting a formulaic answer. In the French context, it is only asked of friends and expects a detailed answer and extended topic, with language inviting interaction. Liddicoat and Crozet's learners were able to include the extended topics into their conversations but not the interactional forms, such as feedback tokens and repetition.

The L2 culture's politeness maxim of modesty realisations can be hard for learners to appreciate. Cook (2001: 80–99) tried to teach learners of Japanese that a display of a humble attitude is valued, and that a lower-status person is expected to sound hesitant, indirect and apologetic. The learners then listened to three job interviews with Japanese speakers, in which two of them humbled their ability using polite hedges, as in 'o-' (honorific prefix on verb stem), '-masu' (honorific suffix) and 'omou' (I think that). The learners did not appreciate how impolite the applicant who did not use the polite forms sounded.

Developmental studies

Some studies show that learners can speak more directly and assertively as they gain confidence. Bardovi-Harlig and Hartford (1993) followed the changes in low-level-proficiency learners of English in discussions with their tutor. Over time, they became more direct, moving from a passive to an active role contradicting the tutor and rejecting advice. They were less likely to use mitigators than native speakers of English, making their comments sound like a fact not negotiable with the tutor:

So, I, I just decided on taking the language structure . . . field method in linguistics.

In the summer I will take language testing.

Other studies show the opposite, that learners became more indirect over time. Kasper and Rose (2002: 134–48) ran a project that showed that at the beginning of training, learners used routine formulae as in 'Let's play the game', whereas at the end, they used analysed, productive language and indirectness such as 'Can I see it so I can copy it?' and 'Is there any more white?'

Learners can be trained to use conversational routines and interactive language. Rose and Kasper (2001) studied the development of American learners of Japanese in their use of acknowledgement expressions, which indicate attentiveness and alignment. They found that at the beginning of training, the learners used only 'aa soo desu ka' ('oh really?') when prompted by the teacher, but that by the end they could use spontaneously a whole range of expressions, including, for example, 'soo desu ne' ('it is, isn't it').

Learner beliefs and attitudes

The extent to which learners adopt the L2 pragmatic dimensions and features depends in part on their beliefs and attitudes.

Learners' attitudes to the native speakers and L2 culture can affect their acquisition of the pragmatic features. Schumann (1986) said that development depends a) on the learners' social distance from the native speakers, seen in the power relations between them, the learners' sense of identity and the native speakers' attitude to the learners, and b) on the learners' psychological distance from native speakers, seen in language shock, culture shock and motivation. The theory is that low socio-psychological distance leads to high integration of the learner with the native speaker group, which in turn leads to acquisition. An awareness of the importance of acculturation has led to companies such as *Lingualearn*, specialising in language learning and intercultural communications, to realise the economic implications and run a Business Culture Training for China course. Their homepage has this notice:

> Failure to take into account linguistic and cultural differences can lead to lost business via misunderstandings, errors, culture shock, suspicion, bad will and poor relationships. The physical distance between China and Western countries accentuates the risk – good understanding of conducting business in China can lead to increased competitiveness and success.
>
> (http://www.lingualearn.co.uk/managers/businessculture.htm)

Identity is a highly influential social factor. Learners may either act the foreigner so as not to be judged as an in-group member, or actively disidentify themselves from the culture to assert their own identity. Barron (2002: 248) carried out a study with Irish learners of German and asked them if they should adopt German directness norms. Half answered affirmatively and half negatively:

If directness is what they understand, you have to cater for that and act accordingly.

At 21 years, I've developed my personality and nature and I don't believe I should have to become direct/more abrupt when speaking a foreign language. I don't want to be German – I want people to still notice that I'm Irish.

Native speaker attitude to learners affects learners. Some native speakers have low expectancies pragmatically when learners have a low L2 proficiency, and show lenience vis-à-vis politeness norms; others have negative views, preferring learners to act as foreigners and not claim in-group membership. Kasper and Rose (2002: 234–5) found that pragmatic stereotypes can inhibit acquisition, for example, if learners are perceived as direct and impolite, the native speakers will not encourage them to use self-humbling formulaic expressions; if learners perceive native speakers to be impolite, they will not notice politeness strategies when they meet language containing them. Web2 (the internet as a platform for communication and collaboration) might improve international understanding. Take for example this blog from the blogspot site of Lynne Murphy, from the Department of Linguistics and English Language, The University of Sussex:

> How often one should thank others is something that differs from culture to culture, and something that people tend to notice as over- or under-present in cultures that are not their own. British expats in America are <u>often heard to say</u> that they miss people saying *please* and *thank you*. For what it's worth, as an American in Britain, I miss people saying (AmE) *Excuse me* or *sorry* when they knock into me in shops or on the street. (Whenever my mother comes to England, she has cause to exclaim *But I thought the English were supposed to be polite!*)
>
> (31 March 2007 http://separatedbyacommonlanguage. blogspot.com/search/label/politeness)

A7.6

Teaching intercultural pragmatics

Closely related to interlanguage pragmatics is the field of **teaching intercultural pragmatics**. Using classroom interaction data, this investigates whether pragmatics should be taught and how to teach it. It looks at the best teaching approach for pragmatic principles, for example, how to teach Mandarin speakers to understand apologies in English.

Studies on teaching intercultural pragmatics began in the 1990s and are still developing in the 2000s. Research reflects Teaching English as a Foreign Language (TEFL) methodology.

Whether to teach it

Some theorists believe that there is no need to teach intercultural pragmatics. The writers of Communicative Language Teaching coursebooks do not generally feel the need: they include texts with cultural content but only use them to teach skills or register. There is a widespread myth that the only way to achieve pragmatic fluency is to go to the country where the language is spoken. This blog from Japan Forum ('a friendly online community dedicated to all things Japanese') reflects this:

Japantvhost

The best way to learn Japanese is immersion. Books and videos are fine but to really understand how to live and breathe the language, go to some small town where there are no foreigners and do a home stay. You will be a talking Japanese in no time.

(10 December 2006 http://www.jref.com/forum/showthread.php?p=438169)

There is no research to substantiate this.

Other theorists (Pennycook 1994; Phillipson 1992) believe that the culture of English-speaking countries should not be taught in EFL classes, saying that English is owned by BANA (Britain, Australia and North America), a global hegemonic power promoting the values of its own culture over those of the countries learning English, and that those who impose BANA cultural competence on education are guilty of 'linguistic imperialism'. Graddol (2006: 112) opposes this point of view, saying that it 'does not wholly explain the current enthusiasm for English which seems driven primarily by parental and governmental demand, rather than promotion by anglophone countries'.

Yet other theorists think that intercultural pragmatics *must* be taught. They believe that knowledge of the L2 culture is essential if learners want to understand subtle meanings in the L2, and that it helps learners to think about the way in which their L1 functions. Followers of the intercultural approach to TEFL say that learning materials should include aspects of L1 culture and that non-native speaker teachers should be valued for their ability to understand both the L1 and the L2 cultures (Corbett 2003). Graddol takes this one stage further, predicting that, because the number of speakers of English as an L2 is growing at such a rate globally, the status of the native speaker will diminish, and EFL will be replaced by English as a Lingua Franca (ELF), reflecting the needs of the non-native speakers of English:

> Unlike traditional EFL, ELF focuses also on pragmatic strategies required in inter-cultural communication. The target model of English, within the ELF framework, is not a native speaker but a fluent bilingual speaker, who retains a national identity in terms of accent, and who also has the special skills required to negotiate under-standing with another non-native speaker.
>
> (Graddol 2006: 87)

Time will tell.

How to teach it

Instruction in pragmatics seems to be better than simply exposing learners to the language in class. Explicit instruction, with the teacher explaining and the learners learning deductively, appears to be better than implicit instruction, with the learners being asked to notice how forms work and learn inductively. Learning is limited if learners are confused because they are given insufficient help in understanding the L2 pragmatics, and if they do not see it as relevant or useful.

It is currently understood that small group discussions give better results in the learning of pragmatic features than teacher-centred classes. In the latter all the Initia-tion and Feedback moves of IRF are the teacher's, so learners cannot develop interac-tional knowledge and have little practice in conversation openings and closings and listener responses. Teacher-centred classes do not bring learners into contact with a variety of social situations, or require them to use a variety of speech acts and politeness strategies.

Error correction is part of TEFL, whatever the approach or classroom set-up. Some feel that it is necessary to correct learners' pragmatic errors because learners tend to be unaware of the reason for the pragmatic failure and unable to repair it. However, sociopragmatic error correction requires sensitivity:

> Sociopragmatic decisions are social before they are linguistic, and while foreign learners are fairly amenable to corrections which they regard are linguistic, they are justifiably sensitive about having their social (or even political, religious, or moral) judgment called into question.
>
> (Thomas 1983: 104)

Section B

DEVELOPMENT:
STUDIES IN PRAGMATICS

B1 ANALYSING THE DISCOURSE IN CONTEXT

B1.1 Analysing text using concepts

❑ Context
❑ Language and the context

Text

How are things going?

Here is another conversation between students. AF, the Scottish woman, comes in and
sees CM, the Canadian man, and DM, the Englishman, sitting with the curtains drawn.
They are joined by BM and MM, English men.

1	AF	God it's hot in here.
2	DM	Is it?
3	AM	Yeah. (1) Really. (0.5) Are you shutting out this lovely sunshine?
4	DM	It's getting in my eyes.
5	AF	Oh no!
6	CM	Yeah. Not used to that are you?
7	DM	No. (6) What's that? Psycholinguistics?
8	AF	Mhm. I have difficulty getting my brain going first thing in the morning.
9	DM	She certainly fills it up, doesn't she? She's got lots of things to tell you I'm sure.
10	AF	Yeah. (yawns) Oh I just want to sit down. (1) You going to get on your bike?
11	DM	Have you got to go?
12	NF	Yeah. I suppose I have. I shouldn't this morning.
13	DM	Yeah right. ((MM and BM enter))
14	MM	Anyone got the key to the photocopier? (1)
15	DM	No.
16	AF	Is it still not there? (2) Oh MM! I (0.5) brought the what what's a name back.
17	MM	Yeah. Tell you what ((unintelligible)).
18	DM	How are you?
19	BM	All right.
20	DM	I haven't seen you very much.
21	BM	No I haven't seen you very much.
22	DM	We must not fit at all.
23	BM	You do you do language planning don't you.
24	DM	Yeah. I've stopped doing that though.
25	BM	Are you er (0.5) are going to do what you thought you'd do about your project.

26	DM	I'm going to give out a questionnaire. And I'll give you one as well
27		Sometime this week I hope t, tomorrow I'll get them all done.
28	AF	What your core project?
29	DM	Yeah. (0.5)
30	CM	Did he like did he like the idea?
31	DM	Well you know what he's like. It's difficult to tell isn't it? Yeah. He
32		said it wasn't terrible anyway. He said go ahead so (0.5) I'm going
		to go ahead.
33	CM	Yeah he said this isn't terrible?
34	DM	No no he didn't tell me that. // (heh heh)

(Students on questionnaire – 1996)

Text analysis

How are things going?

This conversation has all the signs of an exchange between people who know each other well. They are joking and teasing, and their language is informal and assumes a great deal of interpersonal knowledge.

Let us start by analysing the **situational context**. We can see examples of **exophoric** reference to it.

❑ The first is in lines 1–7. AF's 'God it's hot in here' has a **place deixis** demonstrative adverb 'here' pointing to the room that they are in. Her words 'Are you shutting out this lovely sunshine?' contain an exophoric demonstrative adjective 'this' pointing to the sunshine coming through the curtains.

❑ The second example occurs in line 7: 'What's that? Psycholinguistics?' Here we have an exophoric demonstrative pronoun. Presumably, the 'that' points to a book or lecture notes that AF is carrying.

In these two cases, the words do not have to be explicit because the surroundings provide the meaning. Note that AF does not say 'Are you shutting out this lovely sunshine that is coming through the curtains at the window behind you?' and DM does not ask 'What lecture is that file of notes, which is under your arm, for?' It would sound very strange if they did.

Moving on to the **context of the cultural background**, there are three stretches of discourse that show evidence of speakers assuming a common knowledge of the course. Again **exophora** is present.

❑ The first is in lines 8–12. DM infers that AF is making a comment about the lecturer's style and responds showing a similar attitude: 'She certainly fills it up, doesn't she? She's got lots of things to tell you I'm sure'. It is not necessary for DM to name the lecturer, because 'Psycholinguistics' establishes the context of the lecture and presuppositional pool of the lecturer, her style and the materials.

❏ In the second example (lines 13–16), MM asks 'Anyone got the key to the photocopier?' He assumes that all those in the room know which photocopier and key he means. AF implies that she knows about the missing key, with her 'Is it still not there?', the 'still' suggesting that it was already missing before, and the place deixis 'there' showing that she knows where it should be.

❏ In the third example (lines 31–4). They are talking about a lecturer that DM went to see. DM says 'Well you know what he's like. It's difficult to tell isn't it?', assuming that all hearers do indeed know what he is like, and have the same attitude towards him, his 'isn't it?' asking them to agree.

Next, we come to stretches of dialogue assuming knowledge of **interpersonal background context** with **exophora.** There are five instances.

❏ The first is in lines 10–13. It appears that NF stands up to go. AF asks 'You going to get on your bike?' She knows that NF is not going upstairs to the lecture theatre but out of the building, and that she has a bike. DM knows where NF is going and why and that there is some doubt as to whether it is necessary.

❏ The second instance comes in lines 16–17. AF says 'Oh MM! I (0.5) brought the what what's a name back'. MM does not say 'What on earth are you talking about?' He just says 'Yeah' and mumbles something private to her. This is an example of intertextuality: they had possibly had a previous conversation in which MM asked AF to bring something back. It is easier and more private to use the vague expression.

❏ The next example is in lines 21–4. Not only do BM and DM show that they have an interpersonal context of not meeting up because their lectures do not coincide ('We must not fit at all'), but they also know what course options each chose, even though BM's knowledge is out of date.

❏ The fourth instance occurs in lines 25–30. BM refers to the topic of DM's project 'what you thought you'd do'. He may use this inexplicit noun clause because it is convenient, or it may be that he has actually forgotten what DM said he was going to do. Whatever the reason, it is **intertextual**.

❏ The final example is in lines 30–4. CM mentions, out of the blue, an unnamed male person: 'Did he like did he like the idea?' The 'he' gains meaning from the context associated with the project and the questionnaire: it is **intertextual** reference. CM rightly assumed that DM could infer who 'he' refers to.

These stretches of language dependent on the interpersonal context are the most impenetrable to an outsider. The inexplicit reference excludes everyone except people who were present at their last conversation, and it is privileged information, which is just as well as they are gossiping about the lecturers. And the tape-recorder is running.

Now let us look at **cohesion**, and start with **grammatical** cohesion. Even this conversation with all its in-group knowledge and implicitness has plenty of **anaphoric** reference. The conversation has to cohere, and the speakers have to cohere socially:

❏ There is the personal pronoun 'it': in 'It's getting in my eyes' (line 4) it refers to the sunshine; in 'Is it still not there?' (line 16) it refers to 'the key to the photocopier'; and in 'He said it wasn't terrible anyway' (line 31–2) it refers to the 'idea'.

❑ There the demonstrative pronoun 'that': in 'Not used to that are you?' (line 6) it is cohesive with the situation of the 'lovely sunshine' getting in DM's eyes; in 'I've stopped doing that though' (line 24) it is cohesive with 'language planning'; in 'he didn't tell me that' (line 34) it refers to 'this isn't terrible'.

❑ The personal pronoun 'them' in 'I'll get them all done' (line 27) is an interesting case. It is plural and yet it coheres with 'a questionnaire'. This is because it is **associative anaphora.** They know that students produce 20–50 questionnaires.

There is no **cataphoric** reference, but this is hardly surprising. Cataphora is very much a feature of written texts and oral narratives.

Substitution and ellipsis are features of spoken grammar (Carter and McCarthy 2006), but there is only one example of **substitution**: 'I'll give you one as well' (line 26), meaning 'I'll give you a questionnaire'. There are a great number of examples of **ellipsis**, on the other hand:

❑ There is **anaphoric** ellipsis in short questions and answers: 'Is it?' (line 2) means 'Is it hot in here?'; 'Psycholinguistics?' (line 7) asks 'Is it Psycholinguistics?'; 'I suppose I have' (line 12) elides 'got to go'. The 'I shouldn't' could mean 'I shouldn't go' or 'I shouldn't have to go'.

❑ 'What your core project?'(line 28) is incomplete, but, since it is a general orientation question, the non-elided form could be anything from 'Are you talking about your core project?' to 'Are you giving out questionnaires for your core project?'

❑ There are four examples of **situational exophoric** ellipsis, typical of informal spoken discourse: two have no verb – 'You going to get on your bike?' (line 10) and 'Anyone got the key to the photocopier?' (line 14), and two have both verb and subject elided – 'Not used to that are you?' (line 6) and 'Tell you what' (line 17). These examples are also structural, in that the verbs are elided.

Lexical cohesion is practically non-existent. There is no **repetition** and no **synonyms**, because of the low density of nouns and quick change of topic. Only one noun might class as a **superordinate:** 'project' could be said to encompass 'core project' and 'option project'. There are no **general words** with a cohesive function: 'She's got lots of things to tell you' and 'I brought the what's a name back' (lines 9, 16) are exophoric, with no clear indication in the text of their referent.

Further reading →→→→

B1.2

❑ For good examples of the influence of context on meaning, see Mey (1993), Grundy (2000) and Brown and Yule (1983).

❑ For a further exploration of the relationship between context and deixis, see Thomas (1995) and Cruse (2000).

❑ For a simple discussion of reference, substitution, ellipsis and lexical cohesion, see Halliday and Hasan (1976), Brown and Yule (1983), Hatch (1992) and Smith and Leinonen (1992).

❑ Grundy (2000), Cummings (2005) and Huang (2007) offer a complex discussion of deixis, inference and common ground.

❑ Cook (1989) suggests ways to teach language students cohesion.

B2

USING SPEECH ACTS

B2.1

Analysing text using concepts

- ❏ Direct speech acts
- ❏ Felicity conditions
- ❏ Indirect speech acts
- ❏ Interactional/transactional function

Text

Fox-hunting under cover

The following excerpt is taken from the BBC1 thriller series *Dalziel and Pascoe* (6 May 2001). Andrew Dalziel is an older detective of the grumpy-yet-amiable variety. In this scene, Dalziel's boss asks about one of the female police officers, to whom Dalziel had given the job of working under cover as a horse-rider in the fox-hunting world to discover who murdered one of the fox-hunters. Dalziel's boss knows that he is against fox-hunting, partly out of sympathy with the fox, partly out of antipathy for the aristocracy.

1	Boss:	Under cover? This isn't your private army. Is she OK?
2	Dalziel:	She's good. (0.5) In fact she spent half her childhood on a horse.
3	Boss:	How do I know you're lying to me, Andy?
4	Dalziel:	Look, we've even given her a full story; set up a liaison point.
5		Visitors often go on a ride with another hunt. They come for a
6		few days, stay at a local pub, borrow a horse. And since hunting
7		is about drinking as much as it is riding, it shouldn't be long
8		before someone becomes indiscreet. (0.5)
9	Boss:	All right. But don't upset the locals. Hounsden is a nice village.
10	Dalziel:	Pity it's not a bunch of miners – then we could have done what
11		we liked. (1)
12	Boss:	Watch it, superintendent! I'm not asking you to kow-tow to the
13		gentry. I'm telling you to go by the book. (0.5) You see I know
14		how you work.

Text Analysis

Fox-hunting under cover

Let us begin with the macro-function of this excerpt. This is a work conversation and it has a primarily **transactional** function: they are not having a sociable chat, they are negotiating a plan of action. The boss's main aim is to transmit the information that will affect Dalziel's behaviour. She tells him 'Hounsden is a nice village' because she wants him to not 'upset the locals' but 'go by the book'. Dalziel gives his boss a full account of how he has organised the officer's task and cover because she needs the information. Between the factual points, there is language with a primarily **interactional** function. The boss's 'All right' is an expression of agreement; Dalziel's 'Pity it's not a bunch of miners' comment is not essential to the negotiation, it is an attempt to share opinions and make the conversation more sociable.

Let us move on to the **perlocutionary** effect of the speakers' words on the hearers. The boss's 'How do I know you're lying to me, Andy?' makes Dalziel reassure her and convince her that his plan of action in this case is all well-thought out and safe. He has to impress her since she is his superior and has the ultimate say in all his actions. The boss presumably hopes that the perlocutionary effect of her warning 'I'm telling you to go by the book' will be that he *will* work in the conventional way, and not offend any of the gentry.

Let us now analyse the **speech acts**, **direct** and **indirect**, and the **illocutionary force**. The boss gives orders indirectly to Dalziel first, and then they become more and more indirect.

❑ In line 1, her 'This isn't your private army' is, on the surface, a declaration, functioning as a direct representative, a statement describing the people who work for Dalziel. Indirectly, it is a directive with the illocutionary force of forbidding him, as in 'Do not use these people to your own ends'.

❑ When Dalziel answers her enquiry about the police officer under cover, saying that she is an experienced rider, she seems to be using an interrogative to ask a representative question in line 3: 'How do I know you're lying to me, Andy?' Again, this has the illocutionary force of an indirect directive forbidding him to lie as in the imperative 'Don't lie to me, Andy' or 'Tell me the truth'.

❑ When he tells her the theory behind his decision, she becomes more direct, giving him in line 9 a **direct directive**, in the form of a negative imperative, telling him, 'Don't upset the locals'.

❑ When Dalziel makes the point about the miners, she then uses, in line 13, something resembling a **direct declaration** to make her command clear, so that there can be no doubt: 'I'm telling you to go by the book.' It comes across as the explicit performative, 'I hereby command you to go by the book'.

Let us look now at what Dalziel is doing in this brief exchange. He starts by showing respect, with neutral declaratives and indirect expressives, and then follows this with a show of anger, in the form of direct expressives.

❑ His declarative 'In fact she spent half her childhood on a horse' (line 2) is a **direct representative**, but **indirectly**, it is an **expressive** that backs up the previous statement 'She's good', praising her skills. It could also be seen as an indirect commissive, implying 'I promise to you that I know what I'm doing and will not endanger her life'.

❑ Likewise his long story about her cover: lines 4–6 contain direct representatives that carry the **indirect directive** message of 'Don't worry. Everything is in order'.

❑ In lines 10–11, his attitude changes. His words 'Pity it's not a bunch of miners – then we could have done what we liked' bear a reference heavy in cultural background knowledge of the closing of the British coal mines. In the 1980s the Thatcher government destroyed the mining industry, and the miners went on a very long strike; many felt that the closing of the mines was not accompanied by compassion or even consideration for the miners. By making this suggestion, Dalziel is implying an **indirect expressive** deploring the double standards of the country that could be expressed as 'We must make every effort not to upset the aristocracy, but we were not asked to make such efforts with the working class'. What might also be implied is a defiant indirect commissive of 'I'll do what I like'. This is what provokes the boss's 'Watch it, superintendent!' She knows that he refuses to 'kow-tow to the gentry'; what really worries her is that he may do something that does not 'go by the book'. As it happens, later in the programme he does step out of line and join the protesters in obstructing a hunt and saving a fox from being mauled to death by the hounds, a very topical theme for the year 2001, since fox-hunting was made illegal in Scotland and then England and Wales then.

Let us look briefly at the **felicity conditions.** This is closely related to the power structure: the boss's higher social status gives her the right to play the role of telling Dalziel what to do. Interestingly, although he seems to recognise that it is possible for her to carry out the act of directing him, he suggests that he cannot follow her orders and asserts his rights as an individual with opinions. She reminds him in lines 12–14 that she can and will give him orders. It may be the case that other social dimensions are entering into play here. Dalziel is older than his boss and therefore more experienced; it may be this that gives him confidence to defy the felicity conditions. Then, of course, he is a man and is most likely unused to taking orders from a woman; this may be why she has to make it clear that she is boss.

All in all, it is a short but interesting little excerpt, with a great deal going on under the surface.

| B2.2 | **Further reading →→→→** |

❏ For a brief introduction to Speech Act Theory, read Cummings (2005).

❏ For a deeper and more detailed discussion of speech act classifications (slightly different terms), felicity conditions, performative verbs and the performative hypothesis, read Cruse, (2000) and Leech (1983) and Levinson (1983).

❏ For a thorough, yet still accessible, explanation of indirect speech acts, looking at idioms, literal meaning and conventional meaning, with plenty of examples, read Grundy (2000).

❏ Schiffrin (1994) provides an advanced, careful explanation of the development of Austin's and Searle's theories, a discussion of their application to discourse analysis, and demonstrations of sample analysis.

❏ Thomas (1995) and Blakemore (1992) give an advanced, critical discussion of the development of Austin's and Searle's theories, the performative hypothesis and types of performatives, overlaps and cross-cultural differences.

❏ For a clear introduction to the sociolinguistic approach to speech functions, and an exploration of the effect of all cultural differences and contextual constraints, go to Holmes (1992), Spencer-Oatey (2000) and Huang (2007).

□ Tannen (1994) reports on a specialised study report of indirect speech acts in male–female discourse, comparing Greeks and Americans, and the misunderstandings caused by stylistic differences.

□ For those needing suggestions for research projects in speech acts, and the applications to language learning, Hatch (1992) is helpful.

THE PRAGMATICS OF CONVERSATION

B3

Analysing text using concepts

B3.1

□ Exchange moves and IRF Felicity conditions
□ Conversation analysis
□ Interactional sociolinguistics

Text

Scrabble

This extract is taken from British component of the International Corpus of English (ICE-GB). A mother and daughter are at the mother's house, eating, chatting and playing Scrabble ('a game in which players make points by putting rows of separate letters on squares of a board to form words' – Longman Dictionary of Contemporary English, 1978).

1	Mother:	I don't know what you're doing on that.
2	Daughter:	Oh no.
3	Mother:	No.
4	Daughter:	No fear I should say =
5	Mother:	= Well, do it somewhere else. I mean, look there's plenty of other
6		places to put it. How about here? // I like it like that.
7	Daughter:	// Uhm it's OK. Oh God you don't –
8		First of all you don't score so much, and secondly you only
9		get rid of two letters // and you make your chances of picking
		up anything better
10	Mother:	// Uhm
11	Daughter:	that much more reduced by not // you know, getting rid of as
		many as
12	Mother:	// Uhm
13	Daughter:	you can. Two four six – seven twenty-four is eleven. I mean
		you could

14		do so much better than that if // you'd only
15	Mother:	// Yeah. I'm busy eating as a matter of fact
16	Daughter:	Oh.
17	Mother:	I didn't really like that sandwich.
18	Daughter:	(laughs) I wouldn't have noticed (laughs). You've // packed away most
19	Mother:	// No but I
20	Daughter:	of it (laughs) all the same.
21	Mother:	kept hoping it would get better and it got worse. (laughs)
22		Salty. Don't like salty things.
23	Daughter:	No.
24	Mother:	Have some banana bread.
25	Daughter:	Look. I'm not that much of a banana bread eater // and I wish you'd
26	Mother:	// Oh I forgot //
27	Daughter:	stop bothering.
28	Mother:	Never mention it again.
29	Daughter:	Yes, I mean, you know, I know where these things are. If I'm
30		that interested I'll ask if I may have a piece and then you can
31		tell me you haven't made any for months or don't make it any
32		more (laughs) I've got a whole load of my own banana bread in the fridge. I don't know.
33	Mother:	Do we have 'sana' SANA?
34	Daughter:	No. We have 'sauna' SAUNA. Right we have (unclear). A funny game.
35		That's a funny game. 'Go' and 'ox'. And the 'ox' is uh sixteen
36		seventeen eighteen nineteen twenty.
37	Mother:	Mm. Mm.
38	Daughter:	You're now eighty behind. If you'd listened to me (laughs)
39		you'd only be seventy behind. Anyway what else did Linda have to say for herself.
40	Mother:	Oh a lot. Never left off. When she's // finished with the kids, she
41	Daughter:	// Oh.
42	Mother:	goes back to Felicity and all her achievements. Actually you
43		probably wouldn't have enjoyed it here. (laughs)
44	Daughter:	What do you mean about Felicity and her achievements, is it?
45		Oh no // I have been inured to that // for years.
46	Mother:	// How wonderful she is, you know // how she talks.

(ICE-GB: Spoken dialogue, private, direct conversation: S1A – 010, 1991)

B

Text Analysis

Scrabble

The first comment to make about this excerpt is to emphasise that speakers are mother and daughter: they know each other very well and they are alone together in an informal environment. The **interpersonal relations** and the **situational context** have a significant influence on how the conversation flows. They share background knowledge about the daughter's lack of interest in banana bread ('Oh I forgot. Never mention it again') and about the mother's friend Linda and her children ('do you mean about Felicity and her achievements'). They know each other well enough to criticise how they play Scrabble (lines 7–14), to tease about how they eat (lines 18–20), and to pretend to take offence (lines 25–28). The criticisms and teasing are interspersed with laughter and they are not dwelt on.

CA says that this piece of talk shows that they know each other well, but not that their knowing each other well makes them talk like this. Indeed, in a more formal context and talking about less personal topics, the signs of their knowing each other well might not be so obvious. Whereas pragmatics, discourse analysis and interactional sociolinguistics say that all background context influences what interactants say, CA says that only some contexts are relevant in the understanding of the talk.

If we come to this real-life conversation and try to make it fit the a priori **exchange structure**, we find that the conversation is far too 'chaotic', especially as there is not one person with the role or status to initiate (as in teacher, doctor, quizmaster) and the other to respond, and nor does the situational context require it. The only follow-up that stands out is the mother's responses – 'Uhm' (lines 10 and 12), and 'Mm. Mm' (line 37) – and they are more backchannelling and agreeing than evaluating what her daughter is saying.

The 'chaotic' nature of the conversation can be seen if we look at it using **conversation analysis**, which is designed to look at how real data unfold and utterances affect each other. We cannot talk of turn-taking in the sense of respecting **Transition Relevance Places**. Only in the middle of the excerpt, lines 28–39, do the speakers wait till the other has finished talking before they answer or contribute to the conversation. This is because daughter is ranting about not wanting banana bread and telling her mother how far behind she is.

About half of the turns contain **overlaps and interruptions** (indicated with a // in the text), and this is quite a high proportion, even for a casual conversation between familiars:

❑ In lines 7–8, the daughter takes the turn from her mother, with 'Uhm it's OK. Oh God you don't – First of all you don't score so much . . .' and she holds the floor arguing with her 'lesson' on Scrabble tactics, until line 14.

❑ In line 14, the mother interrupts and takes the turn back, with her 'Yeah. I'm busy eating as a matter of fact', and thus does not allow her daughter to extend her 'lesson' any further. The mother overlaps again and seems to take the floor in lines 18–19, with her 'No but I kept hoping it would get better . . .'

❏ In lines 40–45, the daughter interrupts what her mother is saying about Linda and her talking about her children and Felicity, because she cannot and does not want to wait to say that she knows all about it: 'I have been inured to that for years'.

An analysis of the **adjacency pairs** shows that there is not a neat pairing of utterances or turns. The exception could be in lines 18 and 20 in which the daughter 'accuses', with 'You've packed away most of it all the same' and then the mother 'defends' in lines 19 and 21, giving the **preferred** response: 'No but I kept hoping it would get better . . .' More frequent is the **dispreferred** response:

❏ In line 13, the daughter 'advises', with 'I mean you could do so much better than that if only you'd . . .', but the mother neither 'accepts' nor 'rejects' the advice; she justifies her poor playing in line 15: 'Yeah. I'm busy eating as a matter of fact'.
❏ Again, in line 24, the mother 'offers' her daughter some banana bread, but instead of an 'accept', she is faced with a 'reject' ('Look. I'm not that much of a banana bread eater'), and the reject goes on for several lines.

This is not to say that there is a fight going on, to hold the floor. No offence is taken at the interruptions or the dispreferred responses, as it is an amicable exchange. There may, however, be the slightest of power struggles, in the sense that the daughter seems to need to show independence: she knows about Scrabble and she does not have to wait to be asked if she wants to eat. Likewise, the mother ignores the show of independence: her 'I'm busy eating *as a matter of fact*' shows that she is unimpressed, as does her 'Do we have 'sana' SANA'?

Analysis of the **sequences** of the conversation shows that there are no **opening** or **closing** sequences, as this excerpt is part of a longer conversation. There are no **pre-sequences**, which is possibly a reflection of close relationship and the triviality of the task that they are engaged in: neither needs to prepare the other for a suggestion or invitation. It could be said that there are **insertion** sequences, however:

❏ In lines 15–32 the sandwich and the banana bread topics come as an insertion sequence within the main topic of playing Scrabble.
❏ Line 39 onwards about Linda and her family come as another.

Yet, it could also be said that the Scrabble commentaries are the insertions. It depends whether, in their mind, the chat is the background to the Scrabble, or the Scrabble is the background to the chat. The analyst cannot tell.

Returning to the relevance of the interpersonal relations and the situational context, we can analyse the conversation from the **interactional sociolinguistics** point of view and notice that the '**contextualisation cues**' point with imprecise reference to the knowledge that they share. The daughter's 'I know where *these things* are' refers presumably to other foods that the mother tends to offer and to the cupboards or shelves in the refrigerator where they are kept. Similarly, the mother's 'Actually you probably wouldn't have enjoyed *it here*' (lines 42–43) uses exophoric reference with a personal pronoun 'it' and a demonstrative adverb 'here', which only have meaning for them because they know the referring items because of their intertextual knowledge. The mother's 'you know how *she* talks' (line 46) is another example of the way that they refer to their shared knowledge in a way that would exclude an outsider. This interactional talk claiming common ground with vague reference, whether there is a mini-power-struggle or not, is a marker of their friendship.

Further reading →→→→

B3.2

❏ For a simple check on classroom scripts, see Hatch (1992), and for an in-depth analysis of classroom discourse, see Walsh (2006).

❏ For a simple explanation of IRF, see McCarthy and Carter (1994), and for a more thorough discussion, see Coulthard (1985) and Eggins and Slade (1997).

❏ You will find that Levinson (1983), Mey (1993) and Stubbs (1983) provide an in-depth explanation of turn-taking, TRP, adjacency pairs and sequences.

❏ For a comprehensive exploration of the history of conversation analysis and examples of the methodology, go to Schiffrin (1994).

❏ For a classic paper on conversation and book on conversation analysis interactional sociolinguistics, try Sacks, Schegloff and Jefferson (1974), Sacks (1992a and 1992b) and Ochs, Schegloff and Thompson (1996).

❏ For recent developments in conversation analysis and interactional sociolinguistics, try Richards and Seedhouse (2004), Carbaugh (2005) and Liddicoat (2006).

COOPERATION AND RELEVANCE

B4

Analysing text using concepts

B4.1

❏ Observing maxims
❏ Flouting and violating
❏ Relevance Theory

The following text is real data taken from the British National Corpus. It is part of a casual conversation between Lisa, a 30-year-old housewife from the South Midlands, and Melvin, a 29-year-old panel beater. The BNC does not give the situational context; the conversation suggests that the speakers share a certain amount of cultural background knowledge and interpersonal knowledge.

Text

Visiting Louise

1	Lisa:	Oh your mum and dad er popped round last night to see Louise.
2		Guess what time they went round?
3	Melvin:	About nine – ten o'clock?
4	Lisa:	Quarter past eight. She was in bed. She normally goes to bed
5		about half past seven. They said that's the earliest they could
6		get there. I said that's a load of rubbish I said, cos they have fish
		and chips on a Friday night.
7	Melvin:	Yeah.
8	Lisa:	So she didn't have to cook.
9	Melvin:	Ah they would have had to wash up the plates and the knives
10		and forks. But she's just one of those women who don't like
11		leaving stuff around, you know what I mean? Once they've had
12		something, they've got to do it before they go, can you believe?
13		She's a right pain in the arse sometimes, me mum. That's why
14		they don't go anywhere, you see. Yeah, that's why they don't
		come out and visit his brother very often. So why did they want
		to see Louise?
15	Lisa:	It was her birthday.
16	Melvin:	Oh yeah. They should have gone as soon as they got out of
		work.
17	Lisa:	Yeah. And they could have got fish and chips on the way home,
		couldn't they?
18	Melvin:	Yeah

(BNC: kd3 Lisa, 1992)

Text analysis

Visiting Louise

Because Melvin and Louise seem to share such a lot of cultural background knowledge and interpersonal knowledge, we can assume that they know each other and each other's worlds fairly well, and because of their shared knowledge, they can **flout** the maxims freely, in the certainty that they will each be able to infer the other's implied meaning.

❑ When Lisa says that Melvin's mother and father arrived at Louise's house or flat at a quarter past eight, she adds, 'She was in bed. She normally goes to bed about half past seven. They said that's the earliest they could get there' (lines 4–5), which implies that it was not actually 'the earliest they could get there', and she feels that this was inconsiderate of them as they knew that she had to go to bed early and they wittingly disturbed her sleep. All of this information is not mentioned and yet it is can be inferred by Melvin: the maxim of **quantity** is flouted.

❑ The maxim of **relation** may be flouted in the utterances 'They said that's the earliest they could get there. I said that's a load of rubbish I said, cos they have fish and chips on a Friday night' (lines 5–6), since the fact that they have fish and chips does not seem immediately relevant to their getting there early, yet Melvin infers it. Flouting too the maxim of quantity, Lisa omits the reference to the fact that they would have bought fish and chips in a chip-shop, which would have meant that they did not have to spend time preparing, cooking or washing up, which in turn implies that they could have arrived before half past seven. Melvin corrects her, even though she said nothing about washing up: 'Ah they would have had to wash up the plates and the knives and forks. But she's just one of those women who don't like leaving stuff around, you know what I mean?' (lines 9–11).

❑ Melvin flouts the maxim of quantity when he says minimally, 'They should have gone as soon as they got out of work' (line 16). Lisa appears to infer that he means that they could have got there before 7.30, made a special effort for the special occasion and broken with their routine; her answer 'they could have got fish and chips on the way home' (line 17) shows that she is following on his idea.

❑ There is one example of the flouting of the maxim of **quality**: 'She's a right pain in the arse sometimes, me mum. That's why they don't go anywhere' (lines 12–13). This starts with a metaphor that is so well established that it has become a fixed expression and is no longer anything to do with pains or arses. The second part is a hyperbole; it is an exaggeration which his very next utterance would seem to contradict if we did not know that he was flouting the maxim of quality: 'that's why they don't come out and visit his brother very often' (lines 13–14).

A **violation** of the cooperative maxims is much harder to detect. It could be that Louise does not in reality go to bed at 7.30 normally, but that she goes at 9.30, and that Lisa is therefore lying, violating the maxim of quality. Note that Melvin asks if they went at nine or ten o'clock. It could be that the mother is a diabetic and needs to eat at fixed times, and that Melvin knows this but is not saying it, in which case he is violating the maxim of quantity. One would have to know the speakers and their context very well to know if they were trying to deceive each other and intentionally generate a misleading implicature.

There are no obvious examples of a speaker **infringing** a maxim because of imperfect linguistic performance. Nor is there an instance of either speakers **opting out** of a maxim: neither of them refuse to give information, for ethical reasons, and apologise for it, for example.

On the other hand, it could also be said that cooperative maxims are not flouted, violated, infringed or opted out of. For example, Lisa's 'She was in bed. She normally goes to bed about half past seven. They said that's the earliest they could get there. I said that's a load of rubbish I said, cos they have fish and chips on a Friday night' (lines 4–6) shows that she is in fact observing the maxim of quantity and giving Melvin just the amount of information that he needs, just as she is at the end of the excerpt. Sperber and Wilson would say that Lisa's utterances are held together by relevance, and indeed Melvin does not question the connection. **Relevance Theory** holds true for this little passage: Lisa and Melvin communicate successfully, interpreting the connections between utterances as meaningful, making inferences drawing on their own background knowledge of Louise, the parents, birthdays, fish and chips, etc., and selecting the relevant features of context. Each new fact mentioned is relevant to something already known, and the interactants appear to recover the facts effortlessly, understanding each other by drawing on accessible information belonging to the context. This stops what they say being ambiguous and helps them fill in any incomplete parts of the utterance and infer the meaning.

B4.2

Further reading →→→→

❑ For a discussion of conversational implicature, with ample examples and explanations, see Thomas (1995) and Cummings (2005), and for an advanced, critical discussion of the implicature, try Cruse (2000).

❑ Leech (1983), Levinson (1983), Grundy (2000) and Huang (2007) provide an extensive discussion of kinds of implicature and the limitations of each.

❑ Schiffrin (1994) looks at maxims and reference.

❑ For an introduction to Relevance Theory, read Mey (1993), Levinson (2000) and Carston (2002).

❑ For a classic explanation of the Principle of Relevance, read Blakemore (1992).

❑ For an in-depth the most advanced explanation of the Theory of Relevance, study Sperber and Wilson (1982, 1987, 1995).

B5

THE PRINCIPLE OF POLITENESS

B5.1

Analysing text using concepts

❑ Negative politeness
❑ Positive politeness
❑ Maxims of politeness

Text

Imperialism

This excerpt comes from The British Academic Spoken English (BASE) corpus (see Bibliography). This excerpt features a lecture on European imperialism delivered by Dr Iain Smith.

1   Many of you here today are not from Africa but you are, many of you,
2   from parts of the world that have been affected by one of the great global
3   forces at work in world history – what we loosely call imperialism. And
4   that is why I thought what I should try to talk to you about today is this
5   phenomenon of imperialism, not just in terms of the 19th and 20th
6   centuries, and as you will see, not just in terms of the impact of Europe
    on the non-European world.
7   Because what we are grappling with in the phenomenon of imperialism
8   is a phenomenon that in various forms is as old as the formation of state
9   systems by human beings. So I'm going to, er, at considerable risk er to
10 myself, try to set this phenomenon in a much wider, er, more global
11 perspective. I hope that might be of interest to many of you who have
12 either been subjected to what you consider imperialism, or indeed have
13 been part of states and societies that have themselves been imperialistic
    or are still being so. /.../
14 I think we have to begin by facing up to the fact that today we live in an
15 age of anti- imperialism. All over the world there is a reaction against the
16 things which we associate with the phenomenon of imperialism: the
17 domination of the weak countries or societies by the strong; the economic
18 exploitation of the natural resources of often poorer countries er in the
19 world, by the rich industrialised parts of the world; the gross, and in many
20 parts of the world, the widening gap in terms of political, military and
21 economic power and standards of the living between the rich and the poor
22 countries; the belief, in one society, of the absolute superiority of its
23 culture, its values and its beliefs and the attempt to impose these upon
    the people of other cultures and often of different races.
24 Today in Europe and America, in the countries of the ex-Soviet Union and
25 in Asia, as well as in all those areas of what used to be called, the Third
26 World which were until so recently under European influence or indeed
27 colonial rule, imperialism is regarded as a bad thing. To call someone an
28 imperialist is a term of abuse, like calling him a racist or a fascist.
29 The very word imperialism, I think you'll agree, is loaded with emotional
30 and ideological overtones. If I say, for instance, that recently I have been
31 studying and contributing to a new Oxford History of the British Empire,
32 which I have, that is a clear, concrete and perfectly respectable historical
33 subject to study. It was indeed the most powerful and extensive empire
34 in world history. But if I say I'm studying and writing about the history of
35 British Imperialism, that's already a somewhat different thing. The kind of
    books that are written about it are different too.

Text Analysis

Imperialism

At first sight, this text might seem a strange one to use for the analysis of politeness. It is not a dialogue; it is not interactional; nobody is trying to order or suggest or invite; there is nothing said off record and nothing bald on record. Yet there is something friendly about the tone that the lecturer, Dr Smith, sets.

On close analysis, there are elements of what we have been looking at, throughout the excerpt. Let us start by noticing that there are examples of **positive politeness strategies**.

He establishes that his audience may have **common ground** with the topic of his lecture:

❏ referring directly to the students, showing how what he has to say is going to be relevant to them (lines 1–3): 'Many of you here today are not from Africa but you are, many of you, from parts of the world that have been affected by one of the great global forces at work in world history – what we loosely call imperialism';
❏ involving the students by using the pronoun 'you' three times (lines 1, 2 and 3), and emphasising the wide appeal of his lecture by saying 'many of you' twice. In paragraph two, he again addresses them with 'many of you' (line 11);
❏ maintaining his friendly tone of positive politeness throughout this excerpt by the use of the inclusive pronoun 'we': 'Because what we are grappling with . . .' (line 7) and 'I think we have to begin by facing up to the fact that . . .' (line 14);
❏ using 'here today' (line 1) to bring out the closeness and solidarity by drawing their attention to the fact that they have common ground together in time and space.

He then appears to **attend to the hearers' interests, wants and needs**,

❏ by suggesting that it was because of the international and aware characteristic of the students themselves that he chose the topic – 'And that is why I thought what I should try to talk to you about today is . . .' (lines 3–4). Note the repetition of 'today';
❏ by using expressions that capture their attention, as in: 'I hope that might be of interest to many of you . . .' (line 10–11).

He exploits the **politeness maxims**

❏ of **agreement**, by trying to win the students over to his point of view, and even assuming that they already have his point of view: 'as you will see' (line 5) and 'I think you'll agree' (line 29);
❏ of **modesty**, by suggesting tentatively that he is doing his best to serve the students in a very unassuming way: 'I thought what I should try to talk to you about today is . . .' (lines 3–4) and 'I hope that might be of interest to many of you . . .' (lines 10–11); he even plays down the fact that he is writing an important book, adding the information in something that amounts to an 'aside', an afterthought: 'If I say, for instance, that recently I have been studying and contributing to a new Oxford History of the British Empire, which I have . . .' (lines 30–31);

❑ of **generosity**, saying: 'So I'm going to, er, at considerable risk er to myself, try to . . .' (line 9), and maximising the expression of cost to himself, without explaining exactly why it is a risk. It could be that this is in itself a ploy to make what he is saying interesting and intriguing for his audience.

Finally, the lecture contains a liberal sprinkling of **negative politeness**, in the sense that there are hesitation phenomena and hedges, **minimising the imposition** of his information and views, as it were:

❑ 'And that is why I thought what I should try to talk to you about . . .' (lines 3–4);
❑ 'So I'm going to, er, at considerable risk er to myself, try to set this phenomenon in a much wider, er, more global perspective.' (lines 9–10);
❑ 'I think we have to begin by facing up to the fact that . . .' (line 14).

Of course, as an experienced lecturer, Dr Smith is not using these linguistic phenomena by chance. They reflect the friendly, relaxed attitude and welcoming tone that he is intentionally adopting, so as to make his lecture both more enjoyable and easier to understand. However, it is interesting that such an unlikely piece of data contains so many of the positive and negative politeness features and adheres to so many of the polite maxims.

Further reading →→→→

B5.2

❑ For a thorough, yet still accessible, explanation of the relation between the Cooperative Principle and the Politeness Principle, and deeper explanation of the maxims of tact, generosity, approbation and modesty, go to Leech (1983) and Thomas (1995).
❑ For maxims of praise, sympathy and consideration, go to Cruse (2000).
❑ For a full description of strategies and social distance, power, gender and status, as well as other cultural aspects of politeness see Brown and Levinson (1987), Coulthard (1985), Grundy (2000), Mey (1993) and Mills (2003).
❑ For an introduction to the sociolinguistic approach to politeness looking at address forms, read Holmes (1992).
❑ For a cross-cultural approach, try Mizutani and Mituzani (1987), Wierzbicka (1991) Bayraktaroglu and Sifianou (2001) and Reiter and Placencia (2005).

CORPORA AND COMMUNITIES

B6

Analysing text using concepts

B6.1

❑ Corpus linguistics
❑ Corpora, pragmatics and social factors
❑ Corpora, domains and communities

Text

That's right yeah

Here is part of an Oxford WordSmith Tools 4.0 concordance for the search-word 'right' from a corpus of casual conversations of a student community of practice (Cutting 2000). The corpus itself has about 1,750 lines, and there are 105 lines with this word running over three pages of concordance. Space here only permits a short discussion, mainly of the first page (unless otherwise indicated). On the four next pages, there is

❑   'right' in 45 single lines;
❑   'right' in 45 single lines, sorted with the first word to the **left** in reverse alphabetical order;
❑   'right' in 45 single lines, sorted with the first word to the **right** in reverse alphabetical order;
❑   'right' in 10 **five-line** chunks, two lines either side.

Text

That's right yeah

These comments aim to illustrate the sort of analysis that can be done with corpus linguistics; they do not pretend to give a reliable description of the use of 'right' in the corpus. Stenström (1987) found that 'right' evaluated a previous response or terminated an exchange, 'all right' marked a boundary between two stages in discourse, and 'that's right' was an emphasiser (see Unit A7). Analysis of this data shows a slightly different picture, and knowledge of the background context of the interlocutors adds a necessary social dimension.

❑   Impressionistic analysis of 'right' in the 45 single lines suggests that there are many uses of the word. As a pragmatic marker, 'right' is not so much a positive evaluation of a previous response, as a simple backchannel, as in 'That's right yeah' (lines 9–14). It also marks the beginning a new turn, as in 'Right' (lines 22–23, 30–31). In addition, there are examples of 'right' not as a pragmatic marker but as an adjective meaning 'correct' features regularly, e.g. 'a chance of getting everything right with data' (line 17) and 'You're doing the right thing' (line 25). This reflects the anxiety of students checking whether they are doing what is expected of them in their programme. 'All right' is also used to console and reassure: 'You're all right' (line 33). This analysis does not give a picture of the most frequent uses, but does highlight an interactional characteristic of this discourse community of students: the act of checking up and reassuring is typical of their in-group cohesion moves.
❑   Analysis of 'right' with the first word to the left in reverse alphabetical order, suggests that the most frequent two-word cluster is 'that's right' (lines 15–37) and that this occurs at the beginning of a short turn or as the turn itself. Its function seems to be interactive, the student community members supporting and encouraging the interlocutor. This is more frequent than the meaning 'correct'

N Concordance   Set ag

1   parted ways. DM That's right. That's right. Yes. (2) BM We'll have to go out
2   like I'm procrastinating. DM That's right yeah. (2) CM Oh I didn't realise
3   CM = anything about it = DM = That's right. Yeah. (2.5) So I'll just do that
4   // That's right yeah. BF And then anyway I
5   // Oh God right yeah. CM So that's the end of that.
6   BM That was it. (0.5) Well I (2) ah right yeah. (1) I wrote some- some lines
7   it as a steady job could she. DM Yeah. Right. Yeah. ((unintelligible)) APRIL 23
8   My handwriting's pretty awful. CM Oh right yeah. DM I just don't want to get
9   And just screw the classes. DM That's right yeah. BM That's the thing about
10   About sign = AM = Yeah that's // right yeah. Because because er
11   You know. AM Yeah. (1) Yeah that's right yeah. CM They know with their
12   // That's right yeah. CM // Yeah. It is true though.
13   // That's right yeah. (0.5) So they're offering er -
14   you've already had the job. DM That's right yeah. Yeah. Yeah. FEBRUARY 3
15   terms of Structuralism. AM Yeah that's right. X was saying that. CM Yeah. (2)
16   thingy. (0.5) When you can't find the right word. NF // Ah. BF // Right? And it
17   There's a chance of getting everything right with data you know. DM Well yes.
18   you've left the country. AM Yes that's right. When you go through customs.
19   them there. (2) DM Then find what's right what's good. AF Shouldn't've
20   to meet ((unintelligible)) DM That's right. We never did get round to doing
21   remember if we were on the - the right track. (0.5) DM How many people
22   nice to get it over with. CM Yeah. DM Right though I never do things like
23   There's fifteen pages in the article. AM Right. This would be much better than
24   options that I think have I done the right thing. (2) It's now reading week in
25   to do it badly enough. You're doing the right thing. // Do it now yeah. CM //
26   on the bus you get change then. BF Ah right. // That's good. DM // Yeah. AF If
27   your questionnaire. DM Oh that's all right. // That's OK. That's fine. It's still the
28   Wow. We've parted ways. DM That's right. That's right. Yes. (2) BM We'll
29   and the twenty-seventh of April. AM All right so one month later is the em // first
30   any of the other consonants. AM Right. So it all heads it all (0.5)
31   Oh hell. That's what I meant. I just. DM Right. See you later. ater.
32   baby-sitter either even if you have. DM Right. Right. (10) AF Also. I had quite a
33   comments on this. Here's X . You're all right. PERIOD TWO : JANUARY 13 -
34   up. It's almost like bound to make the right outcome they wanted. AM I mean
35   Ah right. CM And it just won't run it. BM Right. // Of I- if I was trying to add
36   have we. CM I've spent the most time right now on all this all this load of er in
37   So Thursday and Tuesday. I wrote that right. Not Thursday. DM And I'll get
38   down and get some coffee. If that's all right? NM Yes. That's all right. BM Well
39   in Applied Linguistics. BM Is that right. NM It's a learned discussion. NF
40   I shouldn't this morning. DM Yeah right. ((MM and BM enter)) MM Anyone
41   // Right. // Mhm. BF // Yeah. (7) BM I had
42   DM Oh no. You've got till next year. All right. It's a project. (1) You'll have a lot
43   (1) M.Litt. is a two-year degree. Right. It's better doing two years on top
44   em X about that MSc thing. DM That's right. I'll go up and see if I can see it.
45   = Yeah = DM = and you think well all // right. I might as well do it yeah. BF

Concordance　　　　　　　　　　　　　　　　　　　　　　Set　ag

1　it. (4) CM Never have to go back. You right (4). I'm not doing any more
2　I shouldn't this morning. DM Yeah right. ((MM and BM enter)) MM Anyone
3　it as a steady job could she. DM Yeah. Right. Yeah. ((unintelligible)) APRIL 23
4　He's just been up too late. DM Yeah right. BF And he's not really up to it you
5　on their little project. DM // Yeah. Yeah. Right. (18)((unintelligible)) DM Hello.
6　them there. (2) DM Then find what's right what's good. AF Shouldn't've
7　oh pick it BM // (heh heh heh) CM up right and he gave him the hole. You said
8　have we. CM I've spent the most time right now on all this all this load of er in
9　the middle of the page or towards // the right CM // Yeah. No I know exactly
10　up. It's almost like bound to make the right outcome they wanted. AM I mean
11　remember if we were on the - the right track. (0.5) DM How many people
12　thingy. (0.5) When you can't find the right word. NF // Ah. BF // Right? And it
13　options that I think have I done the right thing. (2) It's now reading week in
14　to do it badly enough. You're doing the right thing. // Do it now yeah. CM //
15　parted ways. DM That's right. That's right. Yes. (2) BM We'll have to go out
16　And just screw the classes. DM That's right yeah. BM That's the thing about
17　you've already had the job. DM That's right yeah. Yeah. Yeah. FEBRUARY 3
18　em X about that MSc thing. DM That's right. I'll go up and see if I can see it.
19　in two weeks' time? DM Yeah that's right. BM Don't think I can change now.
20　// Ah that's right. CM Do you- go and take a picture
21　terms of Structuralism. AM Yeah that's right. X was saying that. CM Yeah. (2)
22　You know. AM Yeah. (1) Yeah that's right yeah. CM They know with their
23　About sign = AM = Yeah that's // right yeah. Because because er
24　// That's right yeah. (0.5) So they're offering er -
25　wanted after October. BF Yeah that's right. (heh) NOVEMBER 1 DIALOGUE
26　you've left the country. AM Yes that's right. When you go through customs.
27　eggs in Scotland? (0.5) FF That's right.(4) It used not to be a holiday. (1)
28　if you don't know what = DM = That's right = CM = anything about it = DM =
29　CM = anything about it = DM = That's right. Yeah. (2.5) So I'll just do that
30　Wow. We've parted ways. DM That's right. That's right. Yes. (2) BM We'll
31　On Shrove Tuesday. FF Yes. That's right. AM Which // is next NF // Eh
32　instead. // (heh heh heh) AM // That's right. // (heh heh heh) CM // You
33　like I'm procrastinating. DM That's right yeah. (2) CM Oh I didn't realise
34　// That's right yeah. BF And then anyway I
35　// That's right yeah. CM // Yeah. It is true though.
36　I don't really want to. DM Yeah that's // right. CM // That- that shouldn't be a
37　to meet ((unintelligible)) DM That's right. We never did get round to doing
38　So Thursday and Tuesday. I wrote that right. Not Thursday. DM And I'll get
39　in Applied Linguistics. BM Is that right. NM It's a learned discussion. NF
40　simple. But (0.5) he wanted to start right from the beginning. He wanted to.
41　BM // Yeah. NM.// Yes. FF Oh I see right. BM But I mean you obviously er I
42　either even if you have. DM Right. Right. (10) AF Also. I had quite a bad
43　is for your BM // But I- CM next project right? BM OK. Right. (1) CM` Take it em
44　// But I- CM next project right? BM OK. Right. (1) CM` Take it em (1) for get
45　was. DM The questionnaire. CM Oh. Right. DM That it's not um politically

B

N Concordance   Set ag

1   parted ways. DM That's right. That's right. Yes. (2) BM We'll have to go out
2   like I'm procrastinating. DM That's right yeah. (2) CM Oh I didn't realise
3   CM = anything about it = DM = That's right. Yeah. (2.5) So I'll just do that
4   // That's right yeah. BF And then anyway I
5   // Oh God right yeah. CM So that's the end of that.
6   BM That was it. (0.5) Well I (2) ah right yeah. (1) I wrote some- some lines
7   it as a steady job could she. DM Yeah. Right. Yeah. ((unintelligible)) APRIL 23
8   My handwriting's pretty awful. CM Oh right yeah. DM I just don't want to get
9   And just screw the classes. DM That's right yeah. BM That's the thing about
10   About sign = AM = Yeah that's // right yeah. Because because er
11   You know. AM Yeah. (1) Yeah that's right yeah. CM They know with their
12   // That's right yeah. CM // Yeah. It is true though.
13   // That's right yeah. (0.5) So they're offering er -
14   you've already had the job. DM That's right yeah. Yeah. Yeah. FEBRUARY 3
15   terms of Structuralism. AM Yeah that's right. X was saying that. CM Yeah. (2)
16   thingy. (0.5) When you can't find the right word. NF // Ah. BF // Right? And it
17   There's a chance of getting everything right with data you know. DM Well yes.
18   you've left the country. AM Yes that's right. When you go through customs.
19   them there. (2) DM Then find what's right what's good. AF Shouldn't've
20   to meet ((unintelligible)) DM That's right. We never did get round to doing
21   remember if we were on the - the right track. (0.5) DM How many people
22   nice to get it over with. CM Yeah. DM Right though I never do things like
23   There's fifteen pages in the article. AM Right. This would be much better than
24   options that I think have I done the right thing. (2) It's now reading week in
25   to do it badly enough. You're doing the right thing. // Do it now yeah. CM //
26   on the bus you get change then. BF Ah right. // That's good. DM // Yeah. AF If
27   your questionnaire. DM Oh that's all right. // That's OK. That's fine. It's still the
28   Wow. We've parted ways. DM That's right. That's right. Yes. (2) BM We'll
29   and the twenty-seventh of April. AM All right so one month later is the em // first
30   any of the other consonants. AM Right. So it all heads it all (0.5)
31   Oh hell. That's what I meant. I just. DM Right. See you later. ater.
32   baby-sitter either even if you have. DM Right. Right. (10) AF Also. I had quite a
33   comments on this. Here's X . You're all right. PERIOD TWO : JANUARY 13 -
34   up. It's almost like bound to make the right outcome they wanted. AM I mean
35   Ah right. CM And it just won't run it. BM Right. // Of I- if I was trying to add
36   have we. CM I've spent the most time right now on all this all this load of er in
37   So Thursday and Tuesday. I wrote that right. Not Thursday. DM And I'll get
38   down and get some coffee. If that's all right? NM Yes. That's all right. BM Well
39   in Applied Linguistics. BM Is that right. NM It's a learned discussion. NF
40   I shouldn't this morning. DM Yeah right. ((MM and BM enter)) MM Anyone
41   // Right. // Mhm. BF // Yeah. (7) BM I had
42   DM Oh no. You've got till next year. All right. It's a project. (1) You'll have a lot
43   (1) M.Litt. is a two-year degree. Right. It's better doing two years on top
44   em X about that MSc thing. DM That's right. I'll go up and see if I can see it.
45   = Yeah = DM = and you think well all // right. I might as well do it yeah. BF

N Concordance

1 I'm afraid. AF Oh well. DM When are (2) you meeting what time is X coming. AF
   Well she should be coming out of class now. (3) MM There she is now. (2) AF
   Oh hell. That's what I meant. I just. DM Right. See you later. d be coming out of
   class now.   (3)   MM   There she is now.(2)   A   Oh   hell. That'
   what I meant. I just.DM   Right. See you later.

2   Are you wanting here? MM Sort of. Are you waiting for a lecture or something?
   Do you want to go for coffee? DM Well no thank you. You AF? AF I can't no.
   I'm meeting X. MM Oh it's OK. I'll be all right. DM No- no I was- I was going to
   move anyway. Shit. I can't sit here and er be chatting to AF all day. AF (heh heh)
   DM I'm afraid. AF Oh well. DM When are (2) you meeting what time is X

3   are you talking about a project? AF Yeah. DM You're talking about a project.
   AF I'm talking about a project. I don't think I'll do the dissertation this year.
   DM Oh no. You've got till next year. All right. It's a project. (1) You'll have a lot
   to do next year if you don't do // another one this year. AF // I know I know..
   That's why I want to. DM It's in your interest isn't it to do // more than one. AF //

4   one. AF Oh the other possibility I suppose is language attitudes. (3) I thought
   I might survey the parents of the kids in the Gaelic Unit and see why they'd sent
   them there. (2) DM Then find what's right what's good. AF Shouldn't've
   brought them. Yeah I know. I'm not very good at thinking up ideas. Especially in
   Linguistics. There's such a fuzzy field isn't it. DM It's very amorphous er. AF It //

5   can I get change? DM Em (1) What how much do you want. AF I'm not sure
   that I have actually. NF Er. Fifty p. (1.5) AF I think I gave it all away. (3) Well
   no- no I can give you forty-five. NF All right. DM That's how you make profits in
   this world. NF // (heh heh) AF // (heh heh heh heh) DM I can give you I can give
   you thirty. AF Oh we soak off the students actually. NF (heh heh) That's not true

6   why all this came // up. DM // That's right yeah. BF And then anyway I decided
   before (0.5) last week that I wasn't going to do it whether he. (0.5) DM You'd
   work. Yeah. BF got the PhD or not. DM Right. BF Anyway this week he should
   have had his application last Friday and I said to him yesterday well did you get
   your application and he said I can't be- I don't really want to do // it. DM // Aye do

7   DM // That's right yeah. CM // Yeah. It is true though. DM // What about Dave?
   Is he going to be ((sniffs)) BF Well he was going to apply for a PhD. That's
   why all this came // up. DM // That's right yeah. BF And then anyway I
   decided before (0.5) last week that I wasn't going to do it whether he. (0.5) DM
   You'd work. Yeah. BF got the PhD or not. DM Right. BF Anyway this week he

8   = Yeah = DM = and you think well all // right. I might as well do it yeah. BF // You
   may as well do it. CM Yeah then you // begin thinking BF // You didn't really want
   to do it // in the first place DM // That's right yeah. CM // Yeah. It is true though.
   DM // What about Dave? Is he going to be ((sniffs)) BF Well he was going to
   apply for a PhD. That's why all this came // up. DM // That's right yeah. BF And

9   you do the danger of doing what you're suggesting is that you- BF // I'm just DM
   you- you- you do that = CM = You might fall into it = DM = Or you get it = CM
   = Yeah = DM = and you think well all // right. I might as well do it yeah. BF //
   You may as well do it. CM Yeah then you // begin thinking BF // You didn't really
   want to do it // in the first place DM // That's right yeah. CM // Yeah. It is true

10 three days. Then I thought I don't want to do it. DM Yeah. It's a real shame to go
   for it if you're not interested isn't it really. BF Yeah. And especially when like well
   I don't really want to. DM Yeah that's // right. CM // That- that shouldn't be a
   factor in your decision though. BF No I // know. CM // Not at all. BF It isn't really.
   // But sort of sort of CM // Yeah like if that's any part of your decision don't even

possibly reflecting anxiety (lines 10–14), which suggests that repeated patterns of two-word clusters tend to be pragmatic markers.

❑ Looking at 'right' with the first word to the right in reverse alphabetical order, it is not so easy to see clusters, except in the case of 'right yeah' (1–14), which could be what Stenström would call an emphasiser, or it could be another backchannel. A great number of them come at the end of a turn; whether they are terminating an exchange is unclear.

❑ An examination of 'right' in 10 five-line chunks, two lines either side, should provide more information because of the greater co-text, but a subjective analysis is not very rewarding. However, it does show the flow of discourse over an exchange and enables an analysis of the interactive function in conversation. It becomes more evident that 'that's right' (lines 7, 8 and 10 of last page) stands on its own as a backchannel while others are talking at length, and that 'all right' occurs in listener re-formulations of the interlocutor's words, to show interest: see line 42 'All right. It's a project'.

A more general picture of all the 105 lines can be obtained using WordSmith's Patterns and Clusters functions. The following table shows the Patterns (L4 meaning the fourth word to the left of the search-word, R4 the fourth word to the right, and so on) in order of frequency.

L4	L3	L2	L1	Centre	R1	R2	R3	R4
THE	DM	DM	THAT'S	RIGHT	YEAH	THE	I	I
		YEAH	ALL		BF	I		
		THAT'S	DM		DM	CM		
			AH		BM			
			THE		CM			
			AM					

The Patterns function reveals that 'right' usually comes at the end of the turn (it is followed by the name of the next to speak – BF, DM, BM, CM), which is interesting from the point of view of conversation analysis. It also shows that 'that's right yeah' is the most frequent and 'all right' the second most frequent. The Cluster function makes this description more subtle, showing the frequency of each three-word cluster:

DM THAT'S RIGHT	9
THAT'S RIGHT YEAH	8
YEAH THAT'S RIGHT	6
THAT'S ALL RIGHT	5

Both the Patterns and the Clusters draw attention to the fact that DM is the one that uses 'that's right' and 'right' most. Knowledge of the corpus as a whole allows us to suggest that this may be because he is more of a solidarity-giver than the others; it may be because he listens more than he talks or it may just be because this is part of his idiolect. AM also uses it. If we re-visit the concordance lines, we can see that the men (AM, BM, CM and DM) use it more than the women (AF and BF). There may be a gender dimension here that would be worth exploring.

This corpus is annotated for grammatical and lexical features within the text, and each line of data has contextual headers for functional and interactional features. For a section of the annotated version, see Cutting (2000). One of the contextual headers 'Speech Act'; here is a simplified description of this part of the code:

11: NEUTRAL attitude towards SELF
Inform, express own intentions, plans, wants
12: POSITIVE attitude towards SELF
Inform, evaluate positively, reassure/console self
13: NEGATIVE attitude towards SELF
Inform, evaluate negatively, criticise self, apologise
21: NEUTRAL attitude towards INTERLOCUTOR/COMMUNICATION
Check and show comprehension, backchannel and acknowledge
22: POSITIVE attitude towards INTERLOCUTOR/COMMUNICATION
Agree, evaluate positively, reassure, encourage, empathise, advise
23: NEGATIVE attitude towards INTERLOCUTOR/COMMUNICATION
Disagree, decline, refuse, deny, defend
31: NEUTRAL attitude towards SITUATION/THIRD PARTY
Inform, narrate, ask question
32: POSITIVE attitude towards SITUATION/THIRD PARTY
Inform, evaluate positively
33: NEGATIVE attitude towards SITUATION/THIRD PARTY
Inform, evaluate negatively; express apprehension of situation/third party

---

When the annotated data is put in WordSmith concordancer, it reveals that 'right' is used mostly in lines labelled as speech acts involving the interlocutor: in neutral 21 'Check and show comprehension, backchannel and acknowledge' and especially in positive 22 'Agree, evaluate positively, reassure, encourage, empathise, advise'. This shows the particular Politeness Principles of this community of practice.

B6.2 | **Further reading →→→→**

❏ Read Sinclair (1991) if you would like a historical perspective on the beginnings of this field.
❏ Read McEnery, and Wilson (1997) for an accessible description of how corpus linguistics is developing.
❏ For a simple, handy glossary of the terms used in corpus linguistics, see Baker *et al.* (2006).
❏ For a very user-friendly description of spoken and written grammar and usage, based on analysis of the CIC corpus, read Carter and McCarthy (2006).
❏ Koester (2006) offers a detailed analysis of workplace discourse.
❏ Coupland (2000) provides insights into the relational aspects of small talk, based on corpus studies.
❏ Cutting (2007) offers a description of corpus studies into the vague language used by communities of practice.

B

CULTURE AND LANGUAGE LEARNING

B7

B7.1 Analysing text using concepts

B7.1

❏ Cross-cultural pragmatics
❏ Intercultural pragmatics
❏ Interlanguage pragmatics

Text

No time for games

This scene is from *Bend It Like Beckham* (2002), a British film comedy directed by Gurinder Chadha about a young Indian girl, Jasminder or Jess (played by Parminder Nagra), a second-generation immigrant in London. She is football-mad and aims to play for a top women's football team. Her parents want her to study, learn to cook and marry. This scene takes place just after Joe, her coach (played by Jonathan Rhys-Meyers), has learned that she had been coming to football practice without her parents knowing, and she has now stopped because they found out. He comes to their house.

1	Joe	I'm sorry to barge in on you like this Mr and Mrs Bhamra,
2		but I wanted to talk to you in person. I only found out today
3		that you didn't know that Jess is playing for our team.
4	Mrs B	No we didn't.
5	Joe	I apologise. If I'd known, I would've encouraged Jess to tell you.
6		Because I believe that she's got tremendous potential.
7	Mr B	I think we know better our daughter's potential. Jess has no
8		time for games. She'll be starting her university soon.
9	Jess	But playing for the team is an honour.
10	Mrs B	What bigger honour is there than respecting your elders?
11	Mr B	Young man, when I was a teenager in Nairobi, I was the best fast-
12		bowler in our school. Our team even won the East African Cup.
13		But when I came to this country, nothing. I was not allowed to
14		play in any of the teams. And these bloody Goras* in the club-
15		house made fun of my turban, and sent me off packing.
16	Joe	I'm sorry Mr Bhamra. But now it's //
17	Mr B	// Now what? None of our boys are
18		in any of the football leagues. Do you think they will let our girls?
19		I don't want you to build up Jasminder's hopes. She will only
20		end up disappointed like me.
21	Jess	But Dad, it's all changing now. Look at Nasser Hussein. He's
22		captain of the England cricket team. He's Asian.
23	Mrs B	Hussein's a Muslim name. Their families are different.

24	Jess	Oh Mum!
		[Jess sees Joe out to his car]
25	Joe	We've been invited to play in Germany on Saturday. It's a shame
26		you'll miss it.
27	Jess	Wow, Germany . . .
28	Joe	I can see what you're up against. But your parents don't always
29		know what's best for you, Jess.

* Gora = word for fair-skinned people, whether Indian, European, or other.

Text analysis

No time for games

Let us look at the **intercultural pragmatics** of this scene. The Sikh Bhamra family is bilingual, speaking Punjabi and English as a lingua franca. The interaction between these British Indians and Joe, the Irish coach, juxtaposes their **norms** and **values**. There is no miscommunication or pragmalinguistic failure, but the speakers have conflicting **sociopragmatic** priorities.

Joe's opening gambit is a direct, lexicalised apology (lines 1–5). He makes it clear that he is not apologising for the fact that Jess is playing football contrary to her parents' wishes, or saying he is sorry that she was disobedient. He evidently thinks that Jess is mistress of her own destiny, and says, 'If I'd known, I would've encouraged Jess to tell you', not 'If I'd known, I would've encouraged Jess to ask for your permission'. He thinks that he is exhibiting negative politeness, but self-determination, individualism and commitment to self are British, not Indian, values. Joe appears unaware that traditional Indian culture tends to be family-centred and collective.

Joe's next mistake is to suggest that he knows more about what Jess could do with her life than her parents do. His 'I believe that she's got tremendous potential' is an indirect directive, implying that he thinks that the Bhamras should value the advice of an expert. Mr Bhamra picks up the same words competitively: his 'I think we know better our daughter's potential' is an indirect commissive, implying that she is not mistress of her own destiny, and that her family's knowledge about her possible future overrides any opinions of an outsider. Behind his words is the assumption that her behaviour is determined by the family, to which she has obligations. He accepts the inequality of power.

Rejection of the outsider's opinion is not just typical of Indian culture, of course. The scene is reminiscent of the one in the English film *Billy Elliot*, when Billy's ballet teacher goes to his house to see why he missed his audition for the Royal Ballet School. Billy's brother, who knew nothing about this, challenges her with 'What good's it ganna do him?', 'And anyway, what do *you* know about it?' In *Billy Elliot*, the outsider's opinion was rejected because of social class differences.

Jess explains her motivation in terms that her parents will understand, saying 'But playing for the team is an honour' (line 9), in order to win them over. Evaluating something as an honour is something that a non-Indian person would be less likely to do. Her mother sees through the ploy and throws it back in her face with a reminder about the Indian value of respect for the wisdom and experience of age: 'What bigger honour is there than respecting your elders?' (line 10), flouting the cooperative maxim of quantity and implying an indirect directive. For her, respect means obedience.

Living in a society that discriminates against them reinforces the need to preserve their identity and find a certain way to survive. Mr Bhamra tells the tale about not being allowed to play in a British cricket team and the 'bloody Goras in the club-house' making fun of his turban, to explain his protective attitude towards Jess (the cooperative maxim of relevance is understood). He thinks that Jess as a girl will stand even less of a chance and 'only end up disappointed like me' (19–20). His insistence that 'She'll be starting her university soon' (line 8) is most likely based on a belief that perseverance with education, not sport, will give her security, power and dignity that she needs in this racist environment.

Globalisation means that times and culture are changing. Joe tries to tell Mr Bhamra ('But <u>now</u> it's', line 16); Jess does: 'But Dad, it's all changing <u>now</u>' (line 21), reminding him about Nasser Hussein. The football team is multi-racial; Jess knows that she and her white coach are mutually attracted. Jess despairs when her mother says, 'Hussein's a Muslim name. Their families are different', flouting the cooperative maxim of manner: only the Bhamras know what she means and why this exasperates Jess so much. She may feel that it is irrelevant, and she may have heard it many times before. The whole film shows the struggle of a young person fighting against the norms of the older generation.

But in fact Jess is torn between asserting her own individuality and following her passions, and accepting the collectivist power-unequal traditions. She may embody both cultures. When Joe says 'your parents don't always know what's best for you, Jess' (lines 28–9), she is speechless at having her life structure challenged. Later in the film, once her parents have accepted her football career, she is reluctant to go out with Joe because a second culture clash would be too much for them.

In this short extract of scripted speech, the issue at stake is the conflicting socio-pragmatic priorities, not pragmalinguistic failure. Throughout the analysis we have touched on Speech Acts, Politeness Principle and Cooperative Principle to explain the interaction and intentions, but there are no instances of the two cultures having different realisations of acts and maxims. On the other hand, central to the scene is face: protecting culture means protecting the face of self, and challenging culture means threatening the face of other.

Further reading →→→→→   B7.2

❑   For a simple general background on language and culture, start with Kramsch (1998).
❑   You will find detailed studies for cross-cultural comparisons with Japanese in Mizutani and Mituzani (1987), with Spanish in Reiter and Placencia (2005), and with Polish in Wierzbicka (1991).

❏ Thomas (1983), Scollon and Scollon (1995) and Spencer-Oatey (2000) provide excellent collections of studies in intercultural pragmatics.

❏ To take a broader, worldwide view of intercultural pragmatics and the influence of global English, go to Phillipson (1992), Pennycook (1994), Crystal (1999) and Graddol (2006).

❏ For those of you who are interested in interlanguage pragmatics, Barron (2002), and Kasper and Rose (2002) will serve as very through introductions.

❏ Finally, the TEFL and TESOL teachers amongst you may get perspectives that could alter your teaching, when you read Rose and Kasper (2001), Byram and Grundy (2003) and Corbett (2003) on teaching intercultural pragmatics.

Section C

EXPLORATION:
DATA FOR
INVESTIGATION

C1   CONTEXT

C1.1   Studying further and exploring

❑ Context
❑ Language and the context

In this unit, Texts A, B and C are samples of language dependent on knowledge of the context for their full meaning. Text A is from a TV cookery programme and is necessarily based on the situational context. Text B, about an interview with T. S. Eliot, shows a breakdown in communication due to cultural background knowledge wrongly assumed to be shared. Text C, from *Pride and Prejudice*, contains inter-textual references in an interpersonal context.

Texts D and E are for you to think about cohesion. Text D has cohesive devices that work; Text E has ones that do not.

Text A

Cookery class: Unbaked Chocolate Cake

This excerpt comes from a BBC2 programme entitled *Delia's How to Cook: Part Two*. Delia Smith belongs to Britain's heritage of cookery programmes and simple cookery books. The programme (29 October 2000) is subtitled 'A guide to all things chocolate'. She starts by saying that the chocolate should be melted, and that two ounces of butter be beaten into it.

Now the next ingredient that's going to join the melted chocolate and butter is this one here, which is double cream. And it's been sort of lightly whipped to the floppy stage. So I'm just going to add that. And – just clean the bowl – and then I'm just going to stir the chocolate into the cream, combine the two thoroughly. This needs a bit more mixing, it looks sort of marbley, at the moment, and you just need to get all that sort of marble out of it so that it's a nice evenly blended colour.

And then the next ingredient is in my bowl here. It looks a bit peculiar but what it is actually – it's eight ounces of these, and these are oat biscuits that are very lightly sweetened. And what you do with them is you take the eight ounces and just break them up into little pieces. And I would say these are roughly sort of quarter of an inch, third of an inch, it's not vital, but not too small because you're going to get some crunch in this. Now they're going to go in to the cream and the chocolate. And we're just going to give them a little mix to be thoroughly combined.

And then the next ingredient I've got is the dried cherries that we used earlier in the series when we made the duck sauce, the dried sour cherries. I've got two ounces of those and two ounces of fat juicy raisins. And these have been soaked, um, overnight in three tablespoons of rum. So they're going to go in next.

And then finally I've got four ounces of pistachio nuts. You can buy these in packets ready shelled with no salt, er, specially for baking. And what I've done is

I've just roughly chopped them. And they again shouldn't be too small because we want lots of nice crunch.

So we've got cherries, raisins, pistachio nuts and biscuits and now I'm just going to give this another mixing. Now the name of this cake is Unbaked Chocolate Cake. It's sometimes called Refrigerator Cake because the lovely thing about it is that it doesn't need any baking. It's just going to go into the refrigerator.

Text B

T. S. Eliot's Nobel Prize

The following anecdote is taken from *The Cassell Dictionary of Anecdotes*, edited by Nigel Rees (1999). This tale was told by Philip French of the *Observer* (17 April 1994).

When it was announced that T. S. Eliot had been awarded the Nobel Prize for Literature in 1948, he was making a lecture tour of the United States. A Mid-Western reporter asked him if he had been given the prize for his great work *The Waste Land*. 'No', replied Eliot, 'I believe I have been given it in recognition of my whole corpus.' Accordingly, the journalist wrote: 'In an interview with our airport correspondent this morning, Mr Eliot revealed that the Swedish Academy had given him the Nobel Prize not for *The Waste Land* but for his poem *My Whole Corpus*.'

Text C

Elizabeth and Darcy declare their love

This is from Jane Austen's book *Pride and Prejudice* (1813). Elizabeth had loved Darcy for a long time but had always kept a distance because she had found him proud and supercilious. She had rejected his advances in the past because she had heard rumours about him being cruel to her sister's fiancé. Just before this extract, she learns that he had not in fact been cruel, and that he had secretly helped her sister out of serious financial difficulties. This scene takes place at the end of the book. They walk through the grounds of their estates and, finally alone, open their hearts for the first time.

Now was the moment for her resolution to be executed; and, while her courage was high, she immediately said –

'Mr Darcy, I am a very selfish creature; and for the sake of giving relief to my own feelings, care not how much I may be wounding yours. I can no longer help thanking you for your unexampled kindness to my poor sister. Ever since I have known it, I have been most anxious to acknowledge to you how gratefully I feel it. Were it known to the rest of the family, I should not have merely my own gratitude to express.'

'I am sorry, exceedingly sorry,' replied Darcy, in a tone of surprise and emotion, 'that you have ever been informed of what may, in a mistaken light, have given you uneasiness. I did not think Mrs Gardiner was so little to be trusted.'

'You must not blame my aunt. Lydia's thoughtlessness first betrayed to me that you had been concerned in the matter; and, of course, I could not rest until I knew the particulars. Let me thank you again and again, in the name of all my family, for that generous compassion which induced you to take so much trouble, and bear so many mortifications, for the sake of discovering them.'

'If you *will* thank me,' he replied, 'let it be for yourself alone. That the wish of giving happiness to you might add force to the other inducements which led me on, I shall not attempt to deny. But your *family* owe me nothing. Much as I respect them, I believe I thought only of you.'

Elizabeth was too much embarrassed to say a word. After a short pause, her companion added, 'You are too generous to trifle with me. If your feelings are still what they were last April, tell me so at once. My affections are unchanged; but one word from you will silence me on this subject for ever.'

Elizabeth, feeling all the more than common awkwardness and anxiety of his situation, now forced herself to speak; and immediately, though not very fluently, gave him to understand that her sentiments had undergone so material a change since the period to which he alluded, as to make her receive with gratitude and pleasure his present assurances. The happiness which this reply produced was such as he had probably never felt before, and he expressed himself on the occasion as sensibly and as warmly as a man violently in love can be supposed to do. Had Elizabeth been able to encounter his eyes, she might have seen how well the expression of heartfelt delight diffused over his face became him; but, though she could not look, she could listen, and he told her of his feelings which, in proving of what importance she was to him, made his affection every moment more valuable.

Text D

Survival of the fittest: rare Darwin book finds new home

The Sydney Morning Herald (15 March 2007) published an article with this title online (http://www.gaiaguys.net/meier.p6–11,13sb32.htm). Here is the first half.

IT IS a book that changed the world irrevocably – a rare first edition copy of Charles Darwin's *On the Origin of Species*.

First published in 1859, Darwin's masterpiece rocked Victorian society with its theory of natural selection, challenging conventional wisdoms about science and divinity.

Yet Darwin was already formulating his controversial theories 13 years earlier when HMS Beagle sailed into Sydney Harbour for a two-week stop on its history-making voyage of biological discovery.

Now, Sydney has another connection with Darwin. On Monday the State Library of NSW will unveil an immaculate first edition copy that was originally owned by the Darwin family. The library bought it for £78,000 ($191,000) at a London auction – the first big purchase by the new State Librarian, Regina Sutton.

'It's in excellent condition,' Ms Sutton said. 'It looks like a new book, quite frankly.' According to Ms Sutton, the book is the only first edition in its original binding to be owned by any public institution in Australia.

Just 1250 were printed. Legend has it that they sold out on the first day. The library's copy was a gift from Darwin's great grandson, Quentin Keynes, to his physician, Arthur James Lewis.

First editions of the work are considered even more special because Darwin made significant alterations to subsequent editions, Ms Sutton said.

'Darwin inserted a specific phrase – 'by the creator' – into the second edition. He was trying to pacify the fury . . . of those who accused him of being an atheist who didn't believe God had created man,' she said.

'There are a lot of misconceptions about the book. It is not about the origin of man. It's about natural selection and the evolution of species in general.'

Perhaps the most famous phrase associated with Darwin – 'survival of the fittest' – doesn't even appear in the first edition. That was invented by Darwin's contemporary, the economist Herbert Spencer.

Text E

'Grammar Stammers'

The following mini-extracts are taken from Richard Lederer's amusing *More Anguished English* (1987), which he calls 'An exposé of embarrassing, excruciating, and egregious errors in English'. These extracts come from the chapter entitled 'Grammar Stammers', which lists funny cases of ambiguous grammar taken from US newspapers and magazines.

- ❑ During the summer, my sister and I milked the cows, but now that school has started, my father milks the cows in the morning, and us at night.
- ❑ Mrs McAllister watched as the giant airplane taxied out of the gate. Then like some wild beast she pointed her nose down the runway and screamed terrifically into the sky.
- ❑ Mr Yoshiko said the donkey owners should clearly state why they want to keep the animals. 'If they cannot give good reasons why they need the donkeys, then they will be shot.'
- ❑ Please place your garbage in this barrel. It will be here weekends for use.
- ❑ Recent visitors were Jonathan Goldings and their in-laws the Brett Packards, from Lake Placid, NY. Brett had his tonsils removed in Centerville. It was a pleasant surprise to have them for supper.

Activities ⭐

❏ Text A is a TV cookery demonstration assuming very little cultural background knowledge of the art of cooking.

a. Out of all the referring expressions, roughly what proportion have exophoric reference? How much have you lost by reading the script as opposed to actually seeing the TV programme?

b. How explicit is the language? Are there any parts that you would rewrite in a less explicit way if you were to aim at an audience of more experienced cooks?

c. Do a simple experiment; you will need to find nine individuals willing to take part. Choose a series of connected actions to teach each individual (separately, not as a group); for example, you could demonstrate changing the battery for the flash in your camera or calling a friend using the address book in your mobile phone. Ask three of the individuals to watch you, listening to your instructions (using exophoric reference and deixis), and then, once you have finished, copy you exactly. Ask another three to watch and copy you, without you saying anything. Ask the other three to listen to the instructions and then do it, without you giving a demonstration. Compare how well each of the nine carry out the actions. What does this say about situational context and reference in instructions?

❏ Text B is written for those with a little cultural background knowledge of T. S. Eliot's work. It shows a breakdown in communication.

a. The breakdown occurs because the speaker implies one thing and the hearer infers another. Explain it in terms of background knowledge.

b. Would you agree that this humorous piece of writing invites readers to share the attitude of the writer and laugh at those who know less than them, or do you think the humour lies in something more complex than this? To what extent is this typical of jokes, anecdotes and comedy in general? Can you think of any examples?

❏ In Text C, Elizabeth and Darcy finally refer to their intimate interpersonal context.

c. Can you find examples of intertextuality? How are they expressed?

d. We have said that people who are close make vague and implicit reference to entities and events in their interpersonal context. Is this true of Elizabeth and Darcy? Why / why not?

e. Do they have a shared attitude to conventions in their common socio-cultural context?

❏ Text D contains examples of nearly all types of grammatical and lexical cohesion.

a. Which types predominate?

b. Why are they necessary?

❏ Take each of the sentences in Text E.

a. Explain their ambiguity in terms of cohesion.

b. Rewrite them so that the meaning is clear.

❏ Watch a film or a soap opera on TV, and record it if you can. Choose a ten-minute section of it with a substantial amount of dialogue and make notes on the references to the situational, cultural background and interpersonal background context.

a. Out of the three contexts, which one is referred to most?

b. How often is there an overlap or a mixture of two or all of the contexts at one time, assumed to be known?

c. How much knowledge of the three contexts do you, as a viewer, have? How does the script-writer play on this?

❏ Find a serious piece of online journalism like Text D.

a. List the grammatical and lexical cohesive devices that predominate.

b. Compare the devices that predominate in your texts with the devices that predominate in Text D.

c. To what extent can you say that the genre (type of text) determines the sort of cohesion that is used?

❏ Find a text-book which you have had to read for a course that you are doing or have done, and which you have found particularly difficult you follow.

a. Analyse the cohesive devices of a page or two that you remember having to read and re-read in order to understand.

b. Decide whether you can say your difficulty in understanding is partly due to the presence of some devices or the absence of others.

EXPLORING SPEECH ACTS

C2

Studying further and exploring

C2.1

❏ Direct speech acts
❏ Felicity conditions
❏ Indirect speech acts

The texts and questions in this unit ask you to consider the speech acts and cultural variables. They centre round the fact that the expression of speech acts is affected by the social differences that can dictate the need for indirectness (status, roles, age, gender, education, class, occupation and ethnicity) and the contextual constraints (the size of imposition; formality of situation). This unit also asks you to explore the rules surrounding speech acts and the effect of each country's culture on the choice and expression of speech acts.

Texts A, B and C are examples of speech acts in action. Text A comes from an online news report and contains verbs that describe speech acts. Text B is from a children's book and illustrates the use of indirect speech acts in relations of unequal power. Text C is in fact two texts, both of which show that speech acts are bound by rules.

Text D is not an example of speech acts but a list of cultural dimensions which vary from country to country and reflect a view of life and society.

Text A

Global warming is for real

This is from the NewScientist.com news service, dated 28 February 2007. It comes from an article written by Catherine Brahic entitled 'United Nations' scientists join climate change chorus'. The report follows the UN Intergovernmental Panel on Climate Change.

> As of now, only coal power stations that can accommodate facilities to capture and store their carbon dioxide emissions should be built, scientists advised on Tuesday. Declaring the global warming debate over, the UN-backed team urged the world's nations on to act now to keep climate change from creating a worldwide catastrophe. The group said that in order to avoid 'intolerable impacts' of climate change, global CO_2 emissions must peak at not much above their current level, no later than 2020, and by 2100, they must have declined to about one-third of that value.

Text B

Winnie-the-Pooh

Winnie-the-Pooh is the world-famous teddy bear created by the writer A. A. Milne (1882–1956). The characters of Milne's children's books are based on his son Christopher Robin's nursery toys; their adventures are set in Ashdown Forest, south-east England, where the Milnes lived. This excerpt is from a chapter in *Winnie-the-Pooh* entitled 'In which Eeyore loses a tail and Pooh finds one'. Eeyore is a donkey who has a gloomy outlook on life and humanity; he assumes that someone has taken his tail. Pooh offers to find it and goes to consult Owl. The 'highly educated' Owl gives the highly lovable Bear of Very Little Brain his advice.

> 'Well,' said Owl, 'the customary procedure in such cases is as follows.'
>   'What does Crustimoney Proseedcake mean?' said Pooh. 'For I am a Bear of Very Little Brain, and long words Bother me.'
>   'It means the Thing to Do.'
>   'As long as it means that, I don't mind,' said Pooh humbly.
>   'The thing to do is as follows. First, Issue a Reward. Then –'
>   'Just a moment,' said Pooh, holding up his paw. *What* do we do to this – what you were saying? You sneezed just as you were going to tell me.'
>   'I *didn't* sneeze.'
>   'Yes, you did, Owl.'
>   'Excuse me, Pooh, I didn't. You can't sneeze without knowing it.'
>   'Well, you can't know it without something having been sneezed.'

'What I said was, 'First Issue a Reward'.'

'You're doing it again, ' said Pooh sadly.

'A Reward!' said Owl very loudly. 'We write a notice to say that we will give a large something to anybody who finds Eeyore's tail.'

'I see, I see,' said Pooh, nodding his head. 'Talking about large somethings,' he went on dreamily, 'I generally have a small something about now – about this time in the morning,' and he looked wistfully at the cupboard in the corner of Owl's parlour; 'just a mouthful of condensed milk or what-not, with perhaps a lick of honey –'

'Well, then,' said Owl, 'we write out this notice, and we put it up all over the Forest.'

'A lick of honey', murmured Bear to himself, 'or – or not, as the case may be.' And he gave a deep sigh, and tried very hard to listen to what Owl was saying.

But Owl went on and on, using longer and longer words, until at last he came back to where he started, and he explained that the person to write out this notice was Christopher Robin.

Text C

Invitations

a To garden parties

This text is taken from a fascinating book entitled *Home Management*, by Garth and Wrench, which aims to prepare newly weds to run a household and behave correctly in society. Note that it was published in 1934 (Daily Express Publications, London).

When writing your notes of invitation to a garden party, it is well to mention whether tennis or any other game will be a feature of the afternoon. Guests at a garden party wear their very smartest frocks and hats, and probably carry parasols, but if the tennis players among them know that the tennis court will be in play, they will put on their tennis frocks or flannels, and bring their racquets with them.

Answers to all formal invitations must be in the third person: 'Mr. and Mrs. Dugdale accept with pleasure Mrs. Wynston's kind invitation for Wednesday, June 15, at nine o-clock.' Do be careful to avoid that very frequent mistake of writing '*will be*' pleased to accept. You are referring, remember, to the pleasure you feel at the moment of accepting, not to some future pleasure. Never answer an informal note in the third person. When the letters *R.S.V.P.* are not on an invitation card, an answer is neither expected nor necessary, but when they are, it is essential that a reply be sent – and PROMPTLY.

b *To dinner parties*

This text is from website of the Office of International Students Affairs, the University of Illinois, USA, which aims to prepare students to interact with their American hosts.

> You may receive a verbal or written invitation from an American to visit his or her home. You should always answer a written invitation, especially if it says R.S.V.P. Do not say that you will attend unless you plan to do so. It is acceptable to ask your host about appropriate clothing. It is polite to arrive on time for special dinners and parties. If you will be late, call your host to explain. When you visit an American, especially for dinner, you will be asked what you would like to drink. You do not need to drink an alcoholic beverage. If you have any dietary restrictions you should tell the host at the time you accept the invitation.

Activities ✪

❑ Looking at the texts individually
  a. Which macro-class, direct speech acts and indirect speech acts are involved the most, in Texts A, B and C?
  b. In the three texts, what reasons can you see for the indirect speech acts being used? Consider the social differences and contextual constraints.
  c. In Text A, 'Global warming is for real', why do you think there are so many verbs actually describing the speech acts? Find other online news reports and decide whether 'verbs naming speech acts' is part of the news report genre.
  d. Would you say that Text B, 'Winnie-the-Pooh' shows a power-struggle? Is the indirect speech act and the way it is responded to appropriate for a book for children?

❑ Speech acts are governed by social conventions dependent on the context of culture.
  a. The two Text C 'Invitations' excerpts are about the speech acts of inviting and accepting invitations, and contain examples of a series of ways of expressing directives, giving advice. They illustrate how the social conventions for vary from country to country, and from time to time. Compare the text's conventions and how they are expressed indirectly.
  b. Think of another situation in which a speech act is governed by conventions; write a description of it. You may want to look at the words used to ask someone out, or the words used to compliment someone on their clothes and the response of the complimented one, or the words used to apologise. The speech act situations and realisations are endless: the choice is yours.
  c. Ask 20 people to tell you what the conventions are. You can either write a questionnaire of responses for them to label true or false or you can give them a relatively free questionnaire in which you describe a situation and leave the respondents free to write what the participants would say.
  d. Write a brief description of your results and add a discussion, explaining why you think you got the answers that you did.

❑ Remember that Speech Act Theory has limitations.

a. As you were identifying the speech acts in Texts A, B and C, did you have a problem with overlap, or utterances that did not fit into macro-classes? Which was the greatest problem? Explain the problem and give examples.

b. Do you feel that Speech Act Theory is a satisfactory way of coding the function of language? Can you think of an improvement or better alternative?

❏   Think of a locution that constitutes a declaration speech act in your culture.

a. Explain the felicity conditions using Austin's model and then Searle's.

b. Which model do you prefer? Why?

❏   Think of a language other than English and a culture that you know well and discuss in what way the speech acts and their realisations are different from how they are described in Unit A2. Present your findings to the group.

Text D

Understanding the multi-cultural dimension

The findings summarised below are taken from the Royal Philips Electronic website (http://www.news.philips.com/mondial/archive/1999/august/artike14.html). The summary of the research is provided to guide people doing business with companies from other countries.

Understanding the multicultural dimension

Dutch engineer and social scientist Geert Hofstede has conducted extensive research into the problems of doing business across many cultures. After a comprehensive study of 80,000 IBM employees in 66 countries, he established four dimensions of national culture. These help managers identify areas in which they may encounter cultural difficulties:

❏   **Uncertainty Avoidance**: this dimension refers to how comfortable people feel towards uncertainty. Cultures that ranked low (Great Britain) feel more comfortable with the unknown. Cultures high on uncertainty avoidance (Greece) prefer formal rules.

❏   **Power Distance**: this is defined as 'the extent to which the less powerful members of institutions and organizations accept that power is distributed unequally'. In other words people in high power distance cultures (Philippines) are much more comfortable with a larger status differential than low power distance cultures (Sweden).

❏   **Masculinity-Femininity**: this refers to expected gender roles in a culture. Masculine cultures (Japan) tend to have distinct roles for males and females, while feminine cultures (The Netherlands) have a greater ambiguity in what is expected of the genders.

❏   **Individualism-Collectivism**: this is defined by the extent to which an individual's behavior is influenced and defined by others. Individual cultures (USA) prefer self-sufficiency while collectivists (Indonesia) recognize the obligations to the group.

Activities ⭐ ❑ Text D lists social dimensions that vary from culture to culture and can affect a speaker's choice of direct and indirect speech acts. To what extent would you agree that you can make blanket statements about cultural differences in this way? What difficulties might arise if business people were to take these dimensions as scientifically proven for all occasions?

❑ How often do you use indirect speech acts in the country where you are?

a. Over the next week, do one of the following alternatives:
   ○ make a note of every single direct and indirect *directive* speech act that is addressed to you, word for word if you can, and make a brief note of the context e.g. 'going through a door' or 'at a ticket office';
   ○ write down all written instructions that you see around you on notices e.g. 'No Smoking', and make a brief note of the context e.g. 'at a petrol station' or 'at the entrance to a park'.

b. See which you have more of – direct or indirect.

c. Examine how the indirect directives are expressed, to see which words and grammatical forms are used most.

d. Consider the extent to which the context affects the directness of the act.

e. Draw conclusions.

f. Write up your study.

❑ Make a recording of two friends or relatives having a long casual conversation. You might have to wait until you know that they have settled down in a quiet place to an afternoon's chat over a coffee, or such like, so that you can get about an hours' recording. Do not give them any instructions as to what they should talk about or how; let it be spontaneous and natural.

a. Divide the recording up into three-minute chunks, regardless of what is happening at the three-minute interval; do not bother transcribing all this data.

b. Listen to each three-minute chunk and decide whether its function is primarily transactional or primarily interactional, or a 50/50 mixture.

c. Calculate what proportion of the 20 chunks is primarily transactional, what proportion is primarily interactional, and what proportion a 50/50 mixture, and say which proportion is biggest and why you think so.

d. Look at each of the three groups of chunks and see what direct speech acts are there.

e. Write up your findings under the title 'The Overall Function of a Casual Conversation'.

THE ANALYSIS OF CONVERSATION

Studying further and exploring

❑ Exchange moves and IRF
❑ Conversation analysis
❑ Interactional sociolinguistics

The data in this section are spoken language, since exchange structure and conversation analysis look at how people speak and interact orally. Texts A, B and C are naturally-occurring data. Text A comes from a film documentary of a French primary school. Texts B and C are transcriptions of real conversations in a hospital kitchen and in a lift. By contrast, Text D is from a scripted film; however some of the features of exchange structure and conversation analysis are present, and they are exploited to dramatic advantage.

Text A

Sixes and sevens

This excerpt comes from the film *Être et Avoir* (2002), directed by Nicolas Philibert. It is a documentary of a small school in rural France, where the pupils, aged four to eleven, are taught by one patient, loving teacher (Georges Lopez). This scene comes straight after one in which the lesson was the number seven, and six pupils drew the number on the whiteboard. The teacher then settles down to a quiet one-to-one with a little girl, while the others get on with their work round the table.

1	P1	Un, deux, trois, quatre, cinq, six (1.0) mm
2	T	Après six, qu'est-ce qu'il y a?
3	P1	Mm. (2.)
4	T	Qu'est-ce qu'il y a après six?
5	P1	Mm. Il y a (0.5)
6	T	Qu'est-ce que tu as dessiné? Tout à l'heure, qu'est-ce que tu as coloré à rouge? (1.0)
7		Qu'est-ce qu'on a appris, aujourd'hui? (1.0) Le (0.5)?
8	P1	Le (0.5)
9	T	Elle se rappelle plus. On le demande à Alizé ou à Marie peut-être.
10		appris? Le nombre, le nouveau nombre qu'on a appris?
11	P2	C'est le sept.
12	T	Le sept.
13	P1	Le sept.
14	T	Il est après qui le sept, Marie?
15	P2	Euh (0.5) après qui? Le six. Et après – après le neuf.
16	T	Et bien d'accord. On n'a pas appris le neuf encore.
17	P2	Après le six.
18	P1	Six.

19	T	Et bien un, deux, trios, quatre, cinq, six. Et après on dit?
20	P2	Sept
21	P1	Ss (0.5)
22	T	Qu'est-ce qu'on dit après six? Ella l'a dit Marie. Ella a dit le –
23	P1	Mm.
24	T	Tu te réveilles un petit peu?
25	P1	Oui.
26	T	Le sept.
27	P1	Le sept.
28	T	Raconte maintenant.
29	P1	Un deux trois quatre cinq (0.5)
30	T	Six – qu'est-ce qu'elle a dit, Marie, après le six?
31	P3	[whispered] Sept. [calling out] Il faut l'aider!

* * * * * * * * * * * *

1	P1	One, two, three, four, five, six (1.0) mm
2	T	After six, what is it?
3	P1	Mm. (2.)
4	T	What comes after six?
5	P1	Mm. It's (0.5)
6	T	What did you draw? Just now, what did you colour red? (1.0)
7		What did we learn today? (1.0) The number (0.5)?
8	P1	The number (0.5)
9	T	She can't remember. We'll ask Alizé or Marie perhaps. What did we
10		learn? The number- the new number that we learned?
11	P2	Seven.
12	T	Seven.
13	P1	Seven.
14	T	Who does seven come after, Marie?
15	P2	Um after who? Six. And after – after nine.
16	T	Well yes OK. We haven't done nine yet.
17	P2	After six.
18	P1	Six.
19	T	All right, one, two, three, four, six. And after that we say (0.5)?
20	P2	Seven
21	P1	Ss (0.5)
22	T	What do we say after six? Marie just said it. She said the number –
23	P1	Mm.
24	T	Wakie wakie.
25	P1	Yes.
26	T	Seven.
27	P1	Seven.
28	T	Now say it.
29	P1	One, two, three, four, five (0.5)
30	T	Six – what did Marie say came after six?
31	P3	[whispered] Seven. [calling out] We've got to help her!

❏   Analyse this text from the point of view of IRF. What sort of initiation, response and follow-up is there, in terms of acts? Would you distinguish between the teacher's initiations to S1 and to S2? Can you see what sort of a teacher he is? Finally, how would you classify S3 coming to the rescue at the end?

Text B

Tamara's photos from the fancy dress

This excerpt is taken from a casual conversation in Diana Slade's (1997: 11–12) database. It is a tea-break chat among three Australian women employees in a hospital kitchen. Slade says that the chat contains 'gossip', which 'involves participants engaging in exchanging negative opinions and pejorative evaluations about the behaviour of a person who is absent' and the purpose of which is interpersonal, 'to do with the positioning of participants in relation to each other and to critical issues in their social world'. Note that in Slade's transcription system, = = indicates an overlap, . . . indicates a brief pause, and ( ) is a non-transcribable segment.

Jo	Did she see the photos in her coz*?
Jenny	She walks in . . . She stopped me she stopped me and she said, umm 'Oh, by the way, have you have you seen any photos of = = me?' I thought, you know, you're a bit sort of, you know . . .
Jo	= = No one told her there were photos.
Jenny	She said, 'Have you seen any photos of me at the fancy dress?' And I said, I said, 'Well, as a matter of fact, I've seen one or two, um, of you Tamara, but you know, nothing . . .' And, um, she said 'Do you know of anyone else who's taken = = any photos of me at the fancy dress?'
Donna	= = I wouldn't be taking any photos. = = I mean, I would have asked.
Jenny	= = I mean, if anyone had taken any of me at the fancy dress I'd want to = = burn them.
Jo	Why does she always want to get her picture? ( )
Jenny	She said, 'I just wanted to see how well the costume turned out.'
Jo	She's pretty insecure, that girl.

* As Slade explains 'coz' is common Australian slang for costume.

Text C

Greetings in a lift

This excerpt is from Janet Holmes' (2000: 39) database. Here, Matt and Bob are male colleagues of equal status in a New Zealand government department. They meet and greet in the lift, and the exchange is brought to an end when they reach Bob's floor. This is social talk with a reference to the shared context of work. Note that in Homes' transcription system, there are no capitals, commas or full-stops, and she only uses? to indicate a rising intonation. The symbol + indicates a pause of up to one second.

> M   hi how's things
> B   hi good good + haven't seen you for ages how are you
> M   fine busy though as always + must meet my performance objectives eh [laugh]
> B   [laugh] yeah me too
> *Lift arrives at Bob's floor*
>   ah well see you later
> M   yea bye

Activities

❑   What features of turn-taking can you see in Text B? Why do you think they are present? Try and read it out with someone, and say whether you know of any films written with a script like that, and why.

❑   Describe Text C in terms of sequences and discuss why it has the characteristics that it does. Would you class it as a conversation?

Text D

The Full Monty

This text is from the British comedy film *The Full Monty* (1997). Six unemployed Sheffield steelworkers are driven to prepare a strip show to solve their money problems. As the blurb on the video says, 'Director Peter Cattaneo combines black comedy, roaring hilarity and all the absurdity, heartache and pathos of six men trying to keep body, soul and dignity together.' In this scene, Gaz and his ten-year-old son Nathan are in the post-office. The boy wants to withdraw the £100 that the owner of the club demands to cover his losses. Note the transcription convention of numbers in brackets to indicate the length of pause in seconds.

> G   Nath – Nath – you can't give this, kid! It's your savings!
> N   I can. It just needs your signature. It says in t'book. *[To the assistant at the counter]* I'd like to take out my money out please.
> G   *[To Nathan]* Well you bloody well can't have it. *[To the assistant]* You – you're all right love. It's sorted.
> N   *[To Gaz]* It's my money. I want it. *[To the assistant]* A hundred pounds please.
> G   *[To Nathan]* Well, when you're eighteen, you-you-you you can walk in and get it yourself, can't you?
> N   You said you'd get it back.
> G   I know. (0.5) but you don't want to listen to what I say. (0.5)

> N   You said so. (0.5) I believe you. (0.5)
> G   You do? (1)
> N   Yeah. (2.5)
> G   Blimey, Nath.

❏   Is it possible to look at Text D from the point of view of adjacency pairs and sequences? Discuss why/why not. Analyse, in terms of turn-taking, how the change in dramatic effect half way through this little extract is achieved.

Activities

❏   Going back now to interactional sociolinguistics, you will recall that it takes into account the context, and the fact that social groups have their own varieties or in-group codes. Look again at all four texts and think about how the
    a.   location that the exchange takes place in,
    b.   relationship between the people (look at roles, status and power),
    c.   histories they share,
    d.   purpose in speaking
affects the
    a.   exchange structure,
    b.   turn-taking,
    c.   adjacency pairs,
    d.   sequences,
    e.   grammar,
    f.   lexis.
❏   Record a lesson or seminar and analyse a stretch of it (no more than ten minutes) in which the teacher is talking and interacting with the students. Recording must of course be overt, so you will have to get the authorisation from the teacher before the session. Analyse the ten-minute stretch in terms of IRF.
    a.   What are the factors that determine whether the IRF structure is followed?
    b.   Would you like to suggest a different model for classroom interaction?
❏   Design a questionnaire to see what language people use in pre-sequences. A way to do it would be to describe a situation and ask them what they would say, as in:

> You are in the library sitting next to a colleague whom you do not know very well. The colleague lives near you and has a car. You are feeling tired from your day's reading and want them to run you home (they have never given you a lift before). What might you say, to prepare the ground, before you actually come out with your request?

As you can see, this question is phrased in such a way to ensure that your subjects would use a pre-sequence; otherwise, you may find that they just write their request sequence. Make sure that you include as many types of pre-sequence as possible, for example, pre-requests, pre-invitations, pre-announcements, pre-commands, pre-advice. Your question should also contain the socio-cultural dimensions of situational context, and the context of shared knowledge about speakers, their histories and their purpose in speaking. A list of ten situations should be enough. You will only start to get answers that you can group into trends and typical responses if you give the questionnaire to a minimum of twenty people. Write up your findings about the language that people use in pre-sequences and the socio-cultural factors influencing their choice. Include your questionnaire in an appendix.

C4 FOLLOWING THE COOPERATIVE PRINCIPLE

C4.1 Studying further and exploring

❏ Observing maxims
❏ Flouting and violating
❏ Relevance Theory

You are going to read four quite different scripts. Text A is a theatre's description of a member of staff, taken from its programme. Texts B and C are from the internet: B is a political interview and C is a report about modern-day metaphors; Text D is from a classic play, featuring a dramatic moment between a husband and wife.

Text A

Peter Pan programme

This excerpt is taken from a programme for *Peter Pan*, performed in the Royal Lyceum Theatre, Edinburgh (Christmas 1999). *Peter Pan* is the children's story, written by J. M. Barrie in 1904, but this is a pantomime version. This excerpt is part of the programme's description of the cast and the technical support: it describes Mike Travis, on percussion.

Mike Travis spends his life hitting things of various shapes and sizes. When he is not hitting things, he lives in the country with two dogs, two cats, two goats, twenty-one ducks, five geese, two pigs and eight hens (but not all in the same house, the smell would be minging!*)

He loves playing for the Lyceum Christmas shows (Peter Pan is his twelfth) because he gets to make up funny sounds for people like scratching, creeping, fighting, getting kicked on the bum and getting their noses tweaked.

Mike really likes small children but he couldn't eat a whole one.

* Scots English meaning *smelly*.

Text B

Road pricing

In February 2007, there was a suggestion that the British government might bring in a system called 'road pricing', aimed at reducing the number of vehicles in congested areas. The idea proposed was to track the vehicles, charge them for the number of miles covered and vary the charge according to whether it was a congested area or not. Here is part of an interview that motoring journalist Richard Hammond had with Prime Minister Tony Blair on 1 March 2007. The transcript was published on the British government website http://www.number-10.gov.uk/output/Page11123.asp.

Richard Hammond:

What, so you might get rid of the tax disc*, you might get rid of tax duty on petrol?

Prime Minister:

Well one way you could do it is to say instead of having all these different taxes, right, because you have got your road tax and you have got your fuel duty and all the rest of it, you just have one thing which is the way that you raise the money, right, and you can raise it in all sorts of different ways. Now the reason why this debate is going on here and going on in other countries is because you will have the technology that allows you to do that, but how you decide to set up that system, that is a matter for policy makers in the future to work out.

Richard Hammond:

But could you guarantee though that there would be a commensurate job in the other ways in which we are taxed as motorists if something like road pricing came in?

Prime Minister:

Well this is the point Richard, you have got to take a policy decision. You could decide you were going to get rid of all the other taxes and just have that and you could decide that it is going to be revenue neutral. Now all these are policy decisions that you take in the future. The only issue at the moment is do you want to investigate this technology as a way of dealing with the problem both of congestion and of how you raise money for transport, do you want to do it or not? And you may decide at the end of it you don't want to do it, but all I am saying at the moment is because you have got this additional dimension of congestion, as well as all the complexities of how you tax people in relation to transport, is it not sensible at least to investigate it?

* Tax disc = annual licence on the vehicle.

Text C

Here's a heads up: office jargon doesn't work

This text is from an *AOL News* article by the same title (6 November 2006).

Managers have been lambasted for using needless jargon such as 'blue sky thinking' and 'brain dump' because of the damaging effect it has on British industry.

A survey of almost 3,000 workers showed that management jargon had become a problem and was blamed for widening the divide between the shop floor and the boardroom.

A third of those polled by Investors In People said jargon betrayed a lack of confidence and made them feel inadequate, while others said managers who used it were untrustworthy or were trying to cover something up.

Among the most hated phrases were 'think outside the box', 'joined-up thinking', 'get our ducks in a row' and 'brain dump'.

Most of those questioned would prefer no jargon at all at work and over a third complained it was on the increase.

Nicola Clark, director at Investors In People, which helps firms improve their performance, said many managers were using jargon without thinking of the impact on staff.

'If used inappropriately, jargon can be an obstacle to understanding, which ultimately can impact on an individual's performance and an organisation's productivity.

'Bosses need to lead by example, ditch needless jargon and concentrate on communicating clearly with their employees.'

Text D

Death of a Salesman

This excerpt is from the opening scene from *Death of a Salesman* (1949) by the American playwright Arthur Miller. The characters, Willy and Linda Loman, live in New York. Willy is sixty and has to drive to New England every week to work.

LINDA   [*hearing WILLY outside the bedroom, calls with some trepidation*]:
             Willy!
WILLY: It's all right. I came back.
LINDA: Why? What happened? [*Slight pause.*] Did something happen, Willy?
WILLY: No, nothing happened.
LINDA: You didn't smash the car, did you?
WILLY: [*with casual irritation*] I said nothing happened. Didn't you hear me?
LINDA: Don't you feel well?

WILLY:	I'm tired to death. [*The flute has faded away. He sits on the bed beside her, a little numb.*] I couldn't make it. I just couldn't make it, Linda.
LINDA	[*very carefully, delicately*]: Where were you all day? You look terrible.
WILLY:	I got as far as a little above Yonkers. I stopped for a cup of coffee. Maybe it was the coffee.
LINDA:	What?
WILLY	[*after a pause*] I suddenly couldn't drive any more. The car kept going off on to the shoulder, y'know?
LINDA	[*helpfully*] Oh. Maybe it was the steering again. I don't think Angelo knows the Studebaker.
WILLY:	No, it's me, it's me. Suddenly I realise I'm goin' sixty miles an hour and I don't remember the last five minutes. I'm – I can't seem to – keep my mind to it.
LINDA:	Maybe it's your glasses. You never went for your new glasses.
WILLY:	No, I see everything. I came back ten miles an hour. It took me nearly four hours from Yonkers.
LINDA:	[*resigned*]: Well, you'll just have to take a rest, Willy, you can't continue this way.

Activities

❑   Describe Text A in terms of maxim flouting. How is maxim flouting used to reach the children? Would you say this is typical of programmes and reviews? What about children's literature? Find some examples, to back up your opinion.

❑   Would you agree that children have to be taught to appreciate maxim flouting whereas maxim violating comes to them naturally? Think of examples to support your opinion, in your own experience.

❑   Does Text B contain maxim flouting, violating, infringing or opting out? Which maxims are involved? To what extent is this typical of politician-speak when they are interviewed by the media?

❑   Text C describes about complaints about which maxim(s) being flouted? Why does business flout the maxim(s), do you think? Is this a feature of current business-speak in other countries that you know?

❑   In Text D, a husband violates maxims, talking to his wife. How does she react? Do you feel that this is typical of people who know each other well and for a long time (spouses, close friends, etc.)?

❑   Make a recording of a TV comedy show with well-known actors, or stand-up comedy, and pick out the instances of maxim flouting for comic effect. Which maxim is flouted most, would you say? Why do you think this is?

❑   Test the theory that a lot of what we say contains maxim flouting. Write an essay based on the following:

   a.   Transcribe part of a spontaneous, unguided casual conversation between a husband and wife, or long-term girlfriend and boyfriend.

   b.   Categorise each utterance as 'maxim observing' or 'maxim flouting' (or 'maxim violating' if you know for sure) and calculate the percentage of utterances containing maxim flouting (and maxim violating).

    c. Interview the husband/boyfriend and wife/girlfriend, separately, about what they meant each time they meant more than what they said, why they violated a maxim.

❏ Make a 10-minute recording of a casual conversation between people who know each other well and transcribe it. Are there examples of them infringing or opting out of a maxim? If there are none, why is this? If there are instances,

    d. analyse the language that is used to infringe or opt out, to see if there are any interesting features of note;

    e. have a look at the power relationship between speakers, and describe the social factors involved.

C5   APPLYING POLITENESS

C5.1   Studying further and exploring

❏ Negative politeness
❏ Positive politeness
❏ Maxims of politeness

This unit contains a selection of authentic written texts demonstrating different aspects and uses of politeness strategies and maxims. The majority are written texts with spoken characteristics: Text A is a mobile phone text message, and Texts C and D are emails. Text B is a poem with a particular communicative objective requiring delicacy. Finally, Text E is a film transcript with an idiosyncratic brand of politeness. All the texts have been chosen for you to analyse because each offers an interesting dimension or problem, be it of a cultural nature or a social nature.

Text A

Mobile phone text messages

This is an exchange of text messages on a mobile phone. The names have been changed, and the original telephone number replaced with '07777 888 999' to preserve anonymity. I have updated the software, to preserve credibility. Joan did not know who sent the first text.

Robert:	Hi, any chance of getting a copy of XP today at some point? Rob.
Joan:	You are my first wrong number text message.
Robert:	Why? Who are you? Not pete i assume?
Joan:	No. Do you mean Smith?

Robert:	Yes.
Joan:	I'm Mary's mum.
Robert:	I'm robert, petes mums partner. Sorry to bother you:)))
Joan:	How funny! OK – now tell me what a copy of XP is. *[message sent twice]*
Robert:	Do you want the answer twice?? :)) XP is an operating system for the computer. Just like windows 2000 but better and more secure.
Joan:	I wish I hadn't asked. How did you get my number? Can I put this conversation into a book on linguistics I'm writing?
Robert:	It's the number ive had for peter for a while. Not had call to use it till now. You must have his old phone or sim card. Yes, feel free to use it:))
Joan:	Thanks. This is not his phone or card.
Robert:	Do you have the number he uses now? Sorry to hear about their split.
Robert:	Sorry again. I really dont know where i got your number from.
Joan:	07777 888 999. Have a nice day!
Robert:	Thanks. And you.

❏ In Text A, the mobile phone text message exchange, which predominates – positive politeness or negative politeness? Why? In what way is it similar to a casual conversation? How does it differ and why?

Activity

Text B

To His Coy Mistress

To His Coy Mistress is by Andrew Marvell (1621–78). This 'invitational lyric' (Penguin, 1972) is addressed to his mistress, who is reluctant to consummate their relationship. The poem contains a balance of teasing humour and impatient passion.

> Had we but world enough and time,
> This coyness, lady, were no crime.
> We would sit down and think which way
> To walk, and pass our long love's day.
> Thou by the Indian Ganges' side
> Shouldst rubies find: I by the tide
> Of Humber would complain. I would
> Love you ten years before the Flood;
> And you should, if you please, refuse
> Till the conversion of the Jews.
> My vegetable love should grow
> Vaster than empires, and more slow.
> An hundred years should go to praise

Thine eyes, and on thy forehead gaze;
Two hundred to adore each breast,
But thirty thousand to the rest;
An age at least to every part,
And the last age should show your heart.
For, lady, you deserve this state;
Nor would I love at lower rate.
    But at my back I always hear
Time's winged chariot hurrying near;
And yonder all before us lie
Deserts of vast eternity.
Thy beauty shall no more be found,
Nor, in thy marble vault, shall sound
My echoing song; then worms shall try
That long-preserved virginity;
And your quaint honour turn to dust,
And into ashes all my lust.
The grave's a fine and private place,
But none, I think, do there embrace.
    Now, therefore, while the youthful hue
Sits on thy skin like morning dew,
And while thy willing soul transpires
At every pore with instant fires,
Now let us sport us while we may,
And now, like am'rous birds of prey,
Rather at once our time devour
Than languish in his slow-chapped pow'r.
Let us roll all our strength and all
Our sweetness up into one ball,
And tear our pleasures with rough strife
Thorough the iron gates of life.
Thus, though we cannot make our sun
Stand still, yet we will make him run.

Activity ⭐   ❑ In Text B, which predominates, positive or negative politeness, and why? How do the politeness maxims come into play with cooperative maxims?

Text C

Prospective PhD student

This text is an email from a female Chinese postgraduate student, on an MA in Teaching English to Speakers of Other Languages. It is addressed to one of her female British lecturers, who already has linguistics PhD students in the area of TESOL and pragmatics.

I always consider you as a wise and honest mentor of mine. So, I would like to ask for your opinion about whether or not I am qualified to take up a doctoral study after I finish my MA here. And if your answer is yes, could you give me some suggestions on which schools I should choose for my study.

There are quite a number of fields I am interested in at present.

1. I do love to study pragmatics. I always have great curiosity in finding out how languages work. My dream is that some day I can decode the mystery of how a language is learnt and thus can make it easier for the second language learners.
2. I'm also very interested in the application of new technology (i.e. the Internet or computer or video conferencing) to the field of language teaching and learning. Maybe one day I will successfully run a language school on the Internet!
3. I feel that cultural study is very important for the learning of a second language, especially after students have all the 'correct' grammar in head, but can't communicate. So, I would also like to study how cultures are affecting the learning of a second language.

I know you are very busy, so I would appreciate it if you could give me some advice and directions. Thank you!

❑ What is it about Text C that shows you that the writer has a different culture of politeness maxims from the British culture? What might a British student in the same position have said and why?

Text D

Rejections

These two texts are each the beginnings and ends of emails from journal editors responding to an author's proposal of an article. The *[. . .]* indicates where the central body of the email has been omitted. Neither of the emails brings good news.

Dear *[Name]*

Thank you for your paper *[title]* submitted to *[Journal]*.

I read your paper with interest. It is well and clearly written and argued, the data was interesting and you obviously know what you are writing about.

I must therefore admit that I hesitated a long time whether or not *[Journal]* would be the best forum for this paper, and I finally decided to recommend you to submit it elsewhere. This had little to do with quality, but rather with the fact that its topic is not squarely within the scope our new journal would like to establish in the field.

> [...]
> I am sorry I must recommend you to submit elsewhere, because it is an interesting and good paper, and I hope you'll be back with a paper that is a bit more within the scope of [Journal]
>
> Best wishes [Name]
>
> Dear [Name]
>
> [Name] and I have now had an opportunity to share our reactions to your submission to [Journal], [Title]. I am sorry to say that we think it doesn't reach the Journal's threshold for publication, so we have to decline it.
>   [...]
> I am sorry to have to pass on this disappointing news, but [Name] and I hope the comments may be of some value to you if you decide to revise the paper and submit it to another journal.
>
> With best wishes
> [Name] [Name]

Activity   ❑ Both emails in Text D have the goal of performing a very face-threatening act. Look at the politeness strategies and maxims obeyed and also label the speech acts. Finally, analyse in detail the language used to soften the blow, in terms of grammar and lexis. Are the two emails different in any way?

Text E

A Touch of Class

Basil Fawlty, of BBC TV's *Fawlty Towers*, is a master at politeness and deference pushed to obsequiousness. In this episode, 'A Touch of Class' (1975), the hotel owner sets out to attract a higher class of customer. In this scene, he is trying to impress an upper-class guest calling himself Lord Melbury, and to make up for having made him fall off his chair. When Melbury asks if Fawlty will cash a cheque for £200 (about £1,000 today), he tries to cover up his shock.

> Melbury: I was wondering, can you cash me a small cheque? I – I'm playing golf // this afternoon //
> Fawlty: // Oh delighted! //
> Melbury: // and I'd rather not go into the town =
> Fawlty: = Absolutely! I mean, er, how much? If – if it's not a rude question . . .
> Melbury: Could you manage – fif – er – oh – er a hundred?
> Fawlty: A hun- ! (0.5) Oh! (laughs) Absolutely! Oh yes, I mean, a hundred and fifty? Two hun- a hundred and sixty? Or . . .

> Melbury: Oh yes, well, let's see. Dinner tonight, a few tips, oh and it's the
>   weekend, isn't it? Would two hundred be all right?
> Fawlty: Oh, ha, ha, ha, ha, ha. Oh please! Oh tremendous! Oh I'm so happy.
>   I'll send someone out to town straight away and have it here when
>   – when you get back.
> Melbury: Yes, well, that'll be splendid.
> Fawlty: Thank you. Thank you a lot.
> Melbury: Thank you so much *(Exits.)*
> Fawlty: Not at all. I mean, it's my privilege.

❑ In Text E, discuss Fawlty's polite formulae in terms of context and purpose, and
   social status and roles. Explain linguistically why we can say that he is being more
   obsequious than polite.

❑ Take all the texts together and think about politeness and the variables of status
   and roles. Can you see any tendencies emerging?

❑ If you use a mobile phone for text messages, or you use email, or you have an
   answering machine, collect the messages that you receive in the next few days
   and analyse them from the point of view of politeness strategies and maxims.
   Compare the messages that you receive from people whom you consider to be
   good friends and those you would call acquaintances, to find if differences in degree
   of familiarity affect the way that politeness is expressed.

❑ In what way might written communications differ from spoken exchanges, in terms
   of politeness? What are the variables that might influence these differences?

⭐ **Activities**

CORPORA AND COMMUNITIES

C6

Studying further and exploring

C6.1

❑ Corpus linguistics
❑ Corpora, pragmatics and social factors
❑ Corpora, domains and communities

The data in this unit come from a variety of media; some demonstrate the features
that we have been looking at, and others require you to find texts for yourself first.
Text A is an excerpt from a concordance for you to analyse the function of a pragmatic marker. Text B provides a list of corpora websites, for you find and experiment
with, taking into account the social factor of geographical variety. Text C is a script
from an AOL message board, focusing on the social factor of age, for you to convert

'thing'

aab(064(063))	﹔Libyan regime, is that there is no such thing as a surgical military strike against
aab(101(100))	r Lee Chuk-Yan, who said: ` This whole thing of right of abode gives one more cl
ccd(0577)	The first thing?"
chr(0112)	`This thing's heavier than I thought," puffed Da
dch(0347)	﹔fully there, there'd be at least er sort of thing erm in the summary to see what w﹔
ew4(0384)	One thing is certain: no constituency would fc
ew4(1031(1028))	Fiction, however, is one thing and reality is another.
f71(0098)	it's exciting, but that's one thing I really would like to work with
f7j(809(810))	pending discussions but the whole thing Mr chairman really hasn't erm hasr
flk(0238)	The thing is er, you can end up feeling like a
fls(0280)	﹔tually this sort of environmental control thing would be a good idea.
fls(0370)	I mean, that's the sort of thing.
fm4(1541)	Because that thing you did with the fish tank has show
fu7(0429)	But this was evidently the sophisticated thing.
fut(0132)	For one thing they're often in very tiny print.
fut(0461)	﹔ease, or any words that mean the same thing, like no refunds, no money refunde
fuu(0097)	﹔king of retiring as I have done the least thing you want to be bothered about is n
fuu(602(603))	The only thing you have to bear in mind is that if y﹔
fuu(673(674))	﹔t with temperature but it's only a minute thing.
fx5(0099)	seems to be the thing they're all looking for.
fx5(0233)	open a li little bit for er air, and the next thing there's a boy half way through the `
fxr(0697)	This is just a sort of first list, the one thing erm you were going to ask Jimmy?
fxr(0926)	And probably the best thing to do is say is say, Trumpet plays ﹔
fxr(1597(1596))	﹔which always seems to me a very wrong thing to say, I I'm sure it's quite incorrec﹔
fy8(0064)	﹔as interested in doing the same kind of thing.
fy8(540(542))	Gonna be one thing or the other.
fy8(746(748))	﹔ to cope with the family, erm you know, thing things like that, they're very difficul﹔
fyj(0062)	mixed up, it was all mixed up, the funny thing is, er whilst he was many years my
fyj(0488)	Oh there was no such thing if they gave you the money, you mi﹔
g0a(2865(2859))	How's this new project thing coming along?"
g1v(0183)	Is a created thing, and has sensation,
g1v(0869)	One thing they undertake,
g3u(0280)	Which comes on really to the second thing.
g4n(0049)	wanted, you know and er all that sort of thing and erm I hadn't used to do any, m﹔
g4n(0190)	﹔ly and er it was more trouble getting the thing through the pan to get er the case
g4n(0256)	﹔uld turn the knob and it'd get the whole thing going, it'd get you inside, it'd regist﹔
g4n(0407)	You make a thing as is gonna do the job and it's no ﹔
gv1(1165(1147))	The most important thing to remember when treating fish dis﹔
gw5(0887(0884))	Now, there is one more thing.
h47(0594)	And as we brought out first thing this morning, communication withir
h4a(0186)	The other thing that we need to say is that far from
h5d(0853(0851))	﹔ in theory we should be doing the same thing
hdt(0181)	development, and of course, one other thing that they did that this government ﹔
hem(0117)	Breaking the whole thing up.
hem(0282)	﹔ody thought i you know it was the done thing.
hem(0329)	﹔s Ha a length of them, put it around this thing like that, and then when you starte﹔
hm4(0673)	﹔e end of January, and er the interesting thing from your point of view, is that we ﹔
j2g(0070)	﹔ell's roan horse and I remember the first thing he said.
j2g(242(243))	But the only thing I recognized about him right away `
j3w(0016)	` which are new and that's the important thing so about fifteen hundred new and i
j3w(0023)	﹔en to you about and the most important thing probably for the users besides us ﹔
j3w(0293)	The important thing is for people to listen to the genuin
j55(622(620))	﹔ace himself Incidentally he did the same thing when we recorded Peter Grimes a﹔
jja(0421)	﹔usinesses in the area could have er the thing that er response was er this this pa﹔
jng(0138)	﹔hion show and yet again the interesting thing is that the Scottish P G A is actuall﹔

to a corpus. Text D is an email about blogging, to serve as a departure point for the exploration of a blog community of practice.

Text A

The thing

This is an excerpt from the British National Corpus Sampler single-line concordance (using Sara-32 concordancer) for 'thing' without left or right sorting. 'Thing' occurs 1,319 times in the Sampler ('things' occurs 1,295). Here are the first 55 lines.

❑ 'Thing' serves an anaphoric function, in that the speaker can avoid having to repeat a noun, and an exophoric function, with speakers referring vaguely, exclusively, to an entity in the interlocutors' shared world. It can also function as a **pragmatic marker**: examples in this text are 'sort of thing', which is a filler, 'one thing is certain', which is an emphasising pre-sequence, and 'the thing is', which is a filler and hedge.

a. Count up the number of 'thing's in each category: a) referential and b) pragmatic. Is there another category that you would like to add? Which is the biggest category and why?
b. Make sub-categories in the pragmatic category, to find the main pragmatic function. What sort of contexts would you imagine the sub-category 'thing's take place in?
c. What difficulties might you encounter if you were to return to the original corpora and annotate the 'thing's to indicate these categories?
d. What generalisations can you make about the first and second words to the left of 'thing'? What features can you see to the immediate right?
e. To what extent can you relate these conclusions to Speech Act theory, conversation analysis, and the cooperative and politeness principles?

❑ Is corpus linguistics a theory or a method? Is it even a new or separate branch of linguistics? Does the fact that corpus linguistics can be used in conjunction with other approaches to pragmatics make it part of pragmatics or simply something that facilitates data so researchers can carry out the other approaches on it?

Text B

Corpora round the world

This is a list of some of the world's corpus websites. Some are more informative, accessible, navigatable and generous than others. Visit the sites before you go any further.

❑ The Bank of English: http://www.titania.bham.ac.uk/docs/svenguide.html
❑ The British Academic Spoken English corpus (BASE):
   http://www2.warwick.ac.uk/fac/soc/celte/research/base/
❑ The British National Corpus (BNC): http://www.natcorp.ox.ac.uk/

- ❏ The Cambridge and Nottingham Corpus of Discourse in English (CANCODE): http://www.cambridge.org/elt/corpus/cancode.htm
- ❏ The Cambridge International Corpus (CIC): http://www.cambridge.org/elt/corpus/international_corpus.htm
- ❏ The Corpus of Professional Spoken American English (CPSAE): http://www.athel.com/cspa.html
- ❏ The International Corpus of English (ICE): http://www.ucl.ac.uk/english-usage/ice/index.htm
- ❏ The Limerick Corpus of Irish-English (LCIE): http://www.ul.ie/~lcie/homepage.htm
- ❏ The Longman/Lancaster Corpus: http://www.longman.com/dictionaries/corpus/lancaster.html
- ❏ The Michigan Corpus of Academic Spoken English (MICASE): http://micase.umdl.umich.edu/m/micase/
- ❏ The Scottish Corpus of Texts & Speech (SCOTS): http://www.scottishcorpus.ac.uk/
- ❏ The Wellington Corpus of Written New Zealand English (WWC) and The Wellington Corpus of Spoken New Zealand English (WSC): http://www.vuw.ac.nz/lals/corpora/index.aspx
- ❏ Collins WordbanksOnline English: http://www.collins.co.uk/Corpus/CorpusSearch.aspx

Activity

- ❏ Once you have visited the sites, choose some of the following questions
    a. What do you think of the Bank of English advice?
    b. Find an audio sample of BASE corpus and transcribe it. What might you look for in it?
    c. Look for 'know' in BNC home-page search box. Discuss what you can learn about the usage of the words from the search. Compare it to the ready-made concordance sample for 'know' on the CANCODE homepage.
    d. Check out the information about Learner Corpora on the CIC site. Does it sound as if it would be useful to language teachers?
    e. What do you imagine the owners of CPSAE expect you to do with the sample of their corpus?
    f. Listen to the sample sound files in the ICE corpus for Australia, East Africa, Hong Kong, India, Jamaica and the Philippines. Discuss the advantages of having sound files as part of a corpus.
    g. On the LCIE website and look at the IVACS publications. Are they mostly related to pragmatic markers, Speech Act theory, conversation analysis, or the Cooperative or Politeness Principles?
    h. Look at the sample 'hunt' concordance on the Longman/Lancaster Corpus homepage and discuss whether the idiomatic use of is the most common.
    i. Search the MICASE for any pragmatic marker in the different academic contexts. Who uses the marker most? Limit your search to any of social factor that you like and discuss the effect of limiting your search.

j.   Go to the SCOTS corpus and check how females in Aberdeen use 'och'.
k.   Discuss the social factors involved in the WSC.
l.   Conduct three separate searches of the components of the Collins Wordbanks
     Online (British books, American books and transcribed speech) for the word
     'would' and compare how it is used.
❑ Corpora are being explored to discover **varieties** of languages. Compare as many
   corpora as possible in these sites to see if you can detect differences between
   American, Scottish, Irish and New Zealand English.
❑ Look for websites with corpora in **languages other than English**. If your L1 is not
   English, then your L1 might be the most obvious place to start.
     a.   How do the websites compare in terms information, accessibility, navigability
          and generosity?
     b.   How do the corpora compare to the English language corpora, in terms of
          size, age and range of text types?
     c.   Do they show varieties of the language that you are looking at?
     d.   What have they got that the English language corpora do not have?

Text C

Like school or hate school?

Here is a brief look into a discussion on the AOL Teens Message Board (http://
messageboards.aol.co.uk/aol/en_gb/boards.php?boardId=290590), 21 February 2007.
Note that the discussion is written in a simple form of chatroom speak and also contains errors.

Jamieharding123
I hate the work in school, but when i think bout it, im glad i have to go to school
so i can see my mates and chat 2 them, cos sum live far away, so school is da
only chance i get to talk 2 'em. My sister hated school, but now shes left shes
missin it. I'm joinin da army next year (I'll b 16) so thats da year I'll be leavin. I
wont miss school, but I'll miss talkin 2 all ma m8s.
Any1 else Agree

Malibu 105
well most people at my school are horible 2 me. so i dont like it. works is ok. but
in my opinion its the people that make me hate going into school.

Rosiepattis
I tell every1 dat i h8 school but ur right, school is alright. Most lessons r crap but
sum r alright n u get 2 see all ur m8s.

Jones1gareth
i quite like school, there's only 500 there so everyone knows everyone and it's
gr8. U should really just enjoy it. the only thing is our school gives SO MUCH
homework, it's really bad . . . But because it's ridiulous that there's so much no1
takes it seriously so thats OK.

> Meadow Jono
> And another good thing is that if anyone didn't go to school we wouldn't be using computers like we are now

Activity This exchange is held tightly together by theme and lexis.

❑ If you were to do a concordance of 'school', and you wanted to find the most frequent grammatical co-text, would you sort the lines on the right or the left? How many words away?
❑ Would corpus linguistics help you analyse the attitude to their friends at school?
❑ What are the problems of trying to do a concordance with this genre?
❑ How would you check whether other teenagers in Britain wrote this way on message boards? Could you compare them to other teenagers round the world?

Text D

Add to the general sunshine-weekend feeling by adding a comment to the blog . . . !!!!

This is an email from a university lecturer to her current students on the full-time contact MEd TESOL programme (Friday, 12 May 2006, 2.57 p.m.).

> Feel like commenting on things that are happening in the TESOL world of Moray House? There is now a blog where you can add things! A couple of graduate students have posted comments . . .
>   Go to http://tesol.uniblogs.org/
>   You can add your comments to the posts already there, and if you send me your own blog URL I can add you to the list (known as a 'blogroll') so people can easily find our site. If you don't have a blog but would like to try this way of online diaries and comments, you can sign up free to a blog by going to http://uniblogs.org/
>
> A blog can be a way of keeping a journal, noting things that are of interest to you, letting your friends and family know interesting things. People can add comments to your postings. If you discover an annoying posting or someone making inappropriate comments, you can easily delete it. You can also restrict who can make comments.
>   You can also use your blog to keep links to other websites. This could be, for example, where you have uploaded your photos.
>   Go on . . . the sun is shining so add to the general sunshine-weekend feeling by adding a comment to the blog . . . !!!!
>   Ruby

☐ Discuss the implications of this email:

a. Say whether you think this email would achieve its aim.

b. Consider why the lecturer would want students to add blogs to the site.

c. Decide whether bloggers could be considered a virtual community of practice, or whether they are only a physical community.

d. Discuss whether the possible anonymity could undermine a sense of society or community of practice, erasing norms of interaction and allowing for flaming (posting messages that are deliberately hostile and insulting).

e. Analyse whether blogging makes it easier for members of a community of practice at different levels of hierarchy to communicate and come together on relatively equal terms, with their gender, sexual orientation, ethnic origin and physical and mental ability less in evidence?

☐ Visit the *Language Log* http://itre.cis.upenn.edu/~myl/languagelog/. Discuss:

a. Is this a community of practice?

b. What would you have to do in order make a corpus and carry out concordances?

c. How would you look at social factors of gender, age, class and geography of the corpus?

d. Could you look at dimensions related to Speech Act theory, conversation analysis, and the Cooperative and Politeness Principles?

CULTURE AND LANGUAGE LEARNING

C7

Studying further and exploring

C7.1

☐ Cross-cultural pragmatics
☐ Intercultural pragmatics
☐ Interlanguage pragmatics
☐ Teaching intercultural pragmatics

Text A and B in this unit enable you to look at the language of the Spanish speech acts. Text C asks you to think about the Politeness Principles in an intercultural interaction between two Koreans and an African-American. Text D and E focus on interlanguage pragmatics and teaching intercultural pragmatics: you meet a learner corpus and a tutor's feedback.

Text A

No rubber gloves!

The Motorcycle Diaries (Walter Salles, 2004) is a film about the life-changing journey round Latin America undertaken by the Argentinean medical student Ernesto Che

Guevara (played by Gael García) and biochemist Alberto Granado (played by Rodrigo de la Serna). In this scene Doctor Bresciani takes the two of them into the San Pablo leper colony, in the Peruvian Amazon. The Mother Superior reprimands the doctor because they are not wearing the regulation protective rubber gloves.

1	MS	Doctor Bresciani, estos señores llegan y creen que pueden proceder
2		como les parece?
3	DB	Madre San Alberto, estos señores tienen buena experiencia médica en
4		Córdoba y Buenos Aires.
5	MS	Eso no les da ningún derecho para proceder así, romper las reglas.
6	DB	Que le parece si esa discusión la vamos a dejar para mas tarde, si?
7	MS	Eh //
8	DB	// Gracias Madre. Usted es muy comprehensiva

****

1	MS	Doctor Bresciani, these gentlemen just show up and think they can do
2		what they want?
3	DB	Mother San Alberto, these gentlemen have ample medical experience
4		from Cordoba and Buenos Aires.
5	MS	That doesn't give them any right to go around breaking rules.
6	DB	How would it be if we were to leave this discussion till later, OK?
7	MS	Er //
8	DB	// Thank you, Mother. You are most understanding.

Text B

Damn knives!

Garcia Lorca's *Blood Wedding* (1932) is a tragedy of love: Leonardo and the Bride were once in love, but Leonardo married another and the Bride marries in this play. After the wedding, Leonardo and the Bride run away together, but the groom pursues them and kills them.

This is the first scene: the Mother is bitter about talk of the knife because her husband and elder son had been killed.

Habitación pintada de amarillo.
Novio: *(Entrando)* Madre.
Madre: ¿Que?
Novio: Me voy.
Madre: ¿Adónde?
Novio: A la viña. *(Va a salir)*

Madre: Espera.

Novio: ¿Quieres algo?

Madre: Hijo, el almuerzo.

Novio: Déjalo. Comeré uvas. Dame la navaja.

Madre: ¿Para qué?

Novio: *(Riendo)* Para cortarlas.

Madre: *(Entre dientes y buscándola)* La navaja, la navaja . . . Malditas sean todas y el bribón que las inventó.

Novio: Vamos a otro asunto.

Madre: Y las escopetas, y las pistolas, y el cuchillo más pequeño, y hasta las azadas y los bieldos de la era.

Novio: Bueno.

Madre: Todo lo que puede cortar el cuerpo de un hombre. Un hombre hermoso, con su flor en la boca, que sale a las viñas o va a sus olivos propios, porque son de él, heredados . . .

Novio: *(Bajando la cabeza)* Calle usted.

****

Room painted yellow.

Groom: *(Enters)* Mother.

Mother: What?

Groom: I'm going.

Mother: Where?

Groom: To the vineyard. *(Turns to go)*

Mother: Wait.

Groom: Do you want something?

Mother: Your lunch, son.

Groom: Leave it. I'll eat grapes. Give me the knife.

Mother: What for?

Groom: *(Laughing)* To cut them.

Mother: *(Through clenched teeth, looking for it)* The knife, the knife . . . Damn them and the villain that invented them.

Groom: Let's change the subject.

Mother: And guns, and pistols, and the smallest knife, and even hoes and winnowing forks.

Groom: Right.

Mother: Everything that can cut a man's body. A handsome man, in the bloom of youth, who goes out to the vineyard or his own olive groves, because they're his, inherited . . .

Groom: *(Bowing his head)* Be quiet.

Text A is offered to you for analysis, not as a representative sample of all Spanish disagreement language, but for you to:

⭐ **Activity**

C

- ❑ examine the grammar of the Spanish directive;
- ❑ decide whether the reprimand is a direct or indirect speech act and what the other speech act is;
- ❑ analyse it in terms of the Cooperative Principle;
- ❑ discuss the power structure and struggle in it;
- ❑ discuss whether the same scene fragment could take place in the same way in another language that you know or whether it seems typical to Spanish.

Text C

I want you to know me

This intercultural shop service encounter was collected by Bailey (1997: 345) in a Los Angeles convenience store. The cashier and the owner are Korean, and the customer is African-American.

1	cashier	hi {customer approaches counter} (0.2)
2	customer	how's it going partner? euh
3	{cashier nods}	(1.0)
4	customer	you got them little bottles?
5	cashier	(eh?) {customer's gaze falls on the little bottles} (3.5)
6	customer	one seventy-fi:ve! {customer gazes at display on bottles} (2.0)
7		you've got no bourbon? (1.2)
8	cashier	no: you don't have bourbon (1.0)
9	customer	I'll get a beer then {customer talks to his nephew}
10	cashier	two fifty {cashier rings up purchase and bags beer} (4.5)
11	customer	I just moved in the area I talked to you the other day
12		you [remember me]*?
13	cashier	[oh yesterday] last night
14	customer	yeah
15	cashier	[(o:h yeah?)] {cashier smiles and nods}
16	customer	[goddamn shit] [then you don't]
17	owner	[new neighbour huh?]
		{customer turns halfway to the side towards the owner}
18	customer	{loudly, smiling} then you don't KNOW me
19	cashier	[(I know you)] {cashier gets change from the till}
20	customer	[I want you to KNOW] me so when I walk in here
21		you'll know I
22		smoke Winstons your sons knows me
23	cashier	[ye::ah]
24	customer	[the yo]ung guy
25	cashier	there you go {cashier proffers change}

(* Square brackets indicate overlapping text.)

❏ Describe what goes on in this encounter in terms of Politeness Principles (negative
and positive) and macro-functions (transactional and interactional). In what way
do the customer's intentions conflict with the cashier's and owner's. Who 'wins'?

❏ What is the customer's attitude to the Koreans? Would he speak in the same way
to an African-American cashier and owner, do you think?

❏ What is the Koreans' attitude to the African-American? Would they have spoken
in the same way to him if he had been less disposed to reduce the social distance?

Text D

It would be very grateful if you could

The following 18 lines are taken from a concordance for 'would' in the Learner Business
Letter Corpus WM98. This corpus, compiled by Yasumasa Someya, is made up of 1,464
letters written by Japanese business people learning English. A search for 'would' brings
up 46 lines with various meanings; the ones selected here are those used in polite requests
and thanks. (See Chapter A7 for an explanation of concordance.)

3 ur staff members. For the reference, we	would	appreciate if you would send the booklet
4 [WM98:P=00173] In this regard, we	would	appreciate it if you would send us one
5 [WM98:P=00010] I	would	appreciate it very much if you would se
6 ision staff at the moment. Therefor, we	would	appreciate it very much if you would se
7 ing of International Division staffs. I	would	appreciate it very much if you would se
8 [WM98:P=00057] I	would	appreciate your assistance and response
9 [WM98:P=00087] I	would	appreciate your cooperation in this mat
10 [WM98:P=00012] I	would	appreciate your cooperation in this mat
11 0145] Will you mend me one booklet? It	would	be grateful if you could send me it by
12 P=00085] Please send me one booklet. It	would	be grateful if you could send me it till
13 235] Your kind attention to this matter	would	be highly appreciate.
14 ur booklet as one of our references. It	would	be very grateful if I could have one co
15 [WM98:P=00203] It	would	be, therefore, highly appreciated if yo

/.../

28 [WM98:P=00332] I		would	like to thank you again in advance for
29 [WM98:P=00278] We		would	like to thank you in advance for your c
30 [WM98:P=00072] We		would	like to thank you in advance to your hi
/.../			
35 e are very interested in your text. and		would	much appreciate it if you would send us
36 [WM98:P=00315] We		would	much appreciate it if you would send us

 Activity

❏ Look at the lexis and grammar and find what these upper intermediate learners have mastered well in their writing, and what they are still having difficulty with. Think about why this is happening.

❏ To what extent would you say that they had mastered direct and indirect speech acts, Politeness Principles and Cooperative Principles? How easy is it to be sure of your interpretation, given the absence of contextual headers?

❏ What learners' beliefs and attitudes are in evidence in these lines?

❏ Pragmalinguistic routines are the more straightforward than sociopragmatic features to teach, because the latter need the teacher to be sensitive to the learners' own pragmatic background. Learners can memorise chunks such as 'thank you', 'I wonder if you could X'? and 'I would appreciate it if', since they can allow them to sound more fluent. If learners feel uncomfortable about engaging in the target language culture, e.g. expressing requests in such a personal way and maximising benefit to self, they can be taught formulae, e.g. 'I would be grateful if [noun] could' or 'I very much appreciate your [adjective + noun]', as this does not ask the learners to lose their home identity and adopt the values of the target culture. Discuss.

❏ Graddol says that within the English as a Lingua Franca framework, the fluent bilingual speaker is the target model of English. Should these learners be left and not encouraged to polish their writing, so as to preserve their non-native-speaker-of-English identity? Would this encourage native speakers of English to be lenient when it came to pragmatic failure?

Text E

Tidying up their academic English

Here is a selection of excerpts from lecturer feedback comments on three written assignments in the Masters in TESOL (Teaching English to Speakers of Other Languages) of a university in Britain. The students are teachers of English with an IELTS (International English Language Testing System) minimum score of 6.5. Most classify as 'good users', with an operational command of the language, though with occasional inaccuracies, inappropriacies and misunderstandings in some situations, and able to handle complex language well and understand detailed reasoning.

Student 1

❑ It is unclear to me whether you have fully grasped the issues in the literature. You need to tackle them in greater depth and more explicitly and then you need to link them together more coherently.

❑ You would have got a higher mark if you had shown your own opinion more with regards to the literature. You need to evaluate what the writers say and give reasons for your evaluation.

Student 2

❑ You should go into greater depth and explain some things a little more, e.g. pg.10, you say that reading is social progress – this needs explaining. Generally speaking, your rationale could have been contained more discussion and presentation of debates.

❑ You could have indulged in a little more criticality. For example, it would have been interesting if you had included an analysis of how well a discussion of students' personal diaries might go down in a mixed-sex class of self-conscious teenagers.

Student 3

❑ You show an understanding of schema, pre-while-post-reading, skimming and scanning, P-P-P, TBL, multiple intelligences: your grid on pg.3 is interesting and useful. You might have added an explanation of why the task cycle is not part of the practice stage. You mention seven syllabuses: you should say what they are.

❑ Try to take a more critical stance with the theorists, e.g. you could have given an opinion of Harmer's theory that following a syllabus helps to minimise the plateau effect (pg.2). You might experiment with taking a less all-accepting attitude to theories and develop a little theoretically argued scepticism. You have engaged in the debates on the usefulness of cloze test design.

❑ Summarise what is involved in the two main problems (explicitness and criticality) that are being brought up repeatedly here.

❑ To what extent would you say that these problems occur because of different cooperative maxims of quantity and relevance in the cultures that the students come from?

❑ Check your theory by interviewing five university students from non-English-speaking countries who are studying or have studied in an English-speaking university. Make sure that you interview students who are not being interviewed by anyone else. Record your interview. Ask them if

a. they received advice about explicitness and criticality problems similar to that in these samples (and if not, what their main problems were in terms of written academic style);

b. their lecturers showed an understanding of the causes of their problems and offered constructive comments to help adapt;

c. they went to EAP (English for Academic Purposes) classes to learn about British written academic style, and if they benefited from them;

d. they were able to change their written academic style to match English-speaking university requirements;

e. their 'problems' were reflections of written academic style from their home country, where there are different norms vis-à-vis explicitness and criticality;

f. they felt that their identity might be eroded by changing style, and if this made them reluctant to change;

g. they would go back or have gone back to the written academic style of their home country, once home again.

Once you have transcribed your interviews, circulate the transcriptions round the class so that everyone can read them all. Discuss in plenary the main findings.

❏ Propose a solution for those with explicitness/criticality problems, in terms of EAP class texts and tasks. You might like to try information gap activities (student A has some information which B does not, and the task requires B to find out A's information), jigsaw tasks (both students have information, and they put it together to get the whole picture), or tasks that require the learners to copy cultural behaviour.

❏ Would you imagine that native speakers of English brought up in the English-speaking education system could also have these problems? In what way might they differ?

D

SECTION D
EXTENSIONS:
READINGS

CONTEXT: KNOWLEDGE, REPETITION, REFERENCE

Reading and researching

As you will see in this reading, Wardhaugh explains that 'there are differences between the parties in the specific things that they know in contrast to the kinds of background knowledge that they share'. He makes the point that common knowledge varies from group to group.

Ronald Wardhaugh (from *How Conversation Works*, Oxford: Blackwell, 1985: 18–20.)

For any particular conversation it is also possible to show that there are differences between the parties in the specific things that they know in contrast to the kinds of background knowledge that they share. No two people have identical backgrounds, so in any conversation the participants will have different kinds of knowledge about almost any topic that is likely to be mentioned. If only two people, Fred and Sally, are involved, there will be certain matters known to both, some because 'everybody knows such things' and others because both Fred and Sally happen to know them. Then there will be matters known to only one of the speakers, so that Fred will know something that Sally does not know, or Sally something that Fred does not know. In addition, there will be partly known information: Fred or Sally, or both, may partly know something or know parts of something, but not necessarily the same parts. And Fred or Sally, or both again, may believe that the other knows something that the other actually does not know. As we can see, there are numerous possible permutations in who knows what, who believes who knows what, and so on. Again, there are predictable consequences: conversation can proceed only on the basis that the participants share a set of beliefs, that is, certain things must be known to all parties; others may be known; some will have to be explained; questions may be asked for clarification; difficulties will be negotiated or cleared-up somehow; people will be understanding and tolerant; and the various processes that are involved will be conducted decently. If only one participant in a conversation refuses to subscribe to these beliefs and to conduct himself or herself accordingly, the others will become irritated, confused, or frustrated, and may well abandon any attempt to continue what they have begun.

Since most participants in a conversation usually do share a certain amount of background knowledge about 'proper' behaviour and the 'right' way to do things, much of what they say can be understood if we, too, are familiar with the knowledge they share. Their references to places, times, and events, and their accounts and descriptions are related to what they know and what they believe the others know. A participant in a conversation must believe that he or she has access to the same set of reference points that all the other participants have access to; all he or she needs do in conversing is use those points for orientation, and listeners will comprehend. And such a belief is largely justified. What is hardly ever necessary in a conversation is to begin at the very beginning of anything and to treat everyone and everything as unique and somehow without antecedents. In a trivial sense every occasion is unique, but procedures exist which minimize novelty and maximize normality – accepted ways of asking and giving directions, rules for re-gulating who speaks to whom and about what, and basic principles for conducting yourself, for example, with complete strangers.

**Michael
Hoey**

Reading and researching

D1.2

Hoey looks at cohesion from the point of productive skills and how we should write. Hoey understands that since second language learners generally master cohes-ive devices, the teaching of them may be counter-productive and may not produce native style fluency in composition. He says that what distinguishes a mature native speaker writer from a learner is that the former uses repetition devices connecting over a distance in the text, making the sentences relate to each other in non-linear ways.

Note that when he talks of 'cohesion', he means grammatical cohesion, and his 'repetition' only refers to lexical cohesion. His term 'complex repetition' means related words that share a common root or base form, known as a lexical morpheme, e.g. 'drugs' and 'drugging', 'economist' and 'economy'.

Michael Hoey (from *Patterns of Lexis in Text*, Oxford: Oxford University Press, 1991: 242–5.)

One thing seems certain: the traditional advice to avoid repetition needs to be couched with special care if it is not to interfere actively with the development of mature writing skills. The advice grew out of two quite reasonable worries. First, when an inexperienced writer does not know what else to say, they sometimes resort to restating what they have already said. Nothing in this book should have shaken the reader's conviction that this is an unsatisfactory practice; the existence of pat-terns of lexis in text is not to be interpreted as an incitement to padding.

Second, especially among less experienced writers, limitations of vocabulary and ignorance of the means whereby one can repeat in a language may lead a learner to juxtapose else same lexical item clumsily in adjacent sentences. Again, it has been noted in earlier chapters that the tendency for adjacent sentences to bond is not great; the reason is that, in English, care is usually taken to avoid else clumsy juxtaposition just referred to. So, here too, the advice as tradition-ally given still stands.

But it cannot rest there. Reasonable as the worries concerning repetition may be, the advice to avoid repetition may be harmful unless it is immediately supple-mented by something more. To begin with, if a learner is to avoid clumsiness, he or she must be taught how to avoid it. One of the most important ways is by means of complex repetition. So, in the first sentence of the previous paragraph, I used the lexical item **clumsily**; in the following sentence it has become **clumsy** while in the third sentence of this paragraph it appears as **clumsiness**. Similarly, **juxtapose** becomes **juxtaposition**, and **repeat** becomes **repetition**. There is nothing contrived about these examples; my practice is that of most writers need-ing to repeat without making the repetition obtrusive. Stotsky (1983) comments that 'an increase in the use of morphologically complex words [i.e. complex repetition], rather than repetition of a simple word or the use of a cumbersome paraphrase, may be an important index of growth.'

If we need to protect our learners against this aspect of avoiding repetition, still more must we protect them against misuse of the counsel to avoid padding. Learners should not be encouraged to say the same thing over and over again, but they *should* be advised to make connections between what they are currently saying and what they said before. There should, in non-narrative text, be some relationship between sentences at a distance from each other. What this means for learners is that they need to take time out of grappling with the difficulties of composing the sentence they are currently working on to consider its relationship with what they have already written. This may impose on the writer an additional burden but it also relieves him or her of at least some of the task of lexical selection. Indeed, knowledge that it is legitimate to reuse in different combinations lexical items already brought into play, may actually serve to lighten some aspects of the writing task.

The advice a learner needs will vary from person to person and from group to group. For some the main need may be to avoid going around in circles; such learners will need reminding that new information always accompanies repetition in mature writing. For others the need may be to prevent the text drifting; such learners will need telling that repetition usually provides the grounding for new information. In either case, materials may need developing that give the student practice in bonding back to earlier sentences. The well-tried strategy of supplying the learners with an incomplete text and asking them to complete it may be adaptable to this purpose; indeed, there is no reason why more than one text organizing principle at a time might not be practiced in this way.

D1.3   Reading and researching

The short Wodak excerpt is quite different. It is taken from a book that looks at linguistic barriers to communication in a variety of institutional contexts. The excerpt focuses on the discourse of the media, specifically radio broadcasts of the news. Wodak mentions imprecise references in news stories, and says that because little background context is provided for those who do not already know about the news item so that they can identify the referent, the news is inaccessible to parts of the population. She begins by saying that news stories lack features naturally occurring in spoken language.

Ruth Wodak (from *Disorders of Discourse*, London: Longman, 1996: 100–102.)*

Imprecise references, pronominalizations, and a lack of feed-back are thus also characteristics of these texts. Typically they are produced unconstrained by a need for self-justification. Consequently, they cannot really be considered stories, as the latter are normally conceived. The relevance of the story is never really explained, background knowledge and hints as to orientation are absent, no frame is available within which to embed the news item. As a result there is almost no possibility of 'updating' it. This situation was confirmed by Larsen, who analysed the

---

*   For references see the original work.

intelligibility of Danish news spots (Larsen 1983) (see Wodak/Lutz 1986: 202ff). This suggests that it is often impossible to integrate new information into already available knowledge as long as the present form of providing news items pertains. Little or no acquisition of new knowledge takes place. As Larsen writes:

> The main effect of news bulletins apparently is to confirm the listener's view of the current events, or occasionally, to put new topics on a mental list of current events.

(Larsen 1983: 36)

On the one hand, listening to the news is a process of opinion-making, where opinions are formed and then – often misunderstood and unreflected – integrated. Thus stereotypes, clichés and prejudices are confirmed instead of being subjected to critical evaluation.

On the other hand, a large part of the population is excluded altogether from the information provided. To meet its obligations regarding information and education, the Austrian Broadcasting Company (ORF) would have to alter the text and the style of presentation of the news and make it more comprehensible. And even then we would need tests to see whether simpler news reports are 'better understood'. As long as news broadcasts retain their inaccessibility, they will continue to present the large symbolic capital of the elites. The elites possess information, others are excluded (van Dijk 1993a). And even if news texts are made more comprehensible, the elites and better educated profit more from the greater accessibility (see below). As soon as one considers the complete news-cycle – from news agency report to newswriter, to radio reporter or the newspaper that accepts an item, and from there to the uncomprehending reader – one realizes all the more clearly what power there is in the passing of news information.

□ Summarise the Wardhaugh reading, and say whether you agree and why (not).
□ Test Wardhaugh's point that we have common background knowledge about 'proper' behaviour and the 'right' way to do things.
  a. Record a group of people having a casual, natural, spontaneous conversation. The choice of who, where and when is yours.
  b. Make sure that the people know that you are recording them and that they do not mind you doing it. If they do mind, take the machine away and find another group of recordees, another time, another place.
  c. Make sure that there is no extraneous background noise, such as voices off, music or machines running, that is going to make it difficult for you to hear what they said when you are playing it through afterwards.
  d. Do *not* tell them that you are investigating common background knowledge about 'proper' behaviour and the 'right' way to do things, otherwise you might make them talk about topics that they might not have chosen, and in an unnatural way. Just say that you are studying their language in general.
  e. Tell them to talk as naturally as possible, about anything they want. Do not give them a topic or prompt them in any way.

f. Keep out of the conversation, but close enough to the speakers to be able to turn the recorder off if they get particularly uncomfortable with it.

g. Record about 10 minutes' conversation when the speakers are in full flow. If you try to record before they have really got started, it will be stilted and awkward since they are still getting used to having the machine there.

h. When you turn the machine off, and they have finished talking, ask them very briefly what brings them together, how long they have known each other, where they meet, how often and why. Do not overdo this interrogation: all you are trying to find out is 'Is there reason for them sharing substantial cultural knowledge and even a little interpersonal knowledge?'

i. Now go back to Wardhaugh's point about us having common background knowledge about 'proper' behaviour and the 'right' way to do things, and answer the following questions:

   i. Are there any instances of some people knowing more about one particular topic than others do?

   ii. Does this upset the conversation or enhance it for the others, as far as you can see?

   iii. Is there an example of somebody wrongly assuming his/her hearers share knowledge of a context, and giving less information than is needed for people to understand? What happens at this point?

   iv. Is there an example of someone wrongly assuming their hearers do not share knowledge of a context, and giving more information than they need in order to follow him/her? What happens at this point?

   v. When you have tried to answer these questions, play your recording to someone from the group who was actually recorded, and see if you have got your answers 'right'.

   vi. Looking at all your answers above, what seems to be the 'proper' behaviour and the 'right' way to do things in conversations? What are the 'rules' about referring to common knowledge and new knowledge, as far as this conversation seems to show?

   vii. Write up your findings in a short essay. Your essay should contain brief answers to questions i to vii, and then the list of conversation rules that you made up in question viii.

❏ Read the Hoey excerpt:

   a. What two reasons does he give for the desire of linguists and teachers of writing skills to make inexperienced writers avoid repetition?

   b. If we do advise students not to use repetition and padding, what should we tell them to use in their place?

   c. What do you think he means by 'learners will need reminding that new information always accompanies repetition in mature writing'?

❏ Take 10 short essays of native speakers or near native speakers of English (they could be cooperative colleagues in your tutorial or seminar group).

   a. Analyse each essay from the point of view of lexical cohesion, quantifying how many instances there are of repetition, complex repetition, synonyms, superordinates general words, in each.

b.   Give copies of the 10 essays to 10 people, and ask them to rate them (and order them) according to how well they think they are written.

c.   Put the essays in the most popular order, taking into account all the answers, and go back to your analysis of them from the point of view of lexical cohesion.

d.   Discover which features are most used in the most popular essays, which features are most used in the least popular essays, and draw conclusions.

e.   What are implications of your findings and how would this help someone teaching writing to native speakers of English?

f.   Write up your project. You could use the following headings, if you like:
   i.   Introduction: what lexical cohesion is.
   ii. Method: how you analysed the essays, who you gave them to, how you analysed the responses, what difficulties you encountered.
   iii. Results: which device featured in the essays felt to be the best-written.
   iv. Discussion: why you think this is so.
   v.   Conclusion: what the implications are for the teaching of writing.

❑ Look at the Wodak excerpt:
   a.   What exactly does she mean by 'imprecise references, pronominalisations, and a lack of feedback', do you think? Give examples.
   b.   Do you agree that radio news broadcasts are only accessible to the elite? Who are the elite and why are they elite?
   c.   Could the same be said of television news broadcasts?

❑ Take a newspaper article from a quality newspaper (broadsheet), and another from a more popular one (tabloid), and compare them in terms of the reference and the background context knowledge that they assume. Is one more imprecise and inexplicit than another? Do they demand different types of background context knowledge?

SPEECH ACTS AND POWER   D2

Reading and researching   D2.1

Fairclough says that the idea of speech acts, 'uttering as acting', is central to what he calls CLS (Critical Language Study). CLS 'analyses social interactions in a way which focuses upon their linguistic elements', and how language affects and is affected by the system of social relationships (1989: 5).

   In the first extract, Fairclough criticises pragmatics for what he sees as its individualism and its idealism. He says that individuals are not usually free to manipulate language to achieve their goals, but that they are constrained by social conventions. He also says that people do not have equal control in interactions, because there are inequalities of power.

In the second, he looks at the speech act of 'requesting' and the way in which it relates to inequalities of power. He says that indirect requests leave the power relationship implicit, and he shows how the grammar of a request can express varying degrees of indirectness.

In the third extract, Fairclough says that speech acts are a central part of pragmatics, which is in turn concerned with the meanings that participants in a discourse give to elements of a text. He refers to the multi-functionality of speech acts, and then focuses on the way that they are related to the co-text, the intertextual context and the situational and cultural background context. He sees the social factors that influence the use of indirect speech acts in terms of power relations, and concludes that the discourse type dictates the conventions for speech acts, and that the conventions reflect the participants' ideology and social relationships.

Norman Fairclough (from *Language and Power*, Harlow: Longman, 1989: 9 –11, 54–5 and 155–7.)

Pragmatics

Anglo-American pragmatics is closely associated with analytical philosophy, particularly with the work of Austin and Searle on 'speech acts'. The key insight is that language can be seen as a form of action: that spoken or written utterances constitute the performance of speech acts such as promising or asking or asserting or warning; or, on a different plane, referring to people or things, presupposing the existence of people or things or the truth of propositions, and implicating meanings which are not overtly expressed. The idea of uttering as acting is an important one, and it is also central to CLS in the form of the claim, that discourse is social practice.

The main weakness of pragmatics from a critical point of view is its individualism: 'action' is thought of atomistically as emanating wholly from the individual, and is often conceptualized in terms of the 'strategies' adopted by the individual speaker to achieve her 'goals' or 'intentions'. This understates the extent to which people are caught up in, constrained by, and indeed derive their individual identities from social conventions, and gives the implausible impression that conventionalized ways of speaking or writing are 'reinvented' on each occasion of their use by the speaker generating a suitable strategy for her particular goals. And it correspondingly overstates the extent to which people manipulate language for strategic purposes. Of course, people do act strategically in certain circumstances and use conventions rather than simply following them; but in other circumstances they do simply follow them, and what one needs is a theory of social action – social practice – which accounts for both the determining effect of conventions and the strategic creativity of individual speakers, without reducing practice to one or the other.

The individuals postulated in pragmatics, moreover, are generally assumed to be involved in cooperative interactions whose ground rules they have equal control over, and to which they are able to contribute equally. Cooperative interaction between equals is elevated into a prototype for social interaction in general, rather than being seen as a form of interaction whose occurrence is limited and socially constrained. The result is an idealized and Utopian image of verbal interaction which is in stark contrast with the image offered by CLS of a sociolinguistic order moulded in social struggles and riven with inequalities of power. Pragmatics often appears to describe discourse as it might be in a better world, rather than discourse as it is.

Pragmatics is also limited in having been mainly developed with reference to single invented utterances rather than real extended discourse, and central notions like 'speech act' have turned out to be problematic when people try to use them to analyse real discourse. Finally, Anglo-American pragmatics bears the scars of the way in which it has developed in relation to 'linguistics proper'. While it has provided a space for investigating the interdependence of language and social context which was not available before its inception, it is a strictly constrained space, for pragmatics tends to be seen as an additional 'level' of language study which fills in gaps left by the more 'core' levels of grammar and semantics. Social context is acknowledged but kept in its place, which does it less than justice.

Cognitive psychology and artificial intelligence

One of the concerns of pragmatics has been with the discrepancies which standardly exist between what is said and what is meant, and with how people work out what is meant from what is said; but the detailed investigation of the processes of comprehension involved, as well as of processes of production, has been undertaken by cognitive psychologists, and workers in artificial intelligence concerned with the computer simulation of production and comprehension. From the perspective of CLS, the most important result of work on comprehension is the stress which has been placed upon its active nature: you do not simply 'decode' an utterance, you arrive at an interpretation through an active process of matching features of the utterance at various levels with representations you have stored in your long-term memory. These representations are prototypes for a very diverse collection of things – the shapes of words, the grammatical forms of sentences, the typical structure of a narrative, the properties of types of object and person, the expected sequence of events in a particular situation type, and so forth. Some of these are linguistic, and some of them are not. Anticipating later discussion, let us refer to these prototypes collectively as '*members' resources*', or MR for short. The main point is that comprehension is the outcome of interactions between the utterance being interpreted, and MR.

Not surprisingly, cognitive pyschology and artificial intelligence have given little attention to the social origins or significance of MR. I shall argue later that attention to the processes of production and comprehension is essential to an understanding of the interrelations of language, power and ideology, and that this is so because MR are socially determined and ideologically shaped, though their 'common sense' and automatic character typically disguises that fact. Routine and unselfconscious resort to MR in the ordinary business of discourse is, I shall suggest, a powerful mechanism for sustaining the relations of power which ultimately underlie them.

Norman
Fairclough

Conversation analysis and discourse analysis

Power is also sometimes hidden in face-to-face discourse. For instance, there is obviously a close connection between *requests* and power, in that the right to request someone to do something often derives from having power. But there are many grammatically different forms available for making requests. Some are *direct* and mark the power relationship explicitly, while others are *indirect* and leave it more or less implicit. Direct requests are typically expressed grammatically in imperative sentences: *type this letter for me by 5 o'clock*, for instance. Indirect requests can be more or less indirect, and they are typically expressed grammatically in questions of various degrees of elaborateness and corresponding indirectness: *can you type this letter for me by 5 o'clock, do you think you could type this letter for me by 5 o'clock, could I possibly ask you to type this letter for me by 5 o'clock*. There are also other ways of indirectly requesting – through *hints*, for instance: *I would like to have the letter in the 5 o'clock post*.

Why would a business executive (let us say) choose an indirect form to request her secretary to type a letter? It could be, particularly if a hint or one of the more elaborate questions is used, for manipulative reasons: if the boss has been pressurizing the secretary hard all day, such a form of request might head off resentment or even refusal. But less elaborate forms of indirect request (*can you/will you/could you type . . .*) are conventionally used in the sort of situation I have described, so the question becomes why business executives and other powerholders systematically avoid too much overt marking of their power.

Activities ✪

❏   Take a look at the first reading and discuss
    a.   what his criticisms of pragmatics are;
    b.   why he says that notions like 'speech act' are problematic;
    c.   what he means by the term 'members resources' (MR);
    d.   what he says comprehension is;
    e.   whether you agree with what he is saying.

❏   Go now to the second reading and
    a.   summarise what he says about the power holder using both elaborate and less elaborate indirect forms to make a request;
    a.   think of another situation that in which a power holder makes a request, list all the ways that they might express the request, and see if the power holder uses indirect forms. Can we generalise, therefore?

❏   This question aims to help you to write an essay on classroom talk. In order to make comparisons, it would be a good idea if you discussed the questions either with other people in your class or with friends outside class from different educational backgrounds.
    a.   Think back to the teaching approach used in your school.
    b.   Define the teaching approach as traditional or liberal, and the level of education.
    c.   Think about the extent to which indirectness would have been used, and in what situations and to do what.

d. See if your experience confirms Fairclough's theory that indirectness is used in traditional classrooms but not in liberal ones, and less in higher education than in schools.

e. Think about whether there any other factors apart from ideology in the classroom that might have influenced whether indirectness was used.

f. Write about your classroom language and the use of indirectness and say to what extent you agree with Fairclough (be sure not to include anecdotes).

❑ Look at the last paragraph of the third abstract, in which he talks of asymmetries of speech act conventions, and

a. Think of situations in which conventions of speech acts and indirectness reflect asymmetrical social relationships (the second abstract gave a very useful example).

b. Choose one of these situations, and find a video film that contains an example of the situation; make sure that it is a short episode of only about ten minutes; watch it several times.

c. Make a note of who can use what speech act, who can be indirect and who can't, and also transcribe the language used to realise the speech act.

d. Decide whether you agree with Fairclough that the conventions of speech acts embody social relationships.

CONVERSATION AND RACE   D3

Reading and researching   D3.1

The first of the Gumperz excerpts begins with a formulation of 'contextualisation cues' and miscommunications. It describes miscommunications that can occur when a speaker from one social group addresses a member of another social group, and it discusses an exchange that is unsatisfactory because of the differences in variety of English and speech style between the two speakers. The formulaic phrases of any social group usually serve to establish personal contact between members.

The second Gumperz excerpt contains another example of miscommunication in brief encounters. This time it is the intonation that causes the problem because it is misinterpreted as communicating a negative attitude.

John Gumperz (from *Discourse Strategies*, Cambridge: Cambridge University Press, 1982: 133–4 and 173–4.)

The conversational analyses described in this chapter extend the methodological principle of comparing ungrammatical and grammatical sentences, by which linguists

John
Gumperz

derive generalizations about grammatical rules, to the analysis of contextualization phenomena that underlie the situated judgements conversationalists make of
each other. Naturally occurring instances of miscommunication are compared with
functionally similar passages of successful communication in the same encounter
or findings from other situations to derive generalizations about subculturally and
situationally specific aspects of inferential processes.

The following example illustrates the type of miscommunication phenomena
we look for and shows how we begin to isolate possible linguistic sources of misunderstanding. The incident is taken from an oral report by a graduate student in
educational psychology who served as an interviewer in a survey.

(1)   The graduate student has been sent to interview a black housewife in a low
       income, inner city neighborhood. The contact has been made over the phone
       by someone in the office. The student arrives, rings the bell, and is met by
       the husband, who opens the door, smiles, and steps towards him:
       Husband: So y're gonna check out ma ol lady, hah?
       Interviewer: Ah, no. I only came to get some information. They called
                     from the office.
       (Husband, dropping his smile, disappears without a word and calls his wife.)

The student reports that the interview that followed was stiff and quite unsatisfactory. Being black himself, he knew that he had 'blown it' by failing to recognize the significance of the husband's speech style in this particular case. The style
is that of a formulaic opening gambit used to 'check out' strangers, to see whether
or not they can come up with the appropriate formulaic reply. Intent on following the instructions he had received in his methodological training and doing
well in what he saw as a formal interview, the interviewer failed to notice the
husband's stylistic cues. Reflecting on the incident, he himself states that, in order
to show that he was on the husband's wave-length, he should have replied with
a typically black response like 'Yea, I'ma git some info' (I'm going to get
some information) to prove his familiarity with and his ability to understand local
verbal etiquette and values. Instead, his Standard English reply was taken by the
husband as an indication that the interviewer was not one of them and, perhaps,
not to be trusted.

The opener 'So y're gonna check out ma ol lady' is similar to the 'Ahma git
me a gig' discussed elsewhere. Both are formulaic phrases identifiable through cooc-
current selections of phonological, prosodic, morphological and lexical options.
Linguists have come to recognize that, as Fillmore (1976) puts it, 'an enormous
amount of natural language is formulaic, automatic and rehearsed, rather than propositional, creative or freely generated.' But it must be emphasized that although
such formulas have some of the characteristics of common idioms like *kick the
bucket* and *spill the beans*, their meaning cannot be adequately described by lexical
glosses. They occur as part of routinized interactive exchanges, such as Goffman
describes as 'replies and responses' (1981). Their use signals both expectations
about what is to be accomplished and about the form that replies must take. They
are similar in function to code switching strategies. Like the latter they are learned

John
Gumperz

by interacting with others in institutionally defined networks of relationships. Where these relationships are ethnically specific they are often regarded as markers of ethnic background. But, as our example shows, their use in actual encounters is ultimately determined by activity specific pre-suppositions so that failure to react is not in itself a clear sign of ethnic identity. Basically, these formulaic phrases reflect indirect conversational strategies that make conditions favorable to establishing personal contact and negotiating shared interpretations . . .

Interethnic communication

Chapters 6 and 7 outline a perspective to conversation that focuses on conversational inference and on participants' use of prosodic and phonetic perceptions as well as on interpretive preferences learned through previous communicative experience to negotiate frames of interpretation. Using this perspective we can account for both shared grammatical knowledge and for differences in communicative style that characterize our modern culturally diverse societies.

This approach to speaking has both theoretical and practical significance. On the theoretical level it suggests a way of carrying out Garfinkel's program for studying naturally organized activities through language without relying on a priori and generally untestable assumptions about what is or is not culturally appropriate. Although it might seem at first glance that contextualization cues are surface phenomena, their systematic analysis can lay the foundation for research strategies to gain insights into otherwise inaccessible symbolic processes of interpretation.

On the practical level, the study of conversational inference may lead to an explanation for the endemic and increasingly serious communication problems that affect private and public affairs in our society. We can begin to see why individuals who speak English well and have no difficulty in producing grammatical English sentences may nevertheless differ significantly in what they perceive as meaningful discourse cues. Accordingly, their assumptions about what information is to be conveyed, how it is to be ordered and put into words and their ability to fill in the unverbalized information they need to make sense of what transpires may also vary. This may lead to misunderstandings that go unnoticed in the course of an interaction, but can be revealed and studied empirically through conversational analysis.

The main purpose of earlier chapters was to illustrate the nature of the cues and the inferential mechanisms involved. To that end, the discussion largely relied on examples of brief encounters. Miscommunications occurring in such brief encounters are annoying and their communicative effect may be serious. But the social import of the phenomena in question and their bases in participants' cultural background is most clearly revealed through case studies of longer events. The following two chapters present in depth analyses of two such events. To begin with, let me give one more brief example to illustrate the scope of the analysis and the subconscious nature of the interpretive processes involved.

In a staff cafeteria at a major British airport, newly hired Indian and Pakistani women were perceived as surly and uncooperative by their supervisor as well as by the cargo handlers whom they served. Observation revealed that while

John
Gumperz

relatively few words were exchanged, the intonation and manner in which these words were pronounced were interpreted negatively. For example, when a cargo handler who had chosen meat was asked whether he wanted gravy, a British assistant would say 'Gravy?' using rising intonation. The Indian assistants, on the other hand, would say the word using falling intonation: 'Gravy.' We taped relevant sequences, including interchanges like these, and asked the employees to paraphrase what was meant in each case. At first the Indian workers saw no difference. However, the English teacher and the cafeteria supervisor could point out that 'Gravy,' said with a falling intonation, is likely to be interpreted as 'This is gravy,' i.e. not interpreted as an offer but rather as a statement, which in the context seems redundant and consequently rude. When the Indian women heard this, they began to understand the reactions they had been getting all along which had until then seemed incomprehensible. They then spontaneously recalled intonation patterns which had seemed strange to them when spoken by native English speakers. At the same time, supervisors learned that the Indian women's falling intonation was their normal way of asking questions in that situation, and that no rudeness or indifference was intended.

After several discussion/teaching sessions of this sort, both the teacher and the cafeteria supervisor reported a distinct improvement in the attitude of the Indian workers both to their work and to their customers. It seemed that the Indian workers had long sensed they had been misunderstood but, having no way of talking about this in objective terms, they had felt they were being discriminated against. We had not taught the cafeteria workers to speak appropriate English; rather, by discussing the results of our analysis in mixed sessions and focusing on context bound interpretive preferences rather than on attitudes and stereotypes, we have suggested a strategy for self-diagnosis of communication difficulties. In short, they regained confidence in their own innate ability to learn.

The first of the longer case studies examines excerpts from an interview – counselling session recorded in an industrial suburb in London. The participants are both educated speakers of English; one is a Pakistani teacher of mathematics, who although born in South Asia went to secondary school and university in England. The other is a staff member of a center funded by the Department of Employment to deal with interethnic communication problems in British industry. The teacher has been unable to secure permanent employment and having been told that he lacks communication skills for high school teaching, he has been referred to the center. While both participants agree on the general definition of the event as an interview–counselling session, their expectations of what is to be accomplished, and especially about what needs to be said, differ radically. Such differences in expectation are of course not unusual even where conversationalists have similar cultural backgrounds. Conversations often begin with an introductory phase where common themes are negotiated and differences in expectation adjusted. What is unusual about this situation is that participants, in spite of repeated attempts at adjustment over a period of more than an hour, utterly fail to achieve such negotiation. Our analysis concentrates on the reasons for this failure and shows how it is based on differences in linguistic and socio-cultural knowledge.

Activities

John
Gumperz

❑ Read through the first two pages of the first excerpt and summarise
   a. what is meant by 'contextualisation cues';
   b. what Gumperz means by 'miscommunication'.
❑ From your reading of Gumperz, what was it that separated the interviewer
   from the interviewee, socially? Discuss the exchange between them in terms of
   adjacency pairs and say whether you feel that conversation analysis can explain
   what happened, and why. Is it possible to explain it from the point of view of
   interactional sociolinguistics?
❑ Discuss the factors that caused the supervisor and cargo handlers to think that
   the Indian and Pakistani cafeteria assistants were being surly. Do you agree with
   Gumperz's interpretation of what went wrong or do you think that there was more
   to it than that?
❑ Over the next week, make a note of any miscommunication of this sort that you
   happen to overhear. It could be that you have to sit or stand quite close to the
   people who are talking and in a good light because the miscommunications
   may be quite small or ambiguous, and only detectable in a hesitation or a slight
   flinch before the next speaker talks. What linguistic features are involved, and
   what socio-cultural factors? Are the features of overlaps, interruptions and
   pauses, the adjacency pair structure and sequences anything to do with the
   miscommunication?
❑ The miscommunications in the pages selected from Gumperz occur between
   people of different social class and different ethnic groups. Do you think that lessons
   can be learned from these findings? Should courses be designed for social
   workers and immigrants with a different first language from the country that they
   now are, to train them to appreciate the subtleties of language such as formulae
   and intonation and their socio-cultural effect? What sort of exercise could be
   given to sensitise those assistants in the airport cafeteria? Look at some advanced
   course books for teaching English as a Foreign Language and see how much of
   this is sort of thing is included.
❑ Have a look through several novels that you are familiar with and see if the
   writers have made their characters speak with overlaps, interruptions and pauses,
   the adjacency pair structure and sequences. What use do the writers make of
   all these features of natural speech? Is there always supposed to be a meaning
   or significance behind them? Which of the features is most represented in the books?
   Why do you think this is?
❑ Record a casual conversation between two or three people whom you know to be
   friends, and transcribe five minutes from the middle of the recording, including
   the overlaps, interruptions and pauses. Try and label each turn now, as part of
   an adjacency pair. What conclusions can you draw? To what extent would you
   say that the overlaps, interruptions and pauses and the adjacency pair structure
   are a result of the speakers being friends?
❑ Record a cross-cultural programme on the TV or radio; this could be an interview between people from different countries or simply an informal exchange
   of ideas, or maybe even a travel programme. Observe the backchannels of each
   participant and observe the pauses.

a. Are there any differences?
b. What seems to be the function of each?
c. Are there any misunderstandings or breakdown in communication that occur as a result of the differences?
d. Why do you think this is?

RELEVANCE AND INDIRECTNESS

Reading and researching

The Sperber and Wilson extract is more complex than the readings in this book have been so far. They say that Grice's appeals to the maxim of relation are 'no more than dressed-up appeals to intuition'.

Dan Sperber and Deirdre Wilson (from *Relevance*, Oxford: Blackwell, 1995: 36–40.)*

Problems of explanation: Grice's theory of conversation

The Gricean analysis of communication has been discussed almost exclusively by philosophers, whose main concern has been to define the terms 'meaning' or 'communication'. From our current, more psychological point of view, defining communication is not a primary concern. For one thing, communication does not necessarily involve a distinct and homogeneous set of empirical phenomena. Our aim is to identify underlying mechanisms, rooted in human psychology, which explain how humans communicate with one another. A psychologically well-founded definition and typology of communication, if possible at all, should follow from a theoretical account of these underlying mechanisms. We see Grice's analysis as a possible basis for such a theoretical account. From this perspective, the main defect of Grice's analysis is not that it defines communication too vaguely, but that it explains communication too poorly.

The code model has the merit of explaining how communication could in principle be achieved. It fails not on the explanatory but on the descriptive side: humans do not communicate by encoding and decoding thoughts. The inferential model, despite the technical problems discussed earlier, provides a description of human communication which rings true. By itself, however, it explains very little. The temptation to return to the code model will remain powerful as long as the inferential model is not developed into a plausible explanatory account of communication. However, the basis for such an account is suggested by another work of Grice's, his *William James Lectures*, in which he puts forward the view that communication is governed by a 'co-operative principle' and 'maxims of conversation'.

* For references see the original work.

According to the inferential model, communication is achieved by the audience recognising the communicator's informative intention. However, it is not enough to point out, as we have done, that recognising intentions is a normal feature of human cognition. The recognition of informative intentions presents problems which the recognition of other human intentions does not.

How does one recognise another individual's intentions? One observes his behaviour; using one's knowledge of people in general and of the individual in particular, one infers which of the effects of this behaviour he could have both predicted and desired; one then assumes that these predictable and desirable effects were also intended. In other words, one infers the intention behind the behaviour from its independently observed or inferred effects. This pattern of inference is generally not available to an audience trying to recognise a communicator's informative intention. As we have seen, the informative effects of communication are normally achieved, if at all, via recognition of the informative intention. Hence, it seems, the audience cannot *first* observe or infer these effects, and *then* use them to infer the informative intention.

However, the problem is not that it is hard to come up with hypotheses about what the communicator might have intended to convey: it is that too many hypotheses are possible. Even a linguistic utterance is generally full of semantic ambiguities and referential ambivalences, and is open to a wide range of figurative interpretations. For non-coded behaviour there is, by definition, no predetermined range of information it might be used to communicate. The problem, then, is to choose the right hypothesis from an indefinite range of possible hypotheses. How can this be done? First, it is easy enough to infer that a certain piece of behaviour is communicative. Communicative behaviour has at least one characteristic effect which is achieved before the communicator's informative intention is recognised: it overtly claims the audience's attention.

Grice's fundamental idea in his *William James Lectures* is that once a certain piece of behaviour is identified as communicative, it is reasonable to assume that the communicator is trying to meet certain general standards. From knowledge of these general standards, observation of the communicator's behaviour, and the context, it should be possible to infer the communicator's specific informative intention. Grice, talking only of verbal communication, argues,

> Our talk exchanges . . . are characteristically, to some degree at least, cooperative efforts; and each participant recognizes in them, to some extent, a common purpose or set of purposes, or at least a mutually accepted direction . . . at each stage, *some* possible conversational moves would be excluded as conversationally unsuitable. We might then formulate a rough general principle which participants will be expected (*ceteris paribus*) to observe, namely: Make your conversational contribution such as is required, at the stage at which it occurs, by the accepted purpose or direction of the talk exchange in which you are engaged.
>
> (Grice 1975: 45)

This Grice calls the *co-operative principle*. He then develops it into nine *maxims* classified into four categories:

Maxims of quantity
1   Make your contribution as informative as is required (for the current purposes
    of the exchange).
2   Do not make your contribution more informative than is required.

Maxims of quality
Supermaxim: Try to make your contribution one that is true.
1   Do not say what you believe to be false.
2   Do not say that for which you lack adequate evidence.

Maxim of relation
Be relevant.

Maxims of manner
Supermaxim: Be perspicuous.
1   Avoid obscurity of expression.
2   Avoid ambiguity.
3   Be brief (avoid unnecessary prolixity).
4   Be orderly.

This account of the general standards governing verbal communication makes
it possible to explain how the utterance of a sentence, which provides only an
incomplete and ambiguous representation of a thought, can nevertheless express a
complete and unambiguous thought. Of the various thoughts which the sentence
uttered could be taken to represent, the hearer can eliminate any that are incom-
patible with the assumption that the speaker is obeying the co-operative principle
and maxims. If only one thought is left, then the hearer can infer that it is this
thought that the speaker is trying to communicate. Thus, to communicate efficiently,
all the speaker has to do is utter a sentence only one interpretation of which is
compatible with the assumption that she is obeying the co-operative principle and
maxims.

Recall, for instance, our example (16)–(18):

(16)   Jones has bought the *Times*.
(17)   Jones has bought a copy of the *Times*.
(18)   Jones has bought the press enterprise which publishes the *Times*.

There might be situations where only interpretation (17) of the utterance in (16)
would be compatible with the assumption that the speaker does not say what she
believes to be false (first maxim of quality). There might be situations where only
interpretation (18) would be compatible with the assumption that the speaker is
being relevant (maxim of relation). In those situations, the intended interpretation
of (16) can easily be inferred. Hence the maxims and the inferences they give rise
to make it possible to convey an unambiguous thought by uttering an ambiguous
sentence.

Grice's approach to verbal communication also makes it possible to explain
how utterances can convey not just explicit but also implicit thoughts. Consider
dialogue (32):

(32)   *Peter*:   Do you want some coffee?
      Mary: Coffee would keep me awake.

Suppose that Peter is aware of (33). Then from the assumption explicitly expressed by Mary's answer, together with assumption (33), he could infer conclusion (34):

(33)   Mary does not want to stay awake.
(34)   Mary does not want any coffee.

In just the same way, if Peter is aware of (35), he could infer conclusion (36):

(35)   Mary's eyes remain open when she is awake.
(36)   Coffee would cause Mary's eyes to remain open.

Now in ordinary circumstances, Mary would have wanted to communicate (34) but not (36), although both are inferable in the same way from the thought she has explicitly expressed. This is easily explained on the assumption that Mary obeys Grice's maxims. The explicit content of her utterance does not directly answer Peter's question; it is therefore not relevant as it stands. If Mary has obeyed the maxim 'be relevant', it must be assumed that she intended to give Peter an answer. Since he can obtain just the expected answer by inferring (34) from what she said, she must have intended him to draw precisely this conclusion. There is no parallel reason to think that she intended Peter to infer (36). Hence, just as the Gricean maxims help the hearer choose, from among the senses of an ambiguous sentence, the one which was intended by the speaker, so they help him choose, from among the implications of the explicit content of an utterance, the ones which are implicitly conveyed.

    Suppose now that the exchange in (32) takes place in the same circumstances as before, except that Peter has no particular reason beforehand to assume that Mary does not want to stay awake. Without this assumption, no answer to his question is derivable from Mary's utterance, and the relevance of this utterance is not immediately apparent. One of Grice's main contributions to pragmatics was to show how, in the event of such an apparent violation of the co-operative principle and maxims, hearers are expected to make any additional assumptions needed to dispose of the violation. Here Peter might first adopt (33) as a specific assumption jointly suggested by the utterance, his knowledge of Mary, and the general assumption that Mary is trying to be relevant. He might then infer, as in the previous example, that she does not want any coffee. To eliminate the apparent violation of the maxims, Peter would have to assume that Mary had intended him to reason just as he did: that is, that she was intending to convey implicitly both assumption (33) and conclusion (34).

    Grice calls additional assumptions and conclusions such as (33) and (34), supplied to preserve the application of the co-operative principle and maxims, *implicatures*. Like his ideas on meaning, Grice's ideas on implicature can be seen as an attempt to build on a commonsense view of verbal communication by making it more explicit and exploring its implications. In his *William James Lectures*, Grice took one crucial step away from this commonsense view towards theoretical sophistication;

but of course one step is not enough. Grice's account retains much of the vagueness of the commonsense view. Essential concepts mentioned in the maxims are left entirely undefined. This is true of *relevance*, for instance: hence appeals to the 'maxim of relation' are no more than dressed-up appeals to intuition. Thus, everybody would agree that, in ordinary circumstances, adding (33) and (34) to the interpretation of Mary's answer in (32) makes it relevant, whereas adding (35) and (36) does not. However, this fact has itself to be explained before it can be used in a genuine explanation of how Mary's answer is understood.

Grice's view of implicature raises even more basic questions. What is the rationale behind the co-operative principle and maxims? Are there just the nine maxims Grice mentioned, or might others be needed, as he suggested himself? It might be tempting to add a maxim every time a regularity has to be accounted for. However, this would be entirely *ad hoc*. What criteria, then, do individual maxims have to meet? Could the number of maxims be not expanded but reduced?

How are the maxims to be used in inference? Grice himself seems to think that the hearer uses the assumption that the speaker has observed the maxims as a premise in inference. Others have tried to reinterpret the maxims as 'conversational postulates' (Gordon and Lakoff 1975), or even as code-like rules which take semantic representations of sentences and descriptions of context as input, and yield pragmatic representations of utterances as output (Gazdar 1979). The flavour of such proposals can be seen from the following remarks:

> The tactic adopted here is to examine some of the data that would, or should be, covered by Grice's quantity maxim and then propose a relatively simple formal solution to the problem of describing the behaviour of that data. This solution may be seen as a special case of Grice's quantity maxim, or as an alternative to it, or as merely a conventional rule for assigning one class of conversational meanings to one class of utterance.
>
> (Gazdar 1979: 49)

The pragmatic phenomena amenable to this sort of treatment are rather limited: they essentially arise when the utterance of a certain sentence is so regularly correlated with a certain pragmatic interpretation that it makes sense to set up a rule linking the one to the other. For example, the utterance of (37) regularly suggests (38), the main exception being when it is already assumed that (38) is, or might be, false:

(37)   Some of the arguments are convincing.
(38)   Not all of the arguments are convincing.

The proposal is to deal with this by setting up a general rule associating (37) with the pragmatic interpretation (38), and effectively blocking its application in contexts where it is assumed that (38) is, or might be, false (Gazdar 1979: 55–9). However, in most cases of implicature, as for instance in example (32)–(34), the context does much more than filter out inappropriate interpretations: it provides premises without which the implicature cannot be inferred at all. The translation of Grice's maxims into code-like rules would thus reduce them to dealing with a narrow set of interesting but quite untypical examples of implicature.

What, then, are the forms of inference involved in the normal operation of the maxims? If, as seems plausible, non-demonstrative (i.e. non-deductive) inference is involved, how does it operate? Without pursuing these questions in any depth, most pragmatists have adopted one form or another of the Gricean approach to implicatures, and are otherwise content to explain the explicit core of verbal communication in terms of the code model. The results are as can be expected. Although based on an insight which seems quite correct, and although somewhat more explicit and systematic than the intuitive reconstructions supplied by unsophisticated speakers, the analyses of implicature which have been proposed by pragmatists have shared with these intuitive reconstructions the defect of being almost entirely *ex post facto*.

Given that an utterance in context was found to carry particular implicatures, what both the hearer and the pragmatic theorist can do, the latter in a slightly more sophisticated way, is to show how in very intuitive terms there was an argument based on the context, the utterance and general expectations about the behaviour of speakers, that would justify the particular interpretation chosen. What they fail to show is that on the same basis, an equally convincing justification could not have been given for some other interpretation that was not in fact chosen. There may be a whole variety of interpretations that would meet whatever standards of truthfulness, informativeness, relevance and clarity have been proposed or envisaged so far. The theory needs improving at a fundamental level before it can be fruitfully applied to particular cases.

In his *William James Lectures*, Grice put forward an idea of fundamental importance: that the very act of communicating creates expectations which it then exploits. Grice himself first applied this idea and its elaboration in terms of the maxims to a rather limited problem of linguistic philosophy: do logical connectives ('and', 'or', 'if . . . then') have the same meaning in natural languages as they do in logic? He argued that the richer meaning these connectives seem to have in natural languages can be explained in terms not of word meaning but of implicature. He then suggested that this approach could have wider applications: that the task of linguistic semantics could be considerably simplified by treating a large array of problems in terms of implicatures. And indeed, the study of implicature along Gricean lines has become a major concern of pragmatics. We believe that the basic idea of Grice's *William James Lectures* has even wider implications: it offers a way of developing the analysis of inferential communication, suggested by Grice himself in 'Meaning' (1957), into an explanatory model. To achieve this, however, we must leave aside the various elaborations of Grice's original hunches and the sophisticated, though empirically rather empty debates they have given rise to. What is needed is an attempt to rethink, in psychologically realistic terms, such basic questions as: What form of shared information is available to humans? How is shared information exploited in communication? What is relevance and how is it achieved? What role does the search for relevance play in communication? It is to these questions that we now turn.

D4.2

Deborah Tannen

Reading and researching

Tannen combines Cooperative Principle, with Speech Act Theory, critical discourse analysis and intercultural pragmatics, when she suggests that women use indirectness for rapport and solidarity, and for getting their demands met and saving facing at the same time. Her view is that indirectness can be a prerogative of the powerful or even a norm, but that indirectness is not associated with women or with power the world over.

Deborah Tannen (from *Gender and Discourse*. Oxford: Oxford University Press, 1994: 32–4.)*

Indirectness

Lakoff (1975) identifies two benefits of indirectness: defensiveness and rapport. Defensiveness refers to a speaker's preference not to go on record with an idea in order to be able to disclaim, rescind, or modify it if it does not meet with a positive response. The rapport benefit of indirectness results from the pleasant experience of getting one's way not because one demanded it (power) but because the other person wanted the same thing (solidarity). Many researchers have focused on the defensive or power benefit of indirectness and ignored the payoff in rapport or solidarity.

The claim by Conley, O'Barr, and Lind (1979) that women's language is really powerless language has been particularly influential. In this view, women's tendency to be indirect is taken as evidence that women don't feel entitled to make demands. Surely there are cases in which this is true. Yet it can also be demonstrated that those who feel entitled to make demands may prefer not to, seeking the payoff in rapport. Furthermore, the ability to get one's demands met without expressing them directly can be a sign of power rather than of the lack of it. An example I have used elsewhere (Tannen 1986) is the Greek father who answers, 'If you want, you can go,' to his daughter's inquiry about going to a party. Because of the lack of enthusiasm of his response, the Greek daughter understands that her father would prefer she not go and 'chooses' not to go. (A 'real' approval would have been 'Yes, of course, you should go.') I argue that this father did not feel powerless to give his daughter orders. Rather, a communicative system was conventionalized by which he and she could both preserve the appearance, and possibly the belief, that she chose not to go rather than simply obeying his command.

Far from being powerless, this father felt so powerful that he did not need to give his daughter orders; he simply needed to let her know his preference, and she would accommodate to it. By this reasoning, indirectness is a prerogative of the powerful. By the same reasoning a master who says, 'It's cold in here,' may expect a servant to make a move to close a window, but a servant who says the same thing is not likely to see his employer rise to correct the situation and make

* For references see the original work.

him more comfortable. Indeed, a Frenchman who was raised in Brittany tells me that his family never gave bald commands to their servants but always communicated orders in indirect and highly polite form. This pattern renders less surprising the finding of Bellinger and Gleason (1982, reported in Gleason 1987) that fathers' speech to their young children had a higher incidence than mothers' of both direct imperatives (such as 'Turn the bolt with the wrench') *and* implied indirect imperatives (for example, 'The wheel is going to fall off').

The use of indirectness can hardly be understood without the cross-cultural perspective. Many Americans find it self-evident that directness is logical and aligned with power whereas indirectness is akin to dishonesty as well as subservience. But for speakers raised in most of the world's cultures, varieties of indirectness are the norm in communication. In Japanese interaction, for example, it is well known that saying 'no' is considered too face-threatening to risk, so negative responses are phrased as positive ones: one never says 'no,' but listeners understand from the form of the 'yes' whether it is truly a 'yes' or a polite 'no.'

The American tendency to associate indirectness with female style is not culturally universal. The above description of typical Japanese style operates for men as well as women. My own research (Tannen 1981, 1984, 1986) suggests that Americans of some cultural and geographic backgrounds, female as well as male, are more likely than others to use relatively direct rather than indirect styles. In an early study I compared Greeks and Americans with regard to their tendency to interpret a question as an indirect means of making a request. I found that whereas American women were more likely to take an indirect interpretation of a sample conversation, Greek men were as likely as Greek women, and more likely than American men *or women*, to take an indirect interpretation. Greek men, of course, are not less powerful vis-à-vis women than American men.

Perhaps most striking is the finding of Keenan (1974) that in a Malagasy speaking village on the island of Madagascar, women are seen as direct and men as indirect. But this in no way implies that the women are more powerful than men in this society. Quite the contrary, Malagasy men are socially dominant, and their indirect style is more highly valued. Keenan found that women were widely believed to debase the language with their artless directness, whereas men's elaborate indirectness was widely admired.

Indirectness, then, is not in itself a strategy of subordination. Rather, it can be used either by the powerful or the powerless. The interpretation of a given utterance, and the likely response to it, depends on the setting, on individuals' status and their relationship to each other, and also on the linguistic conventions that are ritualized in the cultural context.

❑ Read the whole Sperber and Wilson excerpt.
   a. Summarise all the criticisms that they level against Grice.
   b. Look at the numbered examples that they discuss, and say what concepts they are being used to illustrate.
   c. Say whether you agree with them and why (not).
   d. Write up your summary and point of view in 500 words.

**Deborah
Tannen**

❏ Obtain a copy of the book *Relevance* and read the rest of this chapter. Summarise
the main ideas in five short paragraphs, entitled:
a. 'cognitive environments' and 'mutual manifestness';
b. 'ostension';
c. 'ostensive-inferential communication';
d. 'the informative intention';
e. 'the communicative intention'.
You may prefer to divide the rest of the chapter between the whole group: you
could split into five groups and each mini-group tackle one topic. Each mini-group
could then present it orally to the whole class. Evaluate the concepts critically,
saying whether you agree or not. You may like to refer to L. Cummings (2005)
pages 113–34, for extra support in this endeavour.

❏ What is your opinion as regards Cooperative Principle and Relevance Theory?
Do you think that Sperber and Wilson's theory of communication cancels that
of Grice? Which do you think best describes how exchanges hold together?

❏ Can you think of an alternative principle or set of maxims, other than Cooperative Principle and Relevance Theory, to show how people understand each
other and how conversations run smoothly? Is this set of maxims universal or
country specific?

❏ Summarise the Tannen excerpt in one short paragraph and give your opinion
vis-à-vis her stance. Choose one particular aspect from these pages that you
would like to test. Design a small investigation project to test it. When you have
the results, compare them to Tannen's opinion. If they are different, say why
that may be.

❏ This is a project on indirectness and cultural variables.
a. Choose one of the social factors involved in power and indirectness: status,
role, age, gender, education, class, occupation and ethnicity.
b. Think of a theory or hypothesis that you would like to test. Express it as a
comparison, for example 'When seeking help, women use more indirectness
than men', 'When there is a difference in status, the one in power uses
indirectness more than the one in a less powerful position', 'Indirectness is
used by middle-class people to working-class people, not by working-class to
middle-class'.
c. Check how important the contextual constraints (the size of the imposition and the formality of the situation) are, compared with the social
factor (status, role, age, gender, education, class, occupation, ethnicity) that
you chose.
d. Think of a way that your findings could be of use in society. Who might be
interested in your results or helped by them and why?
e. Write up your project. Describe your method of data collection and analysis
in a way that would allow someone else to reproduce your study.

D

READINGS IN POLITENESS

D5

Reading and researching

D5.1

The Nelson, Al-Batal and Echols article compares Syrian Arabic speakers' and American English speakers' responses to compliments, and shows that, although both groups respond by accepting and mitigating rather than rejecting, the ways that they accept and mitigate are quite different. The authors hope that their article will contribute to an awareness of cross-cultural misunderstandings from pragmatic transfer.

Gayle Nelson

Gayle L. Nelson, M. Al-Batal and E. Echols (from *Applied Linguistics* 18/3, 1996: 411–33.)

This study investigated similarities and differences between Syrian and American compliment responses. Interviews with Americans yielded 87 compliment/compliment response sequences and interviews with Syrians resulted in 52 sequences. Americans were interviewed in English and Syrians in Arabic. Data consisted of demographic information and transcriptions of the sequences. The entire set of data was examined recursively. This examination suggested three broad categories (acceptances, mitigations, and rejections) and subcategories. Two trained raters coded each of the English and Arabic compliment responses as belonging to one of the categories. Intercoder reliability for the American data was 92 per cent and 88 per cent for the Syrian data. Of the American compliment responses, 50 per cent were coded as acceptances, 45 per cent as mitigations, and 3 per cent as rejections. Of the Syrian compliment responses, 67 per cent were coded as acceptances, 33 per cent as mitigations, and 0 per cent as rejections. Results suggest that both Syrians and Americans are more likely to either accept or mitigate the force of the compliment than to reject it. Both groups employed similar response types (e.g. agreeing utterances, compliment returns, and deflecting or qualifying comments); however, they also differed in their responses. US recipients were much more likely than the Syrians to use appreciation tokens and a preferred Syrian response, acceptance + formula, does not appear in the US data at all.

1. INTRODUCTION

Recently, in a conversation with an American who had taught EFL in Damascus for two years, one of the researchers mentioned that she was investigating the strategies Syrians use in responding to compliments. The teacher looked surprised and asked, 'What's there to study? Syrians just say *Shukran* ("thank you"). When I'm complimented in Arabic, that's what I say – *Shukran*.' This teacher was applying a rule from his L1 speech community to an L2 speech community. The rule he was transferring is one that American parents teach their children and one that is taught in etiquette books: 'When you are complimented, the only response necessary is "Thank you"' (Johnson 1979: 43). Compliment responses in Syrian Arabic, as shall become clear later, are much more complex than saying Shukran when praised.

In this paper, we report on a study of Syrian Arabic speakers' and American English speakers' verbal responses to compliments. The purpose of the study is to better understand the strategies used by Syrians and Americans in responding to

Gayle
Nelson

compliments, to discover similarities and differences between the two groups, and to relate the findings to second language acquisition and second language teaching.

2. THEORETICAL FRAMEWORK: CONTRASTIVE PRAGMATICS

In large part due to the theoretical paradigm of communicative competence (Habermas 1970; Hymes 1971, 1972, 1974; Canale and Swain 1980; Wolfson 1981, 1983), research on L2 learning and teaching has been extended to include learners' pragmatic knowledge. Thomas (1983: 92) defines pragmatic competence by contrasting it to grammatical competence. Grammatical competence consists of ' "abstract" or decontexualized knowledge of intonation, phonology, syntax, semantics, etc.', whereas pragmatic competence is 'the ability to use language effectively in order to achieve a specific purpose and to understand language in context' (ibid.: 94). She goes on to point out that if an L1 speaker perceives the purpose of an L2 utterance as other than the L2 speaker intended, pragmatic failure has occurred; the utterance failed to achieve the speaker's goal. The danger of pragmatic failure is that it is likely to result in misunderstandings, embarrassment, frustration, anger, and/or cross-cultural communication breakdowns (Beebe and Takahashi 1989).

Thomas identifies two kinds of pragmatic failure: pragmalinguistic failure and sociopragmatic failure. Pragmalinguistic failure occurs when 'the pragmatic force mapped by S onto a given utterance is systematically different from the force most frequently assigned to it by native speakers of the target language, or when speech act strategies are inappropriately transferred from the H to L2' (Thomas 1983: 99). Sociopragmatic failure refers to 'the social conditions placed on language in use' (ibid.) and includes variables such as gender, social distance, and intimacy of relationship.

In the context of language learning, one cause of pragmalinguistic failure is pragmalinguistic transfer, the use of H speech act strategies or formulas when interacting with members of an L2 speech community (Leech 1983). This transfer has been addressed in a number of speech act/event studies (e.g. Blum-Kulka 1982, 1983; Olshtain 1983; Olshtain and Cohen 1983; Edmonson, House, Kasper, and Stemmer 1984; Thomas 1984, Eisenstein and Bodman 1986; Garcia 1989; Wolfson 1989a; Beebe, Takahashi, and Uliss-Weltz 1990; Takahashi and Beebe 1993). In the anecdote at the beginning of this paper; the American, in responding to Arabic compliments by transferring an appropriate response from his H to an L2, believes that he is politely accepting the compliment. However, if the native Arabic speaker interprets the illocutionary force of the utterance differently (e.g. interprets the response as impolite and inappropriate) pragmatic failure has occurred.

It is, however, difficult, at times, to determine whether the pragmatic failure results from L1 transfer or from other factors. Hurley (1992), for example, notes that pragmatic failure may also result from developmental and proficiency factors or from L2 learners overgeneralizing the use of an L2 form to inappropriate settings. Stated differently, it is sometimes difficult to know why language learners experience certain kinds of pragmatic failure. In order to understand the reasons behind pragmatic failure, it is helpful, and perhaps even necessary, to conduct cross-cultural research to investigate students' H strategies (Wolfson 1989a).

Gayle
Nelson

Speech act and speech event studies have been criticized as being ethnocentric in that most have investigated variations of English (Blum-Kulka, House, and Kasper 1989). Rose (1994) further points out that, in particular, little work has been done in non-Western contexts. The present study is valuable, in part, because it was conducted in Arabic as well as English.

3. COMPLIMENT RESPONSES
Compliment responses were selected for cross-cultural study for two reasons. First, although a body of knowledge exists on the speech act of complimenting (Wolfson 1981, 1983; Manes 1983; Knapp, Hopper, and Bell 1984; Barnlund and Araki 1985; Holmes and Brown 1987; Nelson, El Bakary, and Al-Batal 1993), less research has been conducted on responses to compliments. For non-native English speaking (NNES) students, knowing how to compliment is important, but it is equally important to know how to respond to a compliment. In fact, it could be argued that for NNES students in the United States, appropriately responding to compliments is more important than complimenting because of the frequency with which Americans compliment (Wolfson 1983; Holmes and Brown 1987; Herbert 1988). In other words, ESL students may receive more compliments than they initiate. A second reason is that, although a few studies have been conducted on compliment responses in English-speaking countries (Pomerantz 1978; Herbert 1988; Herbert and Straight 1989), few, if any, cross-cultural studies have investigated compliment responses in an Arabic-speaking country.

For the purpose of this study, a compliment response is defined as a verbal acknowledgement that the recipient of the compliment heard and reacted to the compliment. Compliment/compliment response interactions have been referred to as adjacency pairs (Schegloff and Sacks 1973), action chain events (Pomerantz 1978), interchanges (Herbert 1988), and sequences (Wolfson 1989b). For ease of reference, $Speaker_1$ will refer to the person issuing the compliment and $Speaker_2$ to the recipient of the compliment.

4. PREVIOUS WORK ON COMPLIMENT RESPONSES
Pomerantz (1978) wrote the earliest and perhaps most detailed account of compliment responses among native speakers of English in the United States. She pointed out that, in the United States, compliment responses pose a dilemma for the recipient in that they involve two conversational principles that stand in potential conflict:

Principle I: Agree with and/or accept compliment.
Principle II: Avoid self-praise.

If recipients agree with the compliment, they are, in fact, praising themselves and therefore violating Principle II: Avoid self-praise. If they reject the compliment, they violate Principle I: Agree with and/or accept compliment. Neither of these alternatives, praising oneself or disagreeing with someone, contribute to the social solidarity of the relationship. Pomerantz submitted that compliment responses could be seen as solution types to this dilemma.

Gayle
Nelson

Pomerantz classified compliment responses as belonging to one of four categories: Acceptances, Agreements, Rejections, and Disagreements. Her analysis indicated that Acceptances were relatively infrequent when compared to Rejections and Disagreements (e.g. 'It's just a rag my sister gave me'). She suggested that self-praise avoidance accounts for the frequency of Rejections and Disagreements in compliment responses.

In their studies of complimenting behavior in the United States, Wolfson (1989a) and Manes (1983) included examples of compliment responses. They contended that one function of American compliments is to negotiate solidarity between the interlocutors. For recipients, however, negotiating solidarity is complicated by Pomerantz's (1978) dilemma. Wolfson (1989a) noted that one solution to the dilemma is to downgrade the compliment by referring to another characteristic of the object. In this way, the recipient mitigates the force of the compliment without disagreeing with the speaker and also without praising him/herself. Wolfson (1989a: 116) explained

> In response to a compliment on the beauty of a house, therefore, an American might say, 'Well, we would have liked to have a bigger one' or 'We wish the neighborhood were quieter,' but Americans would be very unlikely to suggest that the speaker was wrong and that the house was not beautiful at all.

The work of Pomerantz (1978), Manes (1983), Wolfson (1989a), and Wolfson and Manes (1980) was helpful in understanding how and why Americans compliment, but it did not provide a quantitative analysis of compliment response types and their frequency.

Herbert (1988) provided such an analysis in a study comparing the compliment/compliment response interchanges from American university students to South African university students. In analyzing his data, he grouped the responses as (a) Agreeing, (b) Nonagreeing, or (c) Requesting interpretation. Overall, nearly 66 per cent of the American compliment responses were broadly classified as Agreements, 31 per cent as Nonagreements, and 3 per cent as Request Interpretations. Of those Agreements (66 per cent), 7 per cent were categorized as Comment Acceptances and 29 per cent as Appreciation Tokens.[1] In contrast, 88 per cent of the South African compliment responses were categorized as Agreements and 43 per cent of those Agreements were categorized as Comment Acceptances. Holmes (1988) studied compliments and compliment responses in New Zealand, another native English speaking (NES) country. She categorized 61 per cent of the responses as acceptances, 29 per cent as deflections/evasions, and 10 per cent as rejections. Her distribution of New Zealand responses closely paralleled Herbert's (1988) study of American responses. The studies by Herbert (1988) and Holmes (1988) were helpful in providing information on the frequency of particular NES compliment response types. They did not, however, compare NES to NNES populations (such comparisons were not the purpose of their studies) and, therefore, did not contribute to an understanding of why a population of L2 learners might respond inappropriately to compliments based on transfer from their L1.

In a study comparing the compliment responses of American and Chinese speakers, Chen (1993) provided this type of explanation. His analysis presented information that helped explain the reasons Chinese speakers might experience pragmatic failure when responding to a compliment given by an American and the reasons Americans might experience pragmatic failure when responding to a Chinese compliment. His findings suggested that the strategies used by the American English speakers were largely motivated by Leech's (1983) Agreement Maxim: maximize agreements between self and others and minimize disagreement between self and others. In Chen's sample, 39 per cent of the US compliment responses were categorized as Acceptances, 19 per cent as Compliment Returns, 29 per cent as Deflections, and 13 per cent as Rejections. The Chinese speaker strategies, on the other hand, were governed by Leech's Modesty Maxim: minimize praise of self and maximize dispraise of self. Of the Chinese compliment responses, 96 per cent were categorized as Rejections: the most common types of rejections were disagreeing and denigrating (51 per cent).

5. THE PRESENT STUDY

The present study also contributes to an understanding of why a population of L2 learners may respond inappropriately to compliments. It builds on the work of Nelson et al. (1993) and their analysis of Egyptian Arabic and American English compliments. In the Egyptian/American study, 20 Egyptians and 20 American university students described in detail the most recent compliment they had given, received, and observed, providing a corpus of 60 Egyptian and 60 American compliments. Interview data were analyzed to determine compliment form and attributes praised. The analysis revealed that both Egyptian and American compliments tended to be adjectival (e.g. 'You look great'). A major difference between Egyptian and American compliments was that Egyptian compliments tended to be longer and contained more comparatives and metaphors than the US compliments (e.g. *shaklak 'ariis innaharda* ['You look like a bridegroom today']).

Both Egyptians and Americans complimented the attributes of physical appearance, personality traits, and skills/work. Because these are attributes complimented in both Arabic-speaking and English-speaking countries (see Holmes and Brown 1987; Holmes 1988 for studies on New Zealand compliments) these were the qualities complimented in this study.

5.1 *Method of data collection*

It is commonly argued that speech acts and events should be studied in their natural contexts using ethnomethodology (Wolfson 1983); however, ethno-methodology is difficult for cross-cultural studies due to problems of comparability (Blum-Kulka, House, and Kasper 1989) and a lack of ethnographers from non-English-speaking speech communities. Although this study did not use ethnomethodology, its method of data collection resulted in naturalistic, yet comparable, data.

In the United States, data were collected during audiotaped interviews. All of the interviewers were graduate students in Applied Linguistics at a large urban university in the southeastern part of the United States. Two were female, one was 26 years old and single and the other 46 and married. The third was male, 32, and single. All were Caucasian and middle class. Before the interviews, interviewers

Gayle
Nelson

asked interviewees if they were willing to be interviewed on audiotape for a soci-olinguistic study. If they agreed, the interviewer began the interview by asking demographic questions (e.g. What part of the United States are you from?). After a few questions, the interviewer complimented the interviewee on an aspect of his or her appearance, on a personality trait, or on a skill or well done job. For instance, one interviewer casually mentioned, 'By the way, you really gave a good presentation to the class last night'. In this way, the compliments were given as an aside, as an utterance not connected to the formal interview, and thus, resulted in naturalistic responses. Eighty-nine Americans were interviewed; two interviews were lost due to a malfunctioning tape recorder. Of the remaining 87 intervie-wees, 47 were female and 40 were male. At the completion of the interviews, interviewees were asked if their responses could be used in this study. All signed a consent form giving their permission. A total of 87 American compliment/com-pliment response interactions were analyzed.

The audiotapes were transcribed in English. The transcriptions included the gender, age, and relationship of the speakers. It is important to point out that the American male interviewer felt uncomfortable complimenting females on appear-ance, believing that the female recipients might interpret the illocutionary force of the compliment differently than he intended. Specifically, he was concerned that Speaker$_2$ might perceive the intent of the compliment as an expression of flirta-tion and a possible first move in the development of an intimate relationship.

The Syrian data were collected by four interviewers from Damascus (i.e. they were Damascenes and spoke Damascene Arabic). Two of the interviewers were female. One was attending college part-time and was 29 years of age, single, and a dental technician. The other was 25, single, a translator and secretary, and an English literature graduate from Damascus University. The other two interviewers were male. One studied English literature at the University, managed his family farm property, was 27 and was single. The fourth also studied English literature at the University and was 22. All four were middle class.

The Syrian compliment/compliment responses were not audiotaped. The Syrian interviewers reported that tape recorders were likely to make the interviewees feel uncomfortable; that, in general, Syrians are not familiar with the practice of conducting sociological or sociolinguistic studies about themselves; and that the tape recording would be culturally inappropriate. The Syrian interviewers praised 32 recipients, 20 males and 12 females, on physical appearance, on personality traits, or on a skill or job; listened to the responses; responded in turn; and after the interaction was completed, wrote down what was said. In some cases, the interviewers felt uncomfortable complimenting a person of a different gender or a person that was older. In these cases, they observed others giving and respond-ing to compliments and wrote down what was said. These observations resulted in an additional 20 compliment/compliment response sequences. In 7 cases, males were complimented, and in 13 cases, females were complimented. These proced-ures resulted in naturalistic data and yielded 52 Syrian compliment/compliment responses from 52 recipients, 27 males and 25 females.

To insure the accuracy of the transcriptions, the Syrian interviewers were trained by one of the researchers. The trainer instructed them (l) to write down the exact words used in the complement/compliment response interaction, and (2) to do so as soon as possible after the interaction took place. In addition, the trainer gave each interviewer note cards and instructed them to write each interaction on a separate card. The trainer met with the interviewers at least once a week. At these meetings, the interviewers reported on their progress and the trainer again emphasized the importance of recording the interactions verbatim.

To native speakers of English, recalling compliment responses word-forward may seem difficult, but the task is less difficult for native speakers of Arabic. Many of the Syrian utterances consist of set formulas. The Syrian interviewers would remember the responses because they exist as formulaic chunks of discourse. The potential for varying the formulas is minimal. For the non-formulaic responses, it is possible that an interviewer might have made a minor change in the wording. However, if such a change occurred, the wording of the compliment response would still be an appropriate Syrian response to the situation.

The Arabic compliment/compliment responses were translated into English, but the primary analysis was based on the Arabic transcripts, not the English translations.

5.2 Analysis

The US data consisted of demographic information and the transcripts of the audiotapes, and the Syrian data consisted of demographic information, the Arabic transcriptions, and the English translations. The entire set of data was examined recursively. This examination suggested classification schemes similar to existing schemes (e.g. Pomerantz 1978; Herbert 1988; Herbert and Straight 1989). In the end, the classification scheme that most appropriately fitted the data was similar to, but still different from, earlier classifications. It consisted of three broad categories (i.e. acceptances, mitigations, and rejections) and subcategories. The specific subcategories are provided in the Results and Discussion section of this article in Tables 1 and 2. Following guide-lines set forth by Krippendorf (1980) and Holsti (1969), the categories were exhaustive (i.e. all data were represented in one of the categories) and mutually exclusive (i.e. a response could belong to only one category).

After the classification scheme was developed, one of the researchers and a graduate research assistant coded each of the English compliment responses as belonging to one of the categories. The Arabic compliment responses were coded by two of the researchers; one of whom is a native Arabic speaker. The coders worked independently and coded all of the compliment responses. Intercoder reliability was determined by comparing both coders' scores. Intercoder reliability was 92 per cent for the American data and 88 per cent for the Arabic. Next, the coders reviewed the coding guide-lines and the items on which there was disagreement. They recoded until they came to a consensus; thus, in the end, agreement on all compliment responses was achieved.

6. RESULTS AND DISCUSSION

This section presents the analysis of the American and Syrian compliment response types.

Gayle Nelson

6.1 *Compliment response types: US English data*

Table 1 provides the frequency and representative examples of the English compliment response types.

Table 1 Frequency distribution of American English compliment response types

	Number	*Percentage*
A. Accept		
1. Appreciation token	25	29
(e.g. Thanks)		
2. Agreeing Utterance	12	14
(e.g. Well, I think so too.)		
3. Compliment Return	6	07
(e.g. Yours are nice. too.)		
4. Acceptance + Formula	0	0
Subtotal	43	50
B. Mitigate		
1. Deflecting or Qualifying Comment	28	32
(e.g. I bought it at REI.)		
2. Reassurance or Repetition Request	11	13
(e.g. Do you really like them?)		
Subtotal	39	45
C. Reject		
1. Disagreeing Utterance	3	03
(e.g. F_1: You look good and healthy.		
F_2: I feel fat.)		
Subtotal	3	03
D. No response	2	02
Total	87	100

(n = 87)

6.1.1 Acceptances

The Acceptance category accounted for 50 per cent of the US compliment responses.

a. *Appreciation Token.* The most common response type in the Acceptance category of the American corpus was Appreciation Tokens. They were 'responses that recognized the status of a previous utterance as a compliment' (Herbert 1988: 11), but were not 'semantically fitted to the specifics of that compliment' (Pomerantz 1978: 83). Examples included 'Thanks' and 'Thank you'.

(1) M_1:   It's a really cool shirt
      M_2:   Thanks (A1)[2]

Gayle
Nelson

For a response to be coded as an Appreciation Token, it included only the statement of appreciation. If additional information was given, the response was coded according to the additional information. Appreciation Tokens accounted for 29 per cent of the compliment responses in this corpus, a frequency identical to the 29 per cent reported by Herbert (1988) and Chen (1993), but one much higher than Pomerantz (1978) reported.

b. *Agreeing Utterance.* As illustrated below, Agreeing Utterances were responses in which Speaker$_2$ accepted 'the complimentary force of Speaker$_1$'s utterance by a response semantically fitted to the compliment' (Herbert 1988: 12). Agreeing Utterances occurred in twelve (14 per cent) of the American responses.

(2) F$_1$: That's really a great shirt.
     F$_2$: See, it matches my shorts. (A7)

(3) M$_1$: Sounds like you're pretty organized.
     M$_2$: Well, I think so. I try to be. Yeah. (A 14)

This response type occurred more frequently in this sample than in the work of other researchers (Herbert 1988; Chen 1993). Pomerantz (1978: 84) found agreeing responses 'very prevalent' in her data; however, her examples suggested that these agreements occurred when two individuals were talking about a third party. In none of her examples did a person agree with a compliment about him or herself.

c. *Compliment Return.* A Compliment Return consisted of two parts – (a) a stated or implied acceptance of the force of the compliment, and (b) praise for the original sender.

(4) M$_1$: Those are nice glasses.
     M$_2$: Yours are nice, too. (A9)

(5) F: You look great.
     M: So do you. (A52)

By returning the compliment, the recipient contributed to the equality of the relationship and maintained rapport. Compliment returns accounted for 7 per cent of the compliment responses in this sample, the same frequency found by Herbert (1988).

d. *Acceptance + Formula.* This type of response did not occur at all in the English sample, but occurred frequently in the Arabic data.

6.1.2 Mitigating Responses
The general category of Mitigating Responses included two distinct compliment response types that shared two features. The first feature was their non-acceptance of the compliment and the second was their non-rejection. These response types in various ways deflected, questioned, or ignored the compliments. In using one of these types, the recipient maneuvered through the straits of Pomerantz's Scylla

Gayle
Nelson

and Charybdis, avoiding both self-praise and other-disagreement. Mitigating responses accounted for 45 per cent of the US corpus.

a. *Deflecting Informative Comment*. This type was the most common of the mitigating responses. In this category, Speaker$_2$ provided additional information about the attribute praised and by doing so, impersonalized 'the complimentary force by giving impersonal details' (Herbert 1988: 13).

(6)   F: I like your jacket.
      M: I bought it at REI. (A47)

(7)   F$_1$:   You look great. ! mean it. You look wonderful.
      F$_2$:   I can hardly believe I'm going to be 54. It sounds very old. I can actually remember when I was going to be 30. (A85)

Herbert (1988: 14) noted that occasionally, in the informative comments that followed the compliment, the recipient ignored 'the praise aspect of the compliment and instead treat[ed] the previous utterances as a mechanism for introducing a topic'. This phenomenon occurred in the example below.

(8)   F$_1$:   That's really a good quality.
      F$_2$:   Well, I read about it in developmental psychology. I can tell what
               people are up to and then
               I usually give them my motivation speech. I mean, like most teachers,
               I don't like people who don't do work, who, at least, don't read the
               material. (A4)

At times, these qualifying comments functioned in a manner that downgrades the compliment, a strategy, as noted by Wolfson (1989a), that further avoids self-praise.

(9)   F: Nice sweater.
       M: It's one of my oldest. (A50)

(10)   F$_1$:   It was very sweet of you.
       F$_2$:   It seemed kinda silly. I don't know. Yeah. Well, but anyway. (A 18)

This category accounted for 32 per cent of the American compliment responses in this study, a frequency similar to Chen's (1993). Chen's category, Deflection comprised 29 per cent of his corpus.

b. *Reassurance or Repetition Request*. At times, Speaker$_2$ requested additional reassurance that the compliment was genuine. Such responses were ambiguous. It was difficult to discern the recipients' intentions in asking the questions. Did they want an expansion or repetition of the original compliment or were they questioning the sincerity of the sender?

(11)   F$_1$:   I like your dress.
       F$_2$:   You don't think it's too bright? (A62)

Gayle
Nelson

(12)   F₁: Nice shoes.
       F₂: Do you really like them? (A54)

Reassurance or Repetition Requests accounted for 13 per cent of the compliment responses.

6.1.3 Rejections

a. *Disagreeing Utterance.* Disagreeing Utterances occurred when Speaker₂ disagreed with Speaker₁'s assertion. This compliment response type occurred infrequently within the present corpus, in 3 interchanges or approximately 3 per cent of the sample.

(13)   M₁: How did you get to be so organized?
       M₂: I'm not organized.
       M₁: I mean neat. You are very neat.
       M₂: I am not. (A11)

(14)   F₁: You look so good and healthy.
       F₂: I feel fat. (A12)

The infrequency of this response type in the United States is consistent with the work of other researchers (Herbert 1988; Chen 1993). By using this response type, Speaker₂ clearly and directly disagrees with the judgment of Speaker₁, thus violating both Pomerantz's (1978) Principle I: Agree with and/or accept compliment and Leech's (1983) Agreement Principle. Americans' preference for not using this response type suggests that, out of all the response types, it may be the most damaging to the solidarity of the relationship between Speaker₁ and Speaker₂, more damaging, for example, than agreeing with Speaker₁ and thus praising oneself, a response type that made up 14 per cent of this sample.

6.2 Compliment responses: gender of US recipient

American males (n = 40) and females (n = 47) employed each of the compliment types, and no compliment response type was used predominantly by one gender. Eleven females and 14 males used Appreciation Tokens, 6 females and 6 males used Agreeing Utterances, and 4 females and 2 males used Compliment Returns. Sixteen females and 12 males employed Deflecting Comments and 7 females and 4 males employed Reassurance or Repetition Requests. Two females and one male disagreed with the compliment. Two recipients did not respond verbally to the compliment they received.

6.3 Compliment response types: Syrian Arabic data

Using the categories described above, this section presents the classification of the Arabic data. The Arabic compliment responses fell into two of the three categories. Recipients either accepted or mitigated the compliments they received. There were no rejections. However, within these categories, the Arabic compliment responses differed from the English responses in several ways. The Arabic compliment responses are summarized in Table 2.

Table 2 Frequency distribution of Syrian Arabic compliment response types

	Number	Percentage
A. Accept		
1. Appreciation Token	1	02
(e.g. *shukran* [thank you])		
2. Agreeing Utterance	6	12
(e.g. *kill taSaamiimi naajHa*		
[All my designs are successful!]		
3. Compliment Return	7	13
(e.g. *w-imi heek yaa Sawsan*		
[And you are the same, Susan])		
4. Acceptance + Formula	21	40
(e.g. *m'addame*		
[it is presented to you])		
Subtotal	35	67
B. Mitigate		
1. Deflecting or Qualifying Comment	13	25
(e.g. M_1: Your body has filled out.		
M_2: I used to work out a long time ago.		
2. Reassurance or Repetition Request	4	08
(e.g. Is that really me?)		
Subtotal	17	33
C. Reject	0	0
Total	52	100

($n = 52$)

6.3.1 Acceptances Sixty-seven per cent of the Syrian compliment responses were coded as Acceptances.

a. *Appreciation Token.* Only 1 of the Arabic compliment responses was coded as an Appreciation Token, a common American response type.

(15) F_1:   *yikhzi l-'een 'ala ha-sh-sha'r! yaa 'eeni, mitl Sundrella.* (May the [evil] eye be thwarted for this hair! My eye, [you look] like Cinderella!)

      F_2:   *shakran!* (Thank you.) (S47)

In this interaction, Speaker$_1$ used the expression *yikhzi l-'een* ('may the evil eye be thwarted') to protect the recipient from the evil eye. In many parts of the world, it is believed that the evil eye can bring harm to people by drawing the attention of evil to them (Maloney 1976).[3] By merely praising a person, Speaker$_1$ might cause harm to come to that person. To counteract this effect, the expression *yikhzi l-'een* ('may the evil eye be thwarted') is used in many countries in the eastern part of the Arab world (e.g. Jordan, Syria, Palestine, and Lebanon).

Gayle
Nelson

b. *Agreeing Utterance.* In the Syrian data, this response type was slightly less frequent than in the US data. Six (12 per cent) of the Syrian interactions were classified as Agreeing Utterances. All six are between males.

(16) M_1: *ft'lan taSmiimak bi-dill 'ala khibirtak w-'ala zaw'ak ir-rafit'.*
(Truly, your design points to your experience and to your exquisite taste.)
M_2: *kill taSaamiimi naajHa.*
(All my designs are successful.) (S43)

(17) M_1: *jismak halla' Saar mniH w-khaaSSatan 'aDalaat ktaafak.*
(Your body now has become fit, especially your shoulder muscles.)
M_2: *ana halla'aHsan waaHid bi-n-naadii.*
(I'm now the best one in the club.) (S3 1)

This response strategy violates Pomerantz's (1978) principle of avoiding self-praise and the social solidarity principle (Herbert 1988; Herbert and Straight t989; Wolfson 1989a). It may be that in Syria agreeing with Speaker$_1$ (and thus praising oneself) is not the kind of egregious error that results in 'a gossip item, an unfavorable character assessment', the kinds of negative behaviors that Pomerantz predicts may result from agreement responses (Pomerantz 1978: 89).

c. *Compliment Return.* The frequency of Compliment Returns hi the Syrian corpus was 13 per cent, slightly higher than the frequency of Compliment Returns in the American data (7 per cent). Examples of Compliment Returns included the following:

(18) F_1: *inti mhandse naajHa, daayman bi-t'addmi shii jdiid w-bi-tkhalli n-naas tiHtirmik, w-khalluu'qa w-shakhSiyytik 'awiyye, ya'ni mitl z-zibdiyye S-Siini, mneen ma rannaytiiha bi-trinn.*
(you are a successful engineer; you always present something new and you make people respect you, and [you are] well-mannered and have a strong personality: in other words you are like a china bowl; from whichever side you hit it, it resonates.)
F_2: *w-inti heck yea Sawsan bass muu Haase b-Haalik.*
(And you are the same, Susan, but you do not know it.) (S2)

(19) F: *inta nashiiT w-shughlak nDiif w-mustaqiim bi-'amalak, maa fii daa'i la-Hada yrnaji' shughlak waraak, zaki w-SariiH w-Habbaab.*
(You are dynamic and your work is well-done and you are straightforward in your work; there is no need for anyone to go over what you do, [you are] smart and honest and amiable.)
M: *shukran, w-inti nafs sh-shii.*
(Thank you, and you are the same.) (S9)

In contrast to Agreeing Utterances, Compliment Returns affirmed the interpersonal connections between the interlocutors; they served to bond the relationship together.

Although the focus of this study is on responses to compliments, the compliments in exchanges 18 and 19 are of interest in that they closely resemble the

Gayle
Nelson

Egyptian compliments in Nelson et al. (1993); they contain more words than US compliments and exchange 18 contains a metaphor. The length of these compliments is related to features of Arabic discourse: (1) repetition of almost the same idea with only a minor change in words, and (2) the use of several adjectives in a series (Shouby 1951). In exchange 18, the person giving the compliment compares the recipient to 'a china bowl; from whichever side you hit it, it resonates'.

d. *Agreement + Formula*. The most common response type in the Syrian sample was Agreement + Formula; it was employed in 40 per cent of the corpus. Responses were coded as Agreement + Formula if they included a particular utterance or saying that is commonly used in Arabic when responding to a particular kind of compliment. These expressions are automatic and often ritualistic. They fulfill a particular social function and should not be interpreted primarily at the semantic level. As far as we know, this response type does not appear in any other language group studied.

One common ritualistic compliment response was *m'addam* ('[It is] presented [to you]'). With this response, Speaker$_2$ offered the object of the compliment to Speaker$_1$. Syrian speakers, in uttering *m'addam* seldom intend for Speaker$_1$ to accept the object. The expression is formulaic, an expected polite response to particular compliments. In the interactions below, the recipients used *m'addam* when complimented on a necklace and a blouse.

(20) F$_1$: *'a'dik ktiir Hilu, Ha-yaakul min ra'btik sha'fe.*
            (Your necklace is very beautiful; it will eat a piece of your neck.)

     F$_2$: *shukran ruuHii! m'addam, maa b-yighla 'aleeki shii.*
            (Thank you my dear! [it is] presented [to you], nothing can be too precious for you.)

     F$_1$: *shukran! 'ala SaaHibtu aHlaa.*
            (Thank you! It looks much nicer on its owner.) (S20)

(21) F$_1$: *Mabruuk! Shu shaarye bluuze jdiide?*
            (Congratulations! Have you bought a new blouse'?)

     F$_2$: *ee waLLa, Marreet bi-S-SaalHiyye w-shifta 'ala l-waajha fa-'ajabitni ktiir, shtareeta, m'addame!*
            (Yes, by God. I was passing through SaalHiyye [district of Damascus] and I saw it in the display window and I liked it very much, so I decided to buy it. [it is] presented [to you].)

     F$_1$: *Tithanni fiiha. InshaaLLaah tihriiha bi-l-hana.*
            (May you enjoy it. May you, God willing, wear it out in happiness.)

     F$_2$: *ALLanh yiHfazik!*
            (May God keep you safe.)[4] (S24)

In both of these interactions, the recipients uttered the formulaic expression *m'addame* ([it is] presented [to you]'), but hi neither case did Speaker$_1$ accept the object offered. In exchange 20, Speaker$_1$ countered with *shukran! 'ala SaaHibtu aHlaa* ('Thank you! It looks much nicer on its owner.') With this utterance, Speaker₁ not only politely rejected the offer of the necklace, but also praised Speaker₂ again ('It looks much nicer on its owner'). In exchange 21, Speaker₂ rejected the offer with the utterance: *Tithanni fiiha. InshaaLLaah tihriiha bi-l-hana* ('May you enjoy it. May you, God willing, wear it out in happiness.')

Three formulaic expressions are illustrated in the interaction below. When complimented on his success, Speaker₂ used the following expressions: *t-tawfii' min aLLa* ('success comes from God'), *min riDa L-Lanh w-riDa l-waaldeen* ('this [success] [comesl] from God's satisfaction and my parents' satisfaction with me'), *li-kuli mujtahidin naSiib* ('He who works hard will have a share [of success]').

(22) M₁: *waLLa inta dayman mwaffa' b-tijaartak yaa abu mHammad.*
            (By God Abu Muhammad If ether of Mohammadl, you are always successful in your trade.)

      M₂: *waLLaahi t-tawfii' min aLLa haada min riDa L-Laah w-riDa l-waaldeen yaa abu SubHii wi-ba'deen yaa siidi li-kuli mujtahidin naSiib.*
            ([I swear] by God, success comes from God. this [success] [comes] from God s satisfaction and my parents' satisfaction [with me], and after all my friend He who works hard will have a share [of success].)

      M₁: *waLLaahi haada Ha' aLLa y'allii maraatbak kamaan w-kamaan.*
            ([I swear] by God this is true, May God raise your stature more and more.) (S4)

In exchanges 20, 21, and 22, the compliment/compliment response sequence continued after Speaker₂ had responded to Speaker₁. The response of Speaker₂ did not signal the end of the compliment/compliment response interaction; it was but part of the repartee, the dialogue, that continued between the two speakers.

In the interaction below, Speaker₁ praised Speaker₂ on her beauty. Speaker₂ responded with the formulaic expression, *inshaaLLa b-tiHla iyyaamik* ('May your days be more beautiful').

(23) F₁: *wishshik Daawi w-mnawwar yaa imm ayman, yimkin la'innik mirtaaHa l-yuum fa-Hilyaane.*
            (Your face is shining today. Um Ayman (mother of Ayman); [this is] perhaps because you are relaxed today, so you look beautiful.)

      F₂: *inshaaLLa b-tiHla iyyaamik haada nuur l-'iimaan yimkin.*
            (May your days be more beautiful, this is perhaps the light of faith.) (S14)

As illustrated below, the expression *haada b-'yuunik bass* ('this is only in your eyes') was also used in response to a compliment on personal beauty.

(24) F: *shuu Halyaan lak Ghayyaath shuu'aamil b-Haalak?*
            (How handsome you have become, Ghayyath, what have you done to yourself?)

      M: *waLLaahi? haada b-'yuunik bass.*
            (Really? This is only in your eyes.) (S 13)

Gayle
Nelson

6.3.2 Mitigating Responses

The general category of Mitigating Responses accounted for 33 per cent of the Syrian data.

a. Deflecting or Qualifying Comment: Thirteen speakers or 25 per cent of the sample employed this response type; it was used by 32 per cent of the Americans.

(25) F: *inta insaan naajiH la-innu shughlak mniiH w-shakhSiyytak 'awiyye maq bi-tkhalli Hada yiHki·'aleek w-bi-lwa't napsuu maHbuub w-waasiq min nafsak.* (You are a successful person because you do your job well and [because] your personality is strong, you do not allow anyone to say anything negative about you and at the same time [you are] amiable and self-confident.

  M: *Yaa sitti shukran hiyye ashya 'andiyye laazim kull insaan ykuun heek biduun takabbur.* (Thank you madam, these are simple things; no one should be conceited.) (S6)

(26) F$_1$: *Bass inti Hilyaane ktiir l-yuum.* (But you look very beautiful today.)

  F$_2$: *laa, muu kill hal'add ma inni ta'baane l-yuum.* (No, not to this extent, [this is] despite the fact I am tired today). (S15)

These Deflecting or Qualifying Comments provide cross-cultural support for Pomerantz's (1978) notion that compliment responses are solution types to the dilemma of avoiding self-praise without disagreeing with Speaker$_1$.

b. *Reassurance or Repetition Request.* This response type accounted for 4 (8 per cent) of the compliment responses, a frequency slightly lower than in the US corpus (13 per cent).

(27) M: *ana Habeetik la-innik unsaa bi-kill ma'na l-kalime w-'indik shakhSiyye mu'assira.* (I have come to like you because you are a woman in the full sense of the word and because you have an impressive personality.)

  F: *haada kullu ana?* (Is that all me?) (S3)

(28) F: *shuu! shu ha-Ta'm l-Hilu haad taariik mizwi' ya Saamir!* (Wow! What a beautiful suit. You have good taste Saamir.)

  M: *leesh ? 'ajabik ?* (Why? Do you like it?) (S22)

6.3.3 Rejection: Disagreeing Utterance

None of the Syrian data was coded as rejections. If, as has been assumed, compliments function as 'social lubricants' and 'increase or consolidate the solidarity between the speaker and the addressee' (Holmes 1988: 486), it may be that, among Syrians, rejecting compliments decreases that solidarity to such a degree that it is seldom used.

Gayle
Nelson

6.4 Compliment responses: gender of Syrian recipients

Both Syrian males (n = 27) and females (n = 25) employed most of the compliment types; one compliment response type, Agreeing Utterances, was used predominantly by one gender. Six males and no females used Agreeing Utterances, one female used an Appreciation Token, 4 females and 3 males used Compliment Returns, and 12 females and 9 males used Acceptance + Formula. Six females and 7 males employed Deflecting Comments, and 2 females and 2 males employed Reassurance or Repetition Requests.

7. LIMITATIONS OF THE STUDY

Data for this study was obtained from one strata of the larger population of Syria and the US. The Syrian compliment responses were uttered by middle class people from an urban area (i.e. Damascus) and most of the American compliment responses were given by Caucasian university graduate students. One cannot assume that these findings generalize to groups within Syria or the US or to other Arabic-speaking or English-speaking countries. Further research is needed to know how generalizable these findings are.

8. FOCUS ON SECOND LANGUAGE LEARNERS

In order for students to become communicatively competent in a second language, they need both grammatical and pragmatic competence (Thomas 1983). However, achieving pragmatic competence may, at times, be complicated due to pragmatic transfer – using the rules governing speech events from one's L1 speech community when interacting with members of an L2 speech community. Pragmatic transfer can lead to pragmatic failure, to not understanding the illocutionary force of an utterance, to not understanding what is meant by what is said (Thomas 1983). Such situations can result in cross-cultural misunderstandings and communication breakdowns. Cross-cultural studies such as this one contribute to our knowledge of appropriate compliment/compliment response competence in Syrian Arabic and American English and also to our understanding of pragmatic transfer as a possible cause for pragmatic failure.

The results of this study suggest similarities and differences in Syrian Arabic and American English compliment responses. Similarities include the overall manner of responding – both Syrians and Americans are much more likely to either accept or mitigate the force of the compliment than to reject it outright. In addition, members of both groups use some similar response types (e.g. Agreeing Utterances, Compliment Returns, Deflecting or Qualifying Comments, and Reassurance or Repetition Requests). Finally, males and females in both groups employ most of the response types. An exception is Agreeing Utterances; Syrian females did not use this response. Students of English and Arabic can use these similarities between Arabic and English compliment responses to their advantage by learning the responses that are similar in both languages. As Kasper and Blum-Kulka (1993) point out, behaviors that are consistent across L1 and L2 usually result in communicative success. However, Hurley (1992) warns that the similarity of an L2 form. to a form in the learner's H can also be a pragmalinguistic

Gayle
Nelson

problem. The danger is that the L2 learner may overgeneralize the form to inappropriate settings.

Although the two groups share similarities in compliment responses, they also differ in important ways. In responding to compliments, US recipients are much more likely than Syrians to use Appreciation Tokens (e.g. thanks). The infrequency of this response in the Arabic data suggests that the utterance *Shukran* ('thank you') by itself is not usually a sufficient response to an Arabic compliment and needs to be supplemented by additional words. By itself, it may sound flat and awkward because it appears to signal the end of the conversation. As illustrated at the beginning of this article, American students of Arabic may respond to a compliment given by a native-speaker of Arabic by saying *Shukran*. If the intent of the American, drawing from his or her L1 strategies, is to respond in an appropriately polite manner and if the native Arabic speaker interprets the force of the utterance differently (e.g. that Speaker$_2$ wants to end the conversation), pragmalinguistic failure has occurred. To avoid this type of misunderstanding, it is important that Arabic as a second language students learn the more extended kinds of Arabic responses illustrated in this study.

ESL students are often taught that an appropriate response to most compliments in American English is 'thank you' (see Levine, Baxter, and McNulty 1987). Wolfson (1989b) points out, however, that the use of 'thank you' in English depends on the status and social distance of the interlocutors. Even though these social variables influence the use of 'thank you' in English, Wolfson (1989a) believes that 'thank you' remains an appropriate response for many compliment situations. ESL teachers of Arabic-speaking students can teach 'thank you' as an appropriate compliment response, but they should be aware that although 'thank you' appears to be a simple and easy response strategy to learn, such plain utterances may be difficult for Arabic speakers because they seem inadequate; they may not appropriately express what the speaker wants to convey.

Another major difference in compliment response strategies is the Syrians' frequent use of formulaic expressions in accepting a compliment; Americans do not use this type of response. One formulate expression that is particularly troublesome to non-native Arabic speakers is *m'addam* ('[it is] presented [to you]'). For non-native Arabic speakers, the illocutionary force of the utterance is ambiguous; (does Speaker$_2$ want Speaker$_1$ to take the object or not?). However, for native Arabic speakers in most contexts, *m'addam* is a polite ritualistic expression not a genuine offer of the object. In response to *m'addam* Speaker$_1$ needs to respond with an appropriate expression (e.g. *'ala SaaHibtu aHlaa* ['It looks much nicer on its owner']). To achieve pragmatic competence in Arabic, American students of Arabic need to learn the specific formulas used in responding to compliments on particular attributes. Additional studies are needed to learn more of these formulate expressions and more about the particular contexts in which they are used.

A final difference between American and Syrian compliment/compliment response sequences is length. A cursory glance at the English and Arabic data reveals that the Arabic sequences are much longer than the English; they contain more words

Gayle
Nelson

and are more likely to continue beyond the initial compliment and corresponding response. This interaction between speakers relates to the sincerity of the compliment and the compliment response; the longer the interaction, the greater the sincerity. The length also relates to the value Arabic speakers place on eloquence. As Nydell (1987: 103) notes, 'the ability to speak eloquently is a sign of education and refinement' and 'how you say something is as important as what you have to say'. If Arabic-speaking ESL/ EFL students, in an attempt to make compliment responses sound sincere to their own ears, use more words than a native English speaker, 'pragmatic failure might result from overindulgence in words', causing native speakers to sense a lack of appropriateness (Blum-Kulka and Olshtain 1986: 175). English-speaking students of Arabic, on the other hand, may have difficulty with the number of words in Arabic compliment/compliment response sequences, particularly with the formulate expressions expected in response to certain compliments. If the length of the sequence results in their feeling phony and insincere, they may fall back on their H strategies. In this case, pragmatic failure may result not from too many words, but from too few.

(*Revised version received October 1995*)

NOTES

1   The remaining 30 per cent were categorized as Comment History, Reassignment, Return, or Praise Upgrade.
2   The M or F in front of the utterances refers to male and female speakers. The (A) or (S) following the interchange refers to American or Syrian.
3   We also have the evil eye phenomenon in the US and Great Britain when we say 'knock on wood' and 'touch wood' to maintain good luck.
4   The Syrian interlocutors frequently used religious expressions, whereas none of the Americans did so.

REFERENCES

Barnlund, D. and S. Araki. 1985. 'Intercultural encounters: The management of compliments by Japanese and Americans.' *Journal of Cross-cultural Psychology* 16: 9–26.
Beebe, L. and T. Takahashi. 1989. 'Sociolinguistic variation in face-threatening speech acts' in M. R. Eisenstein (ed.) 1989: *The Dynamic Inter-language Empirical Studies in Speech Variation*. New York: Plenum Press.
Beebe, L., T. Takahashi, and R. Uliss-Weltz. 1990. 'Pragmatic transfer in ESL refusals' in R. Scarcella, E. Andersen, and S. Krashen (eds.) 1990: *On the Development of Communicative Competence in a Second Language*. New York: Newbury House.
Blum-Kulka, S. 1982. 'Learning how to say what you mean in a second language: A study of speech act performance of learners of Hebrew as a second language.' *Applied Linguistics* 3: 29–59.
Blum-Kulka, S. 1983. 'Interpreting and performing speech acts in a second language. A cross-cultural study of Hebrew and English' in N. Wolfson and E. Judd (eds.) 1983: *Sociolinguistics and Language Acquisition*. Rowley, MA: Newbury House.
Blum-Kulka, S., J. House, and G. Kasper. 1989. 'Investigating cross-cultural pragmatics: An introductory overview' in S. Blum-Kulka, J. House and G. Kasper (eds.) 1989: *Cross-cultural Pragmatics: Requests and Apologies*. Norwood, NJ: Ablex.
Blum-Kulka, S. and E. Olshtain. 1986. 'Too many words: Length of utterance and pragmatic failure.' *Studies in Second Language Acquisition* 8: 165–79.

Gayle
Nelson

Canale, M. and M. Swain. 1980. 'Theoretical bases of communicative approaches to second language teaching and testing.' *Applied Linguistics* 1: 1–47.

Chen, R. 1993. 'Responding to compliments: A contrastive study of politeness strategies between American English and Chinese speakers.' *Journal of Pragmatics* 20: 49–75.

Edmonson, W., J. House, G. Kasper, and B. Stemmer. 1984. 'Learning the pragmatics of discourse.' *Applied Linguistics* 5: 113–25.

Eisenstein, M. and J. Bodman. 1986. 'I very appreciate: Expressions of gratitude by native and nonnative speakers of American English.' Applied Linguistics 7: 167–85.

Garcia, C. 1989. 'Apologizing in English: Politeness strategies used by native and non-native speakers.' *Multilingua* 8: 3–20.

Habermas, J. 1970. 'Introductory remarks to a theory of communicative competence.' *Inquiry* 13: 3. Reprinted in H. P. Dreitzel (ed.) 1970: *Recent Sociology*. London: Macmillan.

Herbert, R. K. 1988. 'The ethnography of English compliments and compliment responses: A contrastive sketch' in W. Oleksy (ed.) 1988: *Contrastive Pragmatics*. Philadelphia: John Benjamins.

Herbert, R. K. and S. Straight. 1989. 'Compliment-rejection versus compliment-avoidance: Listener-based versus speaker-based pragmatic strategies.' *Language and Communication* 9: 35–47.

Holmes, J. 1988. 'Compliments and compliment responses in New Zealand English.' *Anthropological Linguistics* 28: 485–507.

Holmes, J. and D. F. Brown. 1987. 'Teachers and students learning about compliments.' *TESOL Quarterly* 21: 523–46.

Holsti, O. R. 1969. *Content Analysis for the Social Sciences and Humanities*. Reading, MA: Addison-Wesley.

Hurley, D. S. 1992. 'Issues in teaching pragmatics, prosody, and non-verbal communication.' *Applied Linguistics* 13: 259–81.

Hymes, D. 1971. 'Competence and performance in linguistic theory' in R. Huxley and E. Ingram (eds.) 1971: *Language Acquisition: Models and Methods*. London: Academic Press.

Hymes, D. 1972. 'On communicative competence' in J. B. Pride and J. Holmes (eds.) 1972: *Sociolinguistics*. Harmondsworth: Penguin.

Hymes, D. 1974. *Foundations in Sociolinguistics: An Ethnographic Approach*. Philadelphia: University of Pennsylvania Press.

Johnson, D. 1979. *Entertaining and Etiquette for Today*. Washington, DC: Acropolis Books.

Kasper, G. and S. Blum-Kulka. 1993. 'Interlanguage pragmatics: An introduction' in G. Kasper and S. Blum-Kulka (eds.) 1993: *Interlanguage Pragmatics*. New York: Oxford University Press.

Knapp, M. L., R. Hopper, and R. A. Bell. 1984. 'Compliments: A descriptive taxonomy.' *Journal of Communication* 34: 19–31.

Krippendorf, K. 1980. *Content An Introduction to its Methodology*. Beverly Hills: Sage.

Leech, G. 1983. *Principles of Pragmatics*. London: Longman.

Levine, D. R., J. Baxter, and P. McNulty. 1987. *The Culture Puzzle*. Englewood Cliffs, NJ: Prentice Hall.

Maloney, C. 1976. *The Evil Eye*. New York: Columbia University Press.

Manes, J. 1983. 'Compliments: A mirror of cultural values' in N. Wolfson and E. Judd (eds.) *Sociolinguistics and Language Acquisition*. Rowley, MA: Newbury House.

Nelson, G. L., W. El Bakary, and M. Al-Batal. 1993. 'Egyptian and American compliments: A cross-cultural study.' *International Journal of Intercultural Relations* 17: 293–313.

Nydell, M. K. 1987. *Understanding Arabs: A Guide for Westerners*. Yarmouth, ME: Intercultural Press.

Olshtain, E. 1983. 'Sociocultural competence and language transfer: The ease of apology' in S. Gass and L. Selinker (eds.) 1983: *Language Transfer in Language Learning*. Rowley, MA: Newbury House.

Olshtain, E. and A. Cohen. 1983. 'Apology: A speech act set' in N. Wolfson and E: Judd (eds.) 1983: *Sociolinguistics and Language Acquisition*. Rowley, MA: Newbury House.

Pomerantz, A. 1978. 'Compliment responses: Notes in the cooperation of multiple constraints' in J. Sehenkein (ed.) 1978: *Studies in the Organization of Conversational Interaction*. New York: Academic Press.

Rose, K.R. 1994. 'On the validity of discourse completion tests in non-Western contexts.' *Applied Linguistics* 15: 1–14.

Schegloff, E. and H. Sacks. 1973. 'Opening up closings.' *Semiotica* 8: 289–327.

Shouby, E. 1951. 'The influence of the Arabic language on the psychology of the Arabs.' *Middle East Journal* 5: 284–302.

Takahashi, T. and L. M. Beebe. 1993. 'Cross-linguistic influence in the speech act of correction' in G. Kasper and S. Blum-Kulka (eds.) 1993: *Interlanguage Pragmatics*. New York: Oxford University Press.

Thomas, J. 1983. 'Cross-cultural pragmatic failure.' *Applied Linguistics* 4/2: 92–112.

Thomas, J. 1984. 'Cross-cultural discourse as "inequal encounter": Toward a pragmatic analysis.' *Applied Linguistics* 5: 226–35.

Wolfson, N. 1981. 'Compliments in cross-cultural perspective.' *TESOL Quarterly* 15: 117–24.

Wolfson, N. 1983. 'An empirically based analysis of compliments in American English' in N. Woltson and E. Judd (eds.) 1983: *Sociolinguistics and Language Acquisition*. Rowley, MA: Newbury House.

Wolfson, N. 1989a. *Perspectives: Sociolinguistics and TESOL*. New York: Newbury House/ Harper and Row.

Wolfson, N. 1989b. 'The social dynamics of native and nonnative variation in complimenting behavior' in M. R. Eistenstein (ed.) 1989: *The Dynamic Interlanguage: Empirical Studies in Speech Variation*. New York: Plenum Press.

Wolfson, N. and J. Manes. 1980. 'The compliment as social strategy. Papers in Linguistics.' *International Journal of Human Communications* 13: 391–410.

❏   Describe the project that Nelson, Al-Batal and Echols carried out, saying briefly:
   a.   what their hypothesis/theory was;
   b.   what method they used;
   c.   what their results were;
   d.   how they interpreted the results.
   Carry out a similar project to compare the compliment responses of two groups. You may not necessarily want to look at two different nationalities or cultures. You could investigate how people of different genders, classes, and ages respond to compliments.

❏   This is a project on indirectness and cultural variables.
   a.   Choose one of the social factors involved in power and indirectness: status, role, age, gender, education, class, occupation and ethnicity.
   b.   Think of a theory or hypothesis that you would like to test. Express it as a comparison, for example 'When seeking help, women use more indirectness than men', 'When there is a difference in status, the one in power uses indirectness more than the one in a less powerful position', 'Indirectness is used by middle-class people to working-class people, not by working-class to middle-class'.
   c.   Check how important the contextual constraints (the size of the imposition and the formality of the situation) are, compared with the social factor (status, role, age, gender, education, class, occupation, ethnicity) that you chose.

d. Think of a way that your findings could be of use in society. Who might be interested in your results or helped by them and why?

     e. Write up your project. Describe your method of data collection and analysis in a way that would allow someone else to reproduce your study.

❑ Take any other aspect of the politeness strategies or politeness maxims that interests you, and think of a social or cultural variable that might influence how it is expressed. Form a theory. Carry out a project to test your theory.

❑ Think about everything that we have been looking at in this book.

     a. Do you think that in pragmatics, conversation analysis, speech acts, the Co-operative Principle and the Politeness Principle share a common core? Explain in detail your answer with examples.

     b. How does your answer to a. here, relate to the context outside the text, and the context within the text?

D6   CORPORA AND LANGUAGE TEACHING

D6.1   Reading and researching

Hunston looks at the applications of corpora to language teaching, focusing on data-driven learning (DDL) and making suggestions about materials and syllabus design. In DDL, learners can work either with a raw corpus or with concordance lines selected by the tutor. She says that materials using concordances that can work in class are those based on pedagogic corpora (collections of language that learners have been exposed to in class) and the lexical syllabus (the commonest word-forms, the central grammatical patterns of usage and the usual combinations). Finally Hunston enters the debate about native-speaker corpora, cultural saliency and lexical chunks, flagging up issues for consideration.

Susan Hunston (from 'Corpora and language teaching: General applications' in *Corpora in Applied Linguistics*, Cambridge: Cambridge University Press, 2002: 170–97.)*

Data-driven learning

Introduction

As Leech (1997c: 3) comments, the use of corpora in language teaching situations owes much to the work of Tim Johns, who developed data-driven learning (DDL) for use with international students at the University of Birmingham. An often-quoted comment by Johns is that 'Research is too important to be left to the

---

* For full references please see the original article.

Susan
Hunston

researchers' (1991: 2). The theory behind DDL is that students act as 'language detectives' (Johns 1997a: 101), discovering facts about the language they are learning for themselves, from authentic examples. This supports learning, partly because students are motivated to remember what they have worked to find out. In addition, because corpus data can reveal previously unnoticed patterns, a student may well notice something that a teacher has overlooked, or that no textbook covers. As well as being beneficial in teaching specific items, DDL is hypothesised to improve general skills of using context to deduce meaning.[1] DDL involves setting up situations in which students can answer questions about language themselves by studying corpus data in the form of concordance lines or sentences. The questions may arise out of something the student is writing, and may be formulated as 'Is it better to say x or y?' or 'What is the difference between saying x and saying y?' In this case, the questions are the student's own. Alternatively, self-access materials may be written that allow students to explore general issues such as 'that-clauses', using information from a corpus. In this case, the teacher aims to teach items which are known to be problematic or useful for the groups of students concerned. The first kind of study will use a 'raw corpus', in the sense that the student and tutor will look at the corpus together, without either of them necessarily knowing what they will find. For the second kind of study, the tutor has to carefully select and possibly edit the concordance lines in order to demonstrate the target language feature.

The first kind of study has the advantage of maximum student motivation: the student asks a question for which an answer is urgently required (for the student to complete a piece of written work, for example), and is therefore highly motivated to discover information in the corpus data consulted. A possible disadvantage for the teacher is that they have very little control over what happens. If the corpus is consulted and no answer is apparent to student or teacher, or if further difficult questions are raised, the teacher may feel that a loss of expertise has occurred. A more basic problem is that not every teaching situation allows the luxury of one-to-one consultations, or sufficient computer access for students to undertake investigations on their own. In the second kind of study, the teacher, having selected the information, has more control. Materials can be printed on to paper to be used with a whole class. The disadvantage is that, as the teacher has selected the topic for study, the students are potentially less motivated to search for or remember the target information. In these circumstances, DDL may appear to the students to be a tangential activity to the main business of the class.

More recent developments in data-driven learning (e.g. Bernadini 2000) stress the benefits of encouraging students to design their own corpus investigations and to take advantage of the 'serendipity' effect of searching a corpus when the agenda is not too firmly fixed and a student can follow up any interesting observations that they happen across. This Discovery Learning, as it is sometimes called, is most suitable for very advanced learners who are filling in gaps in their knowledge rather

---

[1] The hypotheses about the benefits of DDL have not yet been adequately tested, but see Stevens (1991), Cobb (1997) and Cobb and Horst (2001) for small-scale studies.

Susan
Hunston

than laying down the foundations. At the other end of the scale, Cobb and Horst (2001) describe an experiment to teach large amounts of vocabulary to EAP students, using concordances from a corpus of texts from the students' language course. In this very controlled environment, students learned lists of vocabulary items more successfully when they had access to the concordance lines than using other methods.

DDL with a 'raw' corpus
Advanced learners can safely be encouraged to use a raw (unedited) corpus to make observations about the language. Dodd (1997), for example, describes advanced learners of German using a corpus of German newspapers. Among other activities, the students test out statements made in standard reference books, about grammar, such as rules for the use of particular conjunctions, and lexis, such as differentiation between near-synonyms. The newspaper corpus can also be used to test hypotheses about the use of various key terms in East and West Germany. Many teachers nowadays use the worldwide web to allow students access to a range of corpora, both monolingual and parallel (Foucou and Kübler 2000) or to encourage students to build their own corpora (Pearson 2000).

The challenge for the teacher who wishes to encourage students to do work of this kind is to formulate a task in such a way that the student will obtain maximum benefit from it. If teacher and student are in a one-to-one consultation, the teacher can 'play it by ear'. In other circumstances, however, the teacher will have to do some planning of the activity to be undertaken.

[*Hunston at this point gives two examples of activities which a student may undertake, using an unedited version of the Bank of English corpus. The first is in response to a student who writes an essay,* 'in their efforts to prevent such incidents to ever happen again'. *She says that the teacher can send the student to a corpus to investigate the usage of* 'prevent', *and if possible of* 'prevent' *and* 'incident' *together so that they might note patterns such as* 'prevent something happening' *and* 'prevent something from happening' *and ways of expressing the whole idea, as in* 'prevent such incidents' *or* 'prevent a similar incident'. *The second activity that she describes is to ask the student to check the corpus for* 'there's no' *and* 'there isn't any' *to find what the difference is, which is most frequent, what part of the sentence they come in, what sort of noun follows. Hunston then makes the point that using corpora can give problems if the student finds concordance lines that break the rule that the teacher is trying to present to them. Let us now return to her text.*]

In other words, the corpus information does not seem to accord with native-speaker intuition. Looking at the corpus may therefore confuse the student and undermine the authority of the teacher. Closer examination of lines such as those above suggests a resolution of the problem, in that in each line the past participle is of a verb indicating a specific action (e.g. *vaccines require to be kept, pears require to be pruned, prisoners require to be segregated*) rather than of a general verb such as *do*. In each case the subject of the clause indicates an entity which is the goal of a process, The problem sentence *Further experiments require to be done* is different, not only because the verb is a general one but also because the subject

Susan
Hunston

expresses the range of the verb (in Halliday's terms) rather than the goal. The phrase *do an experiment* expresses a single action rather than an action done to something. Although this may solve Owen's dilemma, it is true that his question 'How many instances in a corpus are enough to show that something is correct English?' becomes a pressing, and awkward, one when learners investigate a corpus for themselves. An extreme example of this is clauses introduced by *like,* such as *They head for me like I'm a magnet or something.* This is usually considered to be 'incorrect' in English, the correct version being *They head for me as if I was a magnet or something.* The Bank of English has numerous examples of the incorrect usage, which is very common, especially in spoken English. Distinguishing between what is said and what is accepted as standard may need the assistance of a teacher or a grammar book.

Designing materials based on corpus data

The alternative to encouraging learners to explore a raw corpus is to select the evidence, that is, to give learners materials based on concordance lines which the teacher has selected, and to add questions which will guide the learners towards noticing relevant information in the lines. Johns (1997a: 101) gives some examples of question types (e.g. 'How many different verbs are shown with this structure?' and 'Which word is present in the right context of citations 1–8 that is not present in the right context of citations 9–16?') and notes that '[s]uch tasks are, of course, "closed" in the sense that the result is known to the teacher in advance'. The advantage of selecting concordance lines is that lines with exceptionally difficult vocabulary can be left out, as can lines that exemplify usages that the teacher would prefer the student to ignore at this stage. This selection allows concordance lines to be used with students who are not advanced enough to benefit from 'raw' concordance data.

The teacher may choose to begin with a word that is already familiar to learners. The following lines illustrate one use of the adjective *angry:*

At first I thought her parents were **angry** with her
But you get so **angry** with me!
how can you be **angry** with the man you love
Ian gets **angry** with the television sometimes

These lines have been selected because they do not contain difficult language and because there is a whole sentence or clause in one line. The lines have been cut so that there is no extraneous information in them. Learners, having identified the sequence *angry with* as the key point here, can be asked to look at other lines with a similar pattern, such as:

I'm more **annoyed with** myself you know
I was **annoyed with** him.
I knew my father would be **annoyed with** me.
But Americans also are **annoyed with** George Bush
He says he's never been **bored with** the job

**Susan
Hunston**

I got a bit **bored with** popular music
I get **bored with** cooking
She's highly intelligent and gets **bored with** television
I was clearly becoming rather **impatient with** rejections.
Charlie could be **impatient with** others.
There are countless times when I get **impatient with** my husband, Ken
increasingly **impatient with** the slow pace of change

A simple exercise is to ask learners to list the adjectives used in this way. If they are able, they might be asked to predict other adjectives that they might expect to have the same pattern, and these can be checked against a corpus, or against a dictionary. Further exercises could include underlining the verbs that come before the adjectives (*BE, GET, BECOME*). If the concordance lines are extended, learners can note a longer phraseology, such as prepositional phrases beginning with *for* that express the reason for anger, as in these extended lines:

Was he not even **angry with** his mother **for** not explaining things t
I do not feel **angry with** him **for** what he has done.
I feel **angry with** her **for** not standing up to him.
looked at him as if she were **annoyed with** him **for** letting it happen.

Learners are building up an extended phrase here that might be expressed as 'be angry with someone for something' or 'be angry with someone for (not) doing something'.

Exercises such as this one can be enjoyable, but they are also time-consuming for the teacher to write, so it is worthwhile bearing in mind this caveat from Dave Willis (personal communication):

One of the major problems with DDL, or with consciousness-raising in general, is what to focus on. Exercises of this kind are very time consuming in the classroom. A sequence like that starting with *angry* and leading on to *angry with someone for something* might not repay the time taken . . . I would not argue that exercises like this are not worth doing. I am saying that time in classrooms is very limited and that there is a danger of spending too long on generalisations which may be of limited value . . .

To avoid a wasteful expenditure of effort, writers of DDL materials frequently focus on items which are known to be difficult for students with a particular language background, or items which are particularly frequent or otherwise important in a given subject area.

DDL exercises can be integrated into the rest of the lesson if the starting point for the activity is a word or phrase met in a reading or listening text, or in another classroom activity. For example, a reading passage with a group of students studying science through the medium of English may contain the sentence *Salt water has a lower freezing point than normal water.* The teacher may consider the phraseology of the phrase *freezing point,* and its close relatives *boiling point, melting point* and so on, to be important enough to warrant the development of DDL materials. It is a simple matter to select some concordance lines:

Susan
Hunston

soil to raise the temperature above **freezing point**, the planetary permafrost
hunt. Temperatures remained at **freezing point**, prompting Kobe doctor
As the temperature dropped below **freezing point** at night, local reside
drops in your area below **freezing point** for seven consecutive
water, still liquid below its **freezing point**, and in a false state
freezer since alcohol has a lower **freezing-point** than water and therefore
imparting taste. They lower the **freezing point** of a food to keep it 1
on runways and aircraft, push the **freezing point** of ice down to 13 degrees
increased pressure lowers the **freezing point** of water. This is the
cold—don't you know what the **freezing point** of alcohol is? As we s
the period never rose above the **freezing point** of water (32F). Certainly
to car antifreeze, to lower their **freezing point**, to prevent large ice
and play in temperatures near to **freezing point**. That's not a whinge
that, sometimes nearly down to **freezing point** on a cold night. And s
reduce the temperature inside to **freezing point** in seconds. 'Imagine

Questions for students could include the following:

- Underline the lines where *freezing point* does not have *a* or *the* or *its* or *their* in front of it. In the lines, which words come before freezing point?
- Complete these sentences:
  The temperature .... dropped freezing point.
  The temperature .... rose freezing point.
  The temperature remained .... freezing point.
  The heater raised the temperature .... near freezing point.
- Look at the lines containing the phrase *the freezing point*. What words come after this phrase?
- Complete these sentences:
  The freezing point of alcohol is .... than the freezing point of water.
  .... will lower the freezing point of water.

The integration of activities of this kind into a lesson and a syllabus will be discussed below.

Reciprocal learning and parallel concordances

Perhaps one of the most exciting innovations in language teaching of recent years is the development of reciprocal learning. Reciprocal learning occurs when two language learners are paired, each helping the other learn their language. For example, a French speaker learning English may be paired with an English speaker learning French. Parallel corpora may be used to aid reciprocal learning, and they are also useful for teaching translation or for more conventional language-learning in situations where all learners share a common first language.

[*Hunston at this point provides sentences extracted from parallel corpora in French and English, which have been identified by searching on the French pronoun 'on'. This pronoun has*

Susan Hunston

several translation equivalents in English, the extracted sentences are used to alert both English and French learners to this fact. The sentences show that 'on' has been translated into English by 'one', 'you', 'I', 'it' and the passive. She provides an example of the French word 'dont', for learners to identify the various ways in which it is expressed in English, and then a task to put missing words into French or English sentences. Let us now return to her text.]

As I mentioned above, I regard reciprocal learning and the use of parallel corpora as two of the most exciting innovations in language teaching and learning in recent years. Learners teaching each other are truly empowered, and are likely to be genuinely motivated to make discoveries about each other's language. The role of the teacher becomes that of materials-provider. My excitement about parallel concordances is a personal response to seeing English–French concordances, and finding from them enormous amounts of information about French. The use of *dont* before a noun phrase, translated as *including* or *among them,* and the use of *dont*+clause in translating 'their heads nodding' and so on were new to me. Moreover, this is not simply a matter of learning how to translate.[2] As a learner of French, having my attention drawn to these examples through their translations gives me a better 'feel' for how the word *dont* is used. The obvious restriction on reciprocal learning, however, is that it can be undertaken only in a context where there are students learning each other's language. This is not the situation in most contexts where English is being taught.

Corpora and language teaching methodology

Many teachers have two main reservations when considering the use of DDL in the classroom. The first is the means by which DDL can be integrated into the plan for an ordinary lesson. The second concerns the language points that seem to be the topic of DDL materials. These tend to deal with the minute details of the phraseology of particular words, and may be difficult to reconcile with the 'big themes' of language teaching, such as 'tenses' or 'articles'. In this section some answers to these questions are offered. The section draws largely on the work of Dave and Jane Willis in considering the place of corpus-based materials in language teaching.

DDL as consciousness-raising
DDL does not 'teach' a language feature, but presents learners with evidence and asks them to make hypotheses and draw conclusions. As an activity, it therefore fits best with a lesson that has such learner-centred activities built into it. An example of such an approach is the framework for task-based learning proposed by J. Willis (1996). Willis defines a task as 'a goal-oriented activity in which learners use language to achieve a real outcome' (1996: 53). She proposes a framework consisting of three stages (1996: 53):

---

[2]   It is interesting that Johns' proposals re-visit traditional grammar-translation methods.

Susan
Hunston

Pre-task: Introduction to the topic and task
Task cycle: Task → Planning → Report
Language Focus: Analysis and practice

For the Language Focus stage, Willis and Willis (1996) propose that 'consciousness-raising activities' should be used, designed to draw learners' attention to some of the language features in the texts (written and spoken) that they have been engaged with when doing the task. Because a particular feature may occur only once or twice in the text, additional corpus material may be useful to help the learner to see a pattern rather than relying on a single occurrence.

As an example, here is one of the texts used as an illustration by Willis and Willis (1996: 71). It is a fairly simple (if frightening) story:

Auto-pilot

The flight ran several times a week taking holiday-makers to various resorts in the Mediterranean. On each flight, to reassure the passengers all was well, the captain would put the jet on to auto-pilot and he and all the crew would come aft into the cabin to greet the passengers.

Unfortunately on this particular flight the security door between the cabin and the flight deck jammed and left the captain and the crew stuck in the cabin. From that moment, in spite of efforts to open the door, the fate of the passengers and crew was sealed.

Willis and Willis suggest a variety of activities designed to encourage students to think about the lexis and grammar of the story. Below is an additional short sequence of activities, each one making use of corpus material in addition to the story itself.

The sequence begins by underlining the phrase: *left the captain and the crew stuck in the cabin*. This phrase from the story has been chosen because the verb *left* here occurs in a useful pattern, in which the verb is followed by a noun group and then by a past participle (*stuck*). Looking at the concordance lines for *LEAVE* in this pattern, it is striking that the past participles are usually words with a negative evaluation, such as *exhausted*, *crippled*, *paralyzed*, *shocked*. Here are some carefully selected examples:

The masked men left her bound and gagged.
A serious operation left her confined to a wheelchair.
A childhood illness has left her crippled . . .
The war left 300,000 homes destroyed.
The bitter winds left many anglers frozen to their seats.
An earthquake . . . killed around 170 people and left thousands homeless.

The subject may be a human being doing something intentionally (*the masked men*) but is more often an inanimate object without intentions (*a serious operation . . . a childhood illness*). The last example above uses a different but very similar pattern, in which the noun group is followed by an adjective instead of a past participle.

Susan
Hunston

The teacher could draw attention to the pattern by asking learners to complete a table which isolates elements of the pattern, thus:

The security door	*left the captain and the crew stuck in the cabin.*	
A serious operation	*left her*	*confined to a wheelchair.*
The bitter winds	*left many anglers*	*frozen to their seats.*
An earthquake	*left thousands*	*homeless.*

This could be taken a step further by looking at other verbs with the same pattern. Here are some examples of *KEEP* and *FIND:*

Russian troops have kept the town sealed off since Saturday.
. . . a social life which kept us and others entertained . . .
I kept myself fit all summer.
She kept that world completely hidden from her friends.
He found himself immediately surrounded by opposing players.
Ray found himself charged with murder.
American soldiers found themselves hopelessly outnumbered.
At some point, he found himself drawn into conversation with Nina and her new friend.

Willis and Willis (1996: 66) refer to the 'grammar of class' as being an important component of pedagogic grammar. Here we are looking at a verb that belongs to a particular 'class': the class of verbs that are followed by a noun and a past participle or adjective.

Another important target of consciousness-raising mentioned by Willis and Willis is collocation. An example of a fixed collocation in the 'Auto-pilot' text is *fate . . . sealed*. This collocation is in danger of being missed by a reader of the text because the individual words are separated by a fairly long noun group: *of the passengers and crew*. (Lewis 1996: 14 makes the point that phenomena like this blur the 'word partnership'.) To make the word partnership, or collocation, clearer, the teacher might show these concordance lines:

```
          These groups, who sealed the fate of President Marcos, have also lo
      night appears to have sealed their fate. Buoyed up by the survival of t
                Mr Wilson had sealed his fate shortly before the murder when he
         nd that politics have sealed his fate—all these features being peculi
     ncer that should have sealed the fate of the tan once and for all, we
            of the border that sealed Collins' fate. And the other directors
   If ever Sir Richard's fate was sealed it was at that moment
to happen. But now my fate was sealed. In the morning the
   rian regimes, and its fate was sealed for a time by the defe
1945, and in 1951 its fate was sealed, even though Labour
      Alas, they cried, our fate is sealed. For the sake
She was convinced her fate was sealed and so she shut her eyes
```

Having been asked to identify the common pattern in these lines, the learners can be asked to find a similar example in the reading text.

Susan
Hunston

The pedagogic corpus
In the examples given above, the concordance lines are taken from the Bank of English. D. Willis (1993, cited in Willis and Willis 1996: 67) suggests an alternative source: what he calls the learner's pedagogic corpus. This consists of all the language that a learner has been exposed to in the classroom – mainly the texts and exercises that the teacher has used. If the teacher has used authentic texts with a class, the corpus will consist of authentic language. If specially written texts have been used, the corpus will consist of invented language. The advantage of a pedagogic corpus is that, when an item is met in one text, examples from previous (and future) texts can be used as additional evidence for the learner to draw conclusions. The disadvantage of the general corpus – the unfamiliarity of the language in it – is overcome. Instead the teacher draws together for the learner aspects of the learner's past language experience to enable the learner to see patterns.

As an example, here are some concordance lines extracted from the first 50 pages of a Malaysian course book in English for postelementary students (Khong et al. 1987). The first set of lines is for the word *at*. These lines are taken from all parts of the course book, that is, from the rubrics to students as well as from the reading samples in the book.

I think we should leave it **at** the office.
Turn right **at** the junction.
ppens around 9:15 am on Saturday mornings **at** the following places?
e lives at 23 Jalan Berenang. Norliza studied **at** the SRJK Jalan Cawang.
Ramlee's family will move into the house **at** No.1 Jalan Kiambang.
The school office is **at** the end of the corridor.
At the end of the corridor, turn left
t time does the afternoon session start? **At** ten minutes past one.
Doesn't the class begin **at** 9 am?
ident that happened one Saturday morning **at** around 9:15 am.
She laughed as she looked **at** the timetable,
notice board. Some students are looking **at** it excitedly,
Look **at** these important benefits.
Read the passage and look **at** the plan of the neighbourhood.
How good are you **at** describing things. Let's find ou
I've one brother, no sisters **at** all.

By this point in the course book, the learners have met *at* in the following contexts:

- to indicate place;
- to indicate time;
- after *look*;
- after *good*;
- in the frame *no . . . at all*.

If a teacher wants to draw attention to the use of *at* in a new text, these concordance lines could be used as supplementary information.

Susan
Hunston

The second example comes from the second 50 pages of the same book. Suppose the learners now meet an '-ing' form following *when* (e.g. *When reading this passage* . . .). The teacher wishes to remind them of this use of *when* and similar words. Here are the examples from the course book:

> Put back the newspapers after reading them.
> Look left, right and left again before crossing the road.
> He has also written down what one should not do while playing the game.
> When asking questions, ask only wh-questions.
> A student dropped her purse when getting into the school bus.

These examples are somewhat stilted because none of the texts in this course book are authentic. They might be supplemented with a few genuine examples:

> When buying a chair, you should first consider its function and the price.
> If you suffer from headaches when reading . . .
> When buying clothes for your baby, I'd definitely go for convenience . . .
> Take care when using traditional remedies.
> Wear rubber gloves when washing up.

Corpora and syllabus design

In this chapter so far we have been taking the view-point of the classroom teacher and materials writer, and we have seen the contribution that materials based on concordances may make to the language class. There are, however, wider issues at stake. If, as Sinclair (1991: 100) says, 'language looks different when you look at a lot of it at once', then the experience of using corpora should lead to rather different views of syllabus design. One type of syllabus whose design is based on concepts arising from corpus studies is the 'lexical syllabus'.

The notion of a 'lexical syllabus' was proposed in a paper by Sinclair and Renouf (1988), and finds its fullest exposition in D. Willis (1990). The term is occasionally (mis-)used to indicate a syllabus consisting only of vocabulary items, but as Sinclair, Renouf and Willis use the term, it comprises all aspects of language, differing from a conventional syllabus only in that the central concept of organisation is lexis. At its most simple, the argument is that it makes sense to teach the most frequent words in a language first. Sinclair and Renouf argue that 'the main focus of study should be on (a) the commonest word forms in the language; (b) the central patterns of usage; (c) the combinations which they usually form' (1988: 148). Their point is that the most frequent words have a variety of uses, so that learners acquire a flexibility of language fairly easily. In addition, the main uses of the most frequent words cover the main points of grammar, if in an unfamiliar form. Sinclair and Renouf quote *MAKE* as an example of a word with many uses, some of which are rarely covered in most beginners' courses. The most frequently occurring use of this verb is in combinations such as *make decisions*, *make discoveries*, *make arrangements*, rather than in the more concrete *make a cake*, etc. In Sinclair's terminology, *MAKE* is used as a delexical verb more

Susan
Hunston

frequently than as an ordinary verb. An English course that focuses only on the concrete sense of *MAKE* denies the learner the opportunity to express sophistic-ated meanings with a simple verb.

Another example of a frequent word with multiple uses is *back*. This is a very frequent word: according to Sinclair 1999, it is 95th in frequency in the Bank of English, ahead of, for example, *get, may, how, think, even* and *us*. The reason for this frequency is that it is used in phrases such as *get the bus back, come/go back, look back, move back, turn back*, as well as as a noun: *behind your back, at the back*. Teaching the typical uses of *back* therefore introduces the learner to a large amount of language though not a massive vocabulary. Sinclair and Renouf make the point:

> Almost paradoxically, the lexical syllabus does not encourage the piecemeal acquisition of a large vocabulary, especially initially. Instead, it concentrates on making full use of the words that the learner already has, at any par-ticular stage. It teaches that there is far more general utility in the recom-bination of known elements than in the addition of less easily usable items. (1988: 155).

Turning to the issue of grammar in a lexical syllabus, Sinclair and Renouf argue that in a lexical syllabus, a separate listing of grammatical items is unnecessary:

> If the analysis of the words and phrases has been done correctly, then all the relevant grammar etc should appear in a proper proportion. Verb tenses, for example, which are often the main organizing feature of a course, are com-binations of some of the commonest words in the language. (1988: 155)

D. Willis (1990) takes up the issue of lexis and grammar (see also chapter 6). He points out that 'English is a lexical language', meaning that many of the con-cepts we traditionally think of as belonging to 'grammar' can be better handled as aspects of 'vocabulary'. For example, the passive can be seen as *BE* plus an adjective or past participle, rather than as a transformation of the active (1990: 17). Conditionals can be handled by looking at the hypothetical meaning of *would,* rather than by proposing a rule about sequence of tenses, that often does not work (1990: 18–19). He also argues that what is traditionally termed 'grammar' can often be called 'pattern' (1990: 51). For example, a pattern consisting of 'noun phrase+*am/are/is* + . . . ing' is what is more usually called the present continu-ous tense. Other patterns that are less often treated as basic grammar might include other frequent words, such as *way*, e.g. '*the*+adjective+*way*+*of*+ . . . ing' (*the best way of getting to Birmingham . . .*), '*the only way*+that-clause+*is/was*+to-infinitive clause' (*the only way you'll do that is to get the train*). In other words, Willis argues that the most productive way to interpret grammar in the classroom is as lexical pat-terning and, conversely, that all patterns involving frequent lexical items are import-ant in the classroom, not only those that are traditionally covered by 'grammar'. Because patterns attach to all lexical items in the language, learning the lexis means learning the patterns and therefore the grammar.

Perhaps Willis' most radical suggestion is that a syllabus can, in effect, consist of a corpus (1990: 70). In other words, if the course designer collects pieces of

Susan
Hunston

authentic language that contain instances of the most frequent patterns of the most frequent words, then that collection (corpus) will exemplify what the learner needs to know. The job of the teacher or materials writer, then, is to devise ways of encouraging the learner to engage with the material in the corpus (e.g. by setting tasks) and of helping the learning to 'notice' (Schmidt 1990; Bernadini 2000) the patterning of language (e.g. by consciousness-raising activities). A description of the syllabus would, in effect, be a description of the corpus. If the syllabus was expressed as a list of items, it would be as a list of the most frequent word-forms in the corpus, along with their most typical phraseologies. As the texts making up the corpus were presented to the learners, the syllabus would inevitably be covered. This alters the respective roles of the syllabus designer and materials writer quite considerably. Instead of the syllabus designer selecting items of language description and the materials writer choosing texts to illustrate them, the materials writer will choose interesting texts and the syllabus designer will keep a check on the balance of the overall collection of texts, ensuring that its most frequent word-forms, and their typical phraseologies, match what the learners require. Here, of course, there is an element of subjectivity. The syllabus designer may aim to mirror the distribution of structures, word frequency and phraseology in a larger, general corpus, or may decide that the learners' age, or specific needs, makes a different target corpus more appropriate. This subjectivity is no more than syllabus designers always employ, however, and has the advantage of making an appeal to principle, rather than to conventional wisdom. A syllabus of this kind would have the advantage of answering Long and Crookes' (1992: 33) objection that a lexical syllabus leads to artificial teaching materials if language is written specially to demonstrate key lexical items. Indeed, Willis' concept of a collection of texts is not dissimilar from the task-based syllabus proposed by Long and Crookes, though it would be a more concrete entity.

One problem in employing a corpus as syllabus is knowing how to describe the relevant frequencies in the corpus. A word-by-word account is very lengthy. One useful piece of supplementary information is a list of frequently occurring sequences. Sequences of this kind are of recent increasing interest to corpus linguists. De Cock et al (1998, also de Cock 1998) compare 'prefabs' in native-speaker and learner corpora, to test the hypothesis that learners tend not to use formulae as frequently as native speakers do. Biber et al (1999: 993–994) examine 'lexical bundles' in conversation and academic prose, using the Longman Grammar Corpus. They find that three-word bundles are much more frequent than four-word, that both kinds of bundles are more frequent in conversation than in academic prose, and that in conversation the bundles comprise more of the total word-count (28%) than they do in academic prose (20%). Some of the very frequent bundles in conversation include: *I don't know, I don't think, do you want, I don't want, don't want to, don't know what, and I said, I was going to, are you going to*; the frequent bundles in academic prose are, unsurprisingly, very different, and include: *in order to, one of the, part of the, the number of, the presence of, in the case of, on the other hand.*

Susan
Hunston

D. Willis (1998) has done a similar study using the somewhat larger Bank of English corpus, but not differentiated by register. Some of the very frequent four-word combinations are:

Phrase	Number of occurrences	Phrase	Number of occurrences
the end of the	2,074	an awful lot of	514
a lot of people	1,834	in the middle of	510
nice to talk to	1,650	in the first place	477
that sort of thing	1,531	that kind of thing	441
a lot of the	1,189	this sort of thing	437
quite a lot of	1,098	per cent of the	392
a bit of a	1,089	got a lot of	389
end of the day	896	a little bit more	382
of the things that	654	a couple of years	366
the rest of the	608	a lot of time	351
a lot of money	595	a lot of things	346
a little bit of	570	most of the time	346
in terms of the	565	used to go to	337
to go to the	549	think a lot of	325
no no no no	536	to make sure that	324

The importance of these bundles or phrases is, firstly, that a syllabus designer working with a pedagogic corpus would wish to ensure that the corpus reflected these sorts of figures, if necessary differentiated by register, and secondly, that a materials designer would wish to draw attention to them as useful formulae for learners to use.

Challenges to the use of corpora in language teaching

Although corpora are widely acknowledged to be a valuable resource in describing language, there is less consensus on the value of corpus findings in the description of language for learners or on the use of corpus-based material in language class-rooms. Among others, Widdowson (2000) and Cook (1998) have spoken against what they term an 'extreme' attitude towards using corpora in language teaching.[3] At the risk of over-simplification, their arguments can be summarised thus:

1. A corpus is 'real language' only in a very limited sense. Language in a corpus is de-contextualised and must be re-contextualised in a pedagogic setting to

[3] For Widdowson, this is part of a more general argument against the uncritical use of theoretical linguistics in applied linguistics. Interestingly, Borsley and Ingham (forthcoming) regard corpora as the preoccupation of Applied Linguistics as opposed to theoretical linguistics.

Susan
Hunston

make it real for learners, In Widdowson's (2000) terms, a corpus comprises traces of texts, not discourse.

2. Teachers (and course book writers etc) should not accept corpus evidence uncritically, but should appraise it in the light of other sources of information about language such as introspection and elicitation. In particular, frequency should not be the only factor in deciding what to teach: how salient a language feature is should also be taken into account, as should how highly valued a language item is. Learners should be encouraged to be creative in their language use, and should not be restricted to clichéd utterances.

3. Corpora tend to comprise the language of native speakers only, whereas many learners will never communicate with a native speaker and/or are not interested in native speaker norms. In particular, the details of phraseology or collocations may be unimportant to a non-native speaker of English. Too strong a dependence on corpora of native-speaker English tends to de-value the language of non-native-speakers and to perpetuate colonialist attitudes towards English.[4]

4. In a similar vein, learners should be allowed to approach language in a way they feel comfortable with. In many cases, this will be via grammatical rules and lists of lexical items. Learners should not be forced to approach English via 'lexical chunks' exclusively.

Some of these points can be taken as common ground. It would be very odd to suggest that language should not be contextualised within the classroom or that teachers should approach corpus evidence uncritically. Previous chapters in this book have stressed the need for caution in extrapolating from a corpus to a language and the importance of careful thought in interpreting corpus evidence. As Barlow (1996: 2) comments, 'using such powerful tools should not cause the researcher to become complacent and imagine that "language" is now in the computer'.

There are, however, three points here that deserve closer attention. These are: the issue of native-speaker corpora; the issue of frequency versus saliency, value and creativity; and the issue of lexis, grammar and 'lexical chunks'. Each of these will be dealt with in turn below.

I would not wish to argue against Cook's (1998) concern that corpora tend to treat native-speaker language as overly valuable.[5] Cook seems to imply, however, that the English of non-native speakers (sometimes called International English, and exemplified by interactions between a Japanese manufacturer and a Turkish wholesaler) does not contain those features that corpus linguists claim for native-speaker English, such as variation between registers, restrictions on co-occurrence, association between pattern and meaning, and so on. Hunston and Francis (1999: 268–270) suggest that although patterning in International English might be different from that found in any native-speaker variety, it would still exist and be worth teaching as patterning. Their argument is that the process of 'doing corpus

---

[4] See, for example, Hall and Eggington (eds.) 2000.
[5] It is worth adding, perhaps, that this argument applies only to English, because of its unique hegemony in the modern world. Learners of French, German, Japanese etc might be less disconcerted by having access to a corpus of language produced by native speakers only.

Susan
Hunston

research' has a value that is independent of the value of the product on which that research is currently carried out. If currently available corpora are inadequate, and in this respect they very clearly are, then there is a strong argument for compiling more adequate corpora, in this case of International English, rather than simply abandoning corpora altogether. I suspect that compiling such a corpus would be fraught with difficulties, ranging from 'Who would consider such an enterprise worth funding?' to 'Whose language should be collected?', but the very existence of such questions, and the problems they raise, is itself usefully revealing of attitudes towards International English.

The second interesting question that Cook raises is that of the importance of frequency. It is very commonly argued by those who advocate using corpus evidence in teaching that what is most frequent should be taught first, and that learners' attention should be drawn most to frequently occurring phenomena. The opposing argument is that certain aspects of English are important even though they are not frequent, either because they carry a lot of information or because they have a resonance for a cultural group or even for an individual. Wray and Perkins (2000, and citing Hickey 1993 and Howarth 1998) make a similar argument when they suggest that a sequence of words may constitute a 'formula' for an individual or a cultural group, even if the sequence is attested only rarely. Items which are important though infrequent seem to be those that echo texts which have a high cultural value. A good example is the co-occurrence of *death* and *adventure* in the following extract from J. K. Rowling's *Harry Potter and the Philosopher's Stone:*

Death is but the next great adventure.

For many (though not all) readers, *death* and *adventure* may effectively be collocates, because of an intertextual reference to the classic children's play *Peter Pan*, by J. M. Barrie, which includes the line:

To die will be an awfully big adventure.

There are a handful of similar instances in the Bank of English, some specifically quoting Barrie, but too few to have statistical significance. The resonance of Rowling's phrase, then, apparently comes from its cultural salience, not its frequency.[6]

In many cases, however, cultural salience is not so clearly at odds with frequency. Examples of salient items sometimes given are: proverbs such as 'Too many cooks spoil the broth'; slogans such as the American Express 'That will do nicely', which has a resonance arising from the frequency with which the advertisement was repeated and mimicked; and headlines such as 'Gotcha!' (the *Sun* newspaper's infamous response to the sinking of the Argentinian ship the Belgrano prior to the Malvinas/Falklands conflict in 1982). In each case, salience does seem to be reflected in statistical measures. *Spoil* is a significant collocate of *broth* (occurring two places to the left of *broth* with a high MI-score of 12, indicating

6   I am grateful to Hsin Chin Lee for bringing this example to my attention.

Susan
Hunston

a strong collocation, and a t-score of 3.3, indicating a certainty just above the cut-off point of 2), and the proverb is not only quoted but exploited with variation, as these concordance lines illustrate:

Too many musical heroes can **spoil** the broth, but not on Bill Laswell's late
    cordon bleu chef might just **spoil** the broth. I don't think anybody really
workers: Too many computers **spoil** the broth. WASHINGTON, DC
    Will one more TV cook **spoil** the broth? Not if it's TODAY columnist
penicillin, and too many cooks **spoil** the book advances. When every other
    part of PR. Too many cooks **spoil** the menu; There's a recipe for

Similarly, *do* occurring immediately to the left of *nicely* has a t-score significance of 10.7, with most examples clearly echoing the advertising slogan, either directly or through exploitations such as *tatt will do nicely, data'll do nicely* or *American Express won't do nicely. Gotcha* occurs in the Bank of English 128 times, including in the phrase *gotcha journalism.*

In these examples, the corpus examples do not explain why a phrase is significant, but the frequency information does seem to follow the salience. The fact that salient phrases are often subject to variation is also illustrated, in turn showing that English is about creativity as well as cliché.

Another aspect of saliency is discussed by Barlow (1996) and Shortall (1999), though not using that terminology. Barlow suggests that learners create schemata for grammatical features of a language, contrasting this with the 'parameter setting' hypothesis. These schemata are based partly on the evidence that the learner meets when experiencing authentic examples of the language, but also on the prototypes or expectations that the learner has about what meaning distinctions might be made. Arguing that both induction and expectation have a role in language learning, Barlow comments: 'the learner is not seen as just a passive pattern extractor, but is, in addition, a cognizer with the ability to make numerous cognitive distinctions' (1996: 17–18). Shortall goes further in relating this to teaching syllabuses. He points out that all language users have 'prototypes' about aspects of language use, and that these may conflict with the evidence of what is most frequent. For example, he finds that, when asked to produce a sentence with *there,* most people use a concrete noun and a prepositional phrase, as in *there are three books on the table,* whereas in the Bank of English corpus *there* constructions are more frequently used with abstract nouns and clauses, as in *there is evidence to suggest that . . .* Shortall expresses the teacher's resulting dilemma in the form of two conflicting statements: 'If concrete nouns are prototypical, and if this is the kind of noun people first think of, perhaps these should be taught first in EFL textbooks' and 'If abstract nouns are more frequent in real language (or in the corpus) perhaps these should be given priority/He argues that prototypes are so strong that learners should be taught them first and only later introduced to the more frequent usages. In this, Shortall demonstrates the discerning attitude towards corpus evidence that Widdowson and Cook advocate.

The third point I wish to debate here is Cook's observation that learners should not be forced to restrict their learning experience to 'lexical chunks'. If a learner wishes to perceive English in terms of grammatical rules supplemented by

**Susan
Hunston**

vocabulary lists, she or he should be allowed to do so, and not be forced into
ignoring rules and learning only phrases. If researchers into corpora did advocate
a 'phrase-book' approach to language learning, then Cook's criticism would be
legitimate, but this is far from the case. The essence of the 'idiom principle' and
of 'units of meaning', as discussed in chapter 6, is that the patterning of language
is more flexible and also more pervasive than the concept of 'lexical chunks' would
suggest. Again, Barlow (1996: 15) expresses this well:

> Part of the motivation for [this] approach . . . is a rejection of the distinction
> between a creative, compositional, productive component of the grammar and
> a component consisting of a collection of fixed idiomatic forms. The claim is
> that *most* of language consists of semi-regular, semi-fixed phrases or units
> . . . [words] have an affinity for each other and are linked together, but not
> so strongly as to form an identifiable lexical unit.

Barlow's discussion of the use of reflexive pronouns illustrates this phenomenon.
Reflexive pronouns are used predominantly with some verbs rather than others
(see Francis et al 1996 for detailed lists), but these do not constitute 'fixed phrases'.

Another point to be made here is that where phrases are advocated as a useful input to language learning (see, for example, the discussion of Willis above),
the notion of language teaching is somewhat different to that apparently envisaged
by Cook. It is not recommended that teachers 'present' phrases as a teaching item,
but that phrases are among the variety of lexical and grammatical features which
are amenable to consciousness-raising (D. Willis, personal communication). Thus,
the learner's predilection for viewing language in a particular way is not thwarted,
but may be encouraged to expand.

Widdowson argues that the importance of corpora 'lies not in the answers
they provide but in the questions they provoke' (2000: 23). I would agree with
the words here, though not in the way Widdowson means them: possibly the most
far-reaching influence of corpora is not the individual observations that have been
made using them, but the radical questions they have raised about the nature of
language itself (see chapter 6). One of the questions provoked for Widdowson
is 'If they do not represent real language for the learner, then what *does?*' (2000:
23). Given the ambiguity of this question, it is one that we can all probably agree
is worth answering.

❏ What does Hunston say are the pros and cons of working with   **★ Activities**
   a. raw corpus?
   b. materials based on concordance lines selected by the tutor?
   c. parallel corpora?
   What methodological guidelines does she suggest might lead to successful use of
   these three in the classroom?
❏ Discuss whether these statements are true or false and why:
   a. DDL teaches a language feature.
   b. DDL can be used in task-based learning.
   c. A pedagogic corpus is a collection of language from coursebooks.
   d. A syllabus can consist of a corpus.

❏ What is your opinion of the four arguments put forward by Widdowson and Cook against the extreme attitude towards corpora in language teaching? Do you agree with what Hunston says about native-speaker corpora, salience and lexical chunks?

❏ Thinking about the idea of International English corpora and recalling your experience of ICE (see Unit C7), do you know of a world English that might represent real language for learners in a context that you know? Does the corpus exist already? If not, how would you go about setting it up? Would you want to combine it with a pedagogical corpus?

❏ Hunston's suggestions for classroom tasks are principally to teach lexis and grammar. Can you think of task types, using her ideas for materials and syllabus design, that would teach features of pragmatics, that is:

   a. speech acts;
   b. Cooperative Principle;
   c. Politeness Principle;
   d. conversation analysis;
   e. exchange structure;
   f. critical discourse analysis;

❏ Find a free corpus or gain access to a commercial one. Design a task for one of the features listed a–f above. Keep in mind the students' location and level.

D7   CULTURE AND LANGUAGE LEARNING

D7.1   Reading and researching

Bardovi-Harlig looks at intercultural pragmatics, which she calls cross-cultural, and interlanguage development. She finds that native speakers (NSs) and non-native speakers (NNSs) can differ observably in the production of speech acts: NNSs may choose different speech acts, have different semantic formulas, and the form and content may be different. She points to studies that show the effect of learner perceptions and judgements on pragmatic errors, conversational implicature, illocutionary force and conversation structure. She discusses the factors that influence L2 pragmatic system development: input, instruction, level of proficiency, length of exposure, and L1 pragmatic transfer. Finally, she debates whether there should be a pedagogy of pragmalinguistic and sociopragmatic features in L2 instruction.

Kathleen Bardovi-Harlig (from 'Evaluating the empirical evidence: grounds for instruction in pragmatics?' in Kenneth R. Rose and Gabriel Kasper (eds), *Pragmatics in Language Teaching*, Cambridge: Cambridge University Press, 2001: 13–32.)*

*   For full references please see the original article.

Introduction

Everyone who works with a second or foreign language, whether learners, teachers, or researchers, knows a funny story about crosscultural pragmatics – or maybe the stories are really not that funny. From the perspective of the speaker, they may be about feeling silly, helpless, or rude; from the perspective of the listener, they may be about feeling confused, insulted, or angry. Anecdotal evidence inspires us to say that we ought to teach, as one of our ESL students said, the 'secret rules' of language. Much research has gone into identifying how speakers of various languages realize speech acts, take turns, and use silence, for example, so that what our student called the secret rules are not unknown; and even if our knowledge is incomplete at this stage, could it form the basis of an informed pedagogy? In other words, is there empirical evidence that warrants the development and implementation of a pedagogy of pragmatics in second and foreign language instruction? In this chapter, I will review the empirical evidence that shows that native speakers (NSs) and nonnative speakers (NNSs) of a given target language appear to have different systems of pragmatics, discuss the factors that influence the development of L2 pragmatics systems, and then address the question of whether differences in pragmatics systems warrant instructional treatment.

The evidence

This review adopts a speech act perspective. Although it is not the only way of viewing pragmatics, speech act research has been well represented in crosscultural and interlanguage pragmatics research, and provides a common analytic framework which facilitates comparison across studies. Although most of the research has focused on production, there are additional studies (although many fewer) that have investigated judgment and perception. The interlanguage pragmatics studies have investigated intermediate to advanced learners from a variety of first language backgrounds, and have used a variety of data collection techniques from different sources, including natural conversations, role-plays, and written questionnaires. Even grammatically advanced learners show differences from target-language pragmatic norms. That is to say, a learner of high grammatical proficiency will not necessarily possess concomitant pragmatic competence. It is equally important to note that at least at the higher levels of grammatical proficiency, learners may also evidence a wide range of pragmatic competence. Advanced NNSs are neither uniformly successful, nor uniformly unsuccessful, pragmatically; however, they are more likely to be less successful as a group than NSs on the same task where contextualized reaction data are available (as in the case of authentic conversations and institutional talk).

Production

There are many ways in which learners can differ from NSs in the production of speech acts. Cohen (1996) identifies three areas for such differences: speech acts, semantic formulas, and form. Blum-Kulka (1982) also notes that speech act realizations may deviate on three levels: social acceptability of the utterance, linguistic acceptability of the utterance, or pragmatic acceptability reflected in shifts of

Kathleen
Bardovi-
Harlig

illocutionary force. In this chapter, I will divide the differences between learners and NSs into four main categories and then give representative examples of each: NSs and NNSs may use different speech acts, or where the same speech acts are used, these may differ in semantic formula, content, or form (Bardovi-Harlig, 1996).

Choice of speech acts. NNSs may perform different speech acts than NSs in the same contexts, or, alternatively, they may elect not to perform any speech act at all. The best examples of this come from authentic conversations and role-plays where speakers have some flexibility in determining what they will say or do. In authentic academic advising sessions, NSs and NNSs favor different speech acts (Bardovi-Harlig & Hartford, 1993). NSs produce more suggestions than NNSs per advising session, whereas NNSs produce more rejections per advising session than NSs do. The two speech acts seem to serve the same function, that of control. NSs exert control over their course schedules by making suggestions; in contrast, the NNSs control their course schedules through rejections, by blocking the suggestions of their advisers (Bardovi-Harlig & Hartford, 1993). Although both groups of students participate in determining what courses they ultimately take, the resulting feeling of harmony in the interview is perceived (by the advisers) to be noticeably different.

A second example comes from role-play data collected by Cohen and Olshtain (1993). The scenario in this example was designed to elicit an apology. However, in the transcript of one Israeli learner of English, we learn that for at least that one learner of English, the conditions for an apology were not satisfied by the scenario.

(1)   Scenario presented to NNS (Cohen & Olshtain, 1993, p. 54)[1]
      You arranged to meet a friend in order to study together for an exam.
      You arrive half an hour late for the meeting.
      Friend (annoyed): I've been waiting at least half an hour for you!
              You: _____

(2)   Transcript of role-play (Cohen & Olshtain, 1993, pp. 54–55)
      Friend: I've been waiting at least half an hour for you!
      Nogah: So what! It's only an – a meeting for –to study.
      Friend: Well. I mean – I was standing here waiting, I could've been sitting in
              the library studying.
      Nogah: But you're in your house. You can – you can study if you wish. You
              can do whatever you want.
      Friend: Still pretty annoying – I mean – try and come on time next time.
      Nogah: OK, but don't make such a big deal of it.
      Friend: OK.

In this exchange, we learn that an appointment with another student to study is not regarded as very important by this learner, and that keeping someone waiting at

---

[1]   There is an error in the original report of the scenario which has been corrected here. Readers may also see Cohen (1997b, p. 259) for the correction. I cite the original study to appropriately place Cohen and Olshtain's innovative research design in 1993.

Kathleen
Bardovi-
Harlig

his or her own house is not a very serious offense. Thus, this respondent may feel that her obligation to apologize is very low. This accords with the findings of Bergman and Kasper's (1993) study of perception, discussed in the section on judgment and perception later in this chapter (see also García, 1989).

As we see in the case of the apology role-plays collected by Cohen and Olshtain (1993), learners may not perform the speech act under investigation. They may also perform a different speech act from NSs in the same context. In the context of the academic advising session, NNSs used rejections rather than suggestions, which were used by NSs. Rejections were found to serve the same function as suggestions in the interviews overall, that of controlling the course schedule. The absence of a particular speech act is often salient. This brings us to the discussion of opting out (Bonikowska, 1988). Opting out is the choice of not performing the speech act under investigation and is particularly difficult to investigate in written questionnaires (Rose, 1994a; Rose & Ono, 1995), but it merits study because it may be an important part of understanding why NSs and NNSs differ in speech act realization (Bonikowska, 1988).

Semantic formulas. A second way in which NSs and NNSs may differ is in the choice of semantic formulas (Hartford & Bardovi-Harlig, 1992; Niki & Tajika, 1994; Bardovi-Harlig, 1996; Murphy & Neu, 1996). Semantic formulas represent the means by which a particular speech act is accomplished in terms of the primary content of an utterance (Fraser, 1981; Olshtain & Cohen, 1983; Beebe, Takahashi, & Uliss-Weltz, 1990). For example, as Olshtain and Cohen (1983) point out, an apology may contain an illocutionary force indicating device (*I'm sorry*), an explanation or account of the situation (e.g., *The bus was late*), an acknowledgment of responsibility (e.g., *It's my fault*), an offer of repair (e.g., *I'll pay for the broken vase*), and/or a promise of forbearance (e.g., *It won't happen again*). Semantic formulas are a superset of specific content which is examined in the following section.

Both NSs and NNSs engaged in authentic advising sessions used more explanations than any other semantic formula when rejecting an adviser's suggestion of a particular course, as in Examples (3)–(5):

Explanations
(3)   That's the one that conflicts with what I have to take. [NS]
(4)   Yeah, but, the books are, probably the books are in German. [NNS] (from Bardovi-Harlig & Hartford, 1991)

Alternative
(5)   Well, I'd kind of thought of taking L541. [NS, DCT (discourse completion task)] (from Hartford & Bardovi-Harlig, 1992)

However, NSs and NNSs differed in their use of alternatives both in actual advising sessions and in response to DCT scenarios based on the advising sessions (Hartford & Bardovi-Harlig, 1992). In the conversational data, alternatives were the second most frequent semantic formula for NSs, whereas alternatives ranked fourth for NNSs, with avoidance as the second ranked strategy. Verbal avoidance is essentially a strategy which diverts attention from the actual force of the student's contribution as a rejection. Besides hedges (e.g., *I don't know*) identified by Beebe et al. (1990), three additional types of verbal avoidance were identified, all questions in form: postponement, questions asking for the repetition of information, and the request for additional information, illustrated in the following examples (Bardovi-Harlig & Hartford, 1991):

(6)   Um . . . Can I decide if next week? I want to think a little bit more.
      [postponement]
      [NNS, L1 Chinese]

(7)   What was that last course?
      [Q requests repetition of information]
      [NNS, L1 Spanish]

During the course of the advising sessions NNSs were often encouraged by the adviser to supply the underrepresented alternative semantic formula as in the following:

(8)   NS Adviser in response to NNS, Korean
      A: Well what would you take if you didn't take phonetics? Have you thought of a replacement? [14 turns]
      All right. Well . . . uh . . . well what, do you suggest? I mean, what you're suggesting is, first you said you want to take phonetics, but now you say you don't want to take phonetics, so . . . what, what do you suggest as an alternative?

In a study of complaints, Murphy and Neu (1996, p. 199) also found a difference in the use of semantic formulas, or what they call 'semantic components.' The NSs, fourteen American men, and the NNSs, fourteen Korean men, all of whom were graduate students, completed an oral discourse completion task in which they were asked to assume the role of a student whose assignment was unfairly graded by his professor. The NSs and NNSs showed relatively high agreement on three of the four semantic formulas used to realize the complaints. All of the subjects except one of the NNSs began the complaint with an explanation of purpose as in Examples (9) and (10).

(9)   Uh, Dr. Smith, I just came by to see if I could talk about my paper. [NS]
(10)   Good afternoon, Professor. Uh, I have something to talk to you about my paper
       . . . [NNS, L1 Korean]

Respondents also showed relatively high agreement on the use of the justification and solution formulas. However, NSs and NNSs differed noticeably on the formula which constitutes the head act. All of the NSs (14/14) used a complaint, as in Example (11), whereas only three of the fourteen NNSs did. The majority of the NNSs used a criticism instead of a complaint, as in Example (12).

(11)   I think, uh, maybe it's my opinion. Maybe the grade was a little low. [NS]
(12)   But you just only look at your point of view and, uh, you just didn't recognize my point. [NNS, L1 Korean]

Kathleen
Bardovi-
Harlig

However, as Murphy and Neu observe, the use of different semantic formulas for the head act constitutes a difference in the choice of speech act rather than in use of semantic formula (a criticism rather than a complaint), and thus this case seems to provide evidence for use of different speech acts as well.

Content. A third way in which NSs and NNSs may differ is in the content of their contribution. Whereas a semantic formula names the type of information given, content refers to the specific information given by a speaker. Even in cases when NSs and NNSs use the same semantic formulas, the content that they encode can be strikingly different (Takahashi & Beebe, 1987; Beebe et al., 1990). A case in point is the content of explanations, a semantic formula found in refusals. In a comparison of the explanations offered by Americans and NSs of Japanese using English, Beebe, Takahashi, and Uliss-Weltz (1990) characterized the explanations of the Americans as providing more details and the explanations of the Japanese as being vague by the American norm. When refusing an invitation, for example, an American might say *I have a business lunch that day,* whereas a Japanese speaker might say *I have something to do.* In a very telling example, Beebe and colleagues report that a Japanese speaker of English declined an invitation by saying *I have to go to a wedding.* The explanation seemed quite definite in its content, and almost led the researchers to reconsider their characterization of Japanese-English explanations as vague – until they learned some weeks later that the wedding had been the woman's own! Thus, when judged by American expectations, the explanation not only seems vague, but perhaps may even be a violation of Grice's (1975) maxim of quantity.

In an experiment designed to test differences in the content of explanations in rejections based on the natural data collected from the advising sessions, Hartford and Bardovi-Harlig (1992) gave NSs reasons for rejecting courses which included several reasons that had been given by NNS graduate students in their advising sessions, but not in NS sessions. These included reasons such as a course being too difficult, or too easy, or even telling the adviser that his or her own course was uninteresting. NSs in the experiment generally avoided using such content and invented other reasons to reject the courses. In contrast, NNSs used the reasons given in the experiment, reflecting their production in the actual advising sessions. Another area of difference is content in compliments. Compliments often reflect cultural values (Manes, 1983). An ethnographic study of compliments in the Kunming dialect of Mandarin Chinese conducted by Yuan (1998) shows that the content of Chinese compliments often differs from that reported for English speakers in the literature (e.g., Manes, 1983; Holmes, 1988). These topics included the behavior or ability of children, desirable personality traits, and the cleanliness of one's house, and the more widely used compliments on appearance.

Form. The fourth way in which NNS production may differ from the NS norm is in the form of a speech act. A longitudinal study of pragmatic development in the context of the academic advising session found that in early sessions NSs and NNSs differed in what speech acts they produced, whereas in subsequent sessions they produced the same speech acts, but these differed in form (Bardovi-Harlig & Hartford, 1993). Learners often did not use the mitigators used by their NS peers;

Kathleen
Bardovi-
Harlig

moreover, they often used aggravators which were never used by NSs. NSs made suggestions as found in (13)–(15).

(13)   Perhaps I should also mention that I have an interest in sociolinguistics and would like, if I can, to structure things in such a way that I might do as much sociolinguistics as I can. [NS]

(14)   I was thinking of taking sociolinguistics. [NS]

(15)   I have an idea for spring. I don't know how it would work out, but . . . [NS]

In contrast, in the NNSs often employed suggestions such as the following:

(16)   In the summer I will take language testing. [NNS]

(17)   So, I, I just decided on taking the language structure. [NNS]

In an experiment employing a written DCT, NS and NNS respondents were given a scenario in which their adviser had suggested that they take a course in which they were not interested (Hartford & Bardovi-Harlig, 1992). Even when the content of the rejection is held constant by using a DCT, there is a striking difference in the form. The NS rejection in Example (18) exhibits the downgraders *I'm not sure* and *really*, whereas the NNS rejection in (19) exhibits an upgrader, *at all*.

(18)   I'm not sure that I'm really interested in the topic. [NS]

(19)   I would rather not take this course because the topic doesn't interest me at all. [NNS]

Researchers have also identified the use of routines or 'typical expressions' (Hudson, Detmer, & Brown, 1995, p. 50) as a difference between realizations of speech acts by NSs and NNSs (Scarcella, 1979; Takahashi & Beebe, 1987; Cohen & Olshtain, 1993; Wildner-Bassett, 1994; Hudson, Detmer, & Brown, 1995; House, 1996). Routines such as *Could you give me a ride/a lift*, as part of a request, or *How clumsy of me*, as part of an apology, make the speech act or semantic formula immediately recognizable to the hearer, and are used more often by NSs than by NNSs.

    In this section I have presented the ways in which NS and NNS speech act realization can differ. However, it is important to note that learners' utterances may exhibit more than one nonnative feature at a time. Nontarget-like semantic formulas may encode nontarget-like content in nontarget-like form. It is also important to note that there may be acquisitional stages in which one feature is more characteristic than another. For example, learners may use the same speech acts preferred by NSs at an earlier stage than acquiring appropriate form (evidencing a so-called U-shaped learning curve). In sum, we have evidence from a variety of sources that learners differ noticeably from identifiable NS norms in at least four areas where the use of speech acts is concerned, producing utterances that reflect the choice of a different speech act, semantic formula, content, or form than those evidenced by NSs.

Judgment and perception

Production studies provide an analysis of differences that are easily observable in L2 speech and written simulations of speech. Perception and judgment studies investigate differences that are no less real, but are somewhat less obvious to an observer. This set of studies is smaller and less cohesive than the production studies; however, it shows that learner judgments and comprehension are often different from those of NSs.

Studies of judgments by learners show how learners may differ from NSs in a number of ways. For example, NNSs may also differentiate more request strategies than NSs, such as identifying seven politeness levels compared to the five levels distinguished by NSs on the same card-sorting task, but at the same time not recognize boundaries between strategies where NSs did (Carrell & Konneker, 1981; Tanaka & Kawade, 1982). A study of the perception of NSs of English and Spanish and Spanish-speaking learners of English revealed differences in perceptions of the degree of imposition involved in a request (Mir, 1995). Learners may also have difficulty identifying the intent of a speech act, as Koike's (1996) study of English-speaking learners of Spanish showed in the case of suggestions. Olshtain and Blum-Kulka (1985) showed that adult learners of Hebrew differ significantly from NS Hebrew respondents to judgment tasks in two areas: tolerance for positive politeness (learners show less tolerance than NSs) and rejection of directness (learners rate directness as less acceptable than NSs). As length of stay increases from 2 years of residence to 2–10 years, and more than 10 years, learners move toward the target-like norm, showing an increase in tolerance for positive politeness and directness. For example, in response to a scenario asking for a loan, an informal optimistic strategy *How about ending me some money* was accepted by Israelis, but rejected by learners. Israelis also accepted the direct *Lend me the money, please,* which learners also rejected. Bergman and Kasper (1993) conducted a study of learner perceptions related to apologies. A group of thirty Thai speakers of English and thirty NSs of English completed an assessment task in which they were asked to rate severity of offense, obligation to apologize, likelihood of the apology being accepted, and offender's loss of face. The NS and NNS responses similarly exhibited high correlations between obligation to apologize and severity of offense, severity and likelihood of acceptance, severity and face-loss, and obligation and face-loss, leading Bergman and Kasper to conclude that the severity of offense is related to the offender's obligation to apologize (see also Olshtain, 1989). However, NSs and NNSs differed most noticeably on their ratings of the obligation to apologize. Out of twenty scenarios, twelve were rated as higher on obligation by the Americans than by the Thai learners of English. If a speaker does not feel the obligation to perform a particular speech act, it is less likely that she or he will. This may account for some of the opting out, or substitution of one speech act for another, as seen earlier.

In a study of perceptions of politeness in requests, Kitao (1990) found differences in Japanese EFL and ESL learners, with ESL learners more closely approximating the NS norms. The study of perceptions is particularly relevant to the issue of what utterances learners take as input and whether learners notice how their own utterances compare to those of other target-language speakers. Bardovi-Harlig and Dörnyei (1998) investigated this question in a study of the identification and rating of pragmatic infelicities and grammatical errors in response to a

Kathleen
Bardovi-
Harlig

videotape with twenty scenarios. In a test of 543 learners and their teachers (N=53) in two countries (Hungary and the United States), the results showed that EFL learners and their teachers consistently identified and ranked grammatical errors as more serious than pragmatic errors, but that ESL learners and their NS English teachers showed the opposite pattern, ranking pragmatic errors as more serious than grammatical errors. They also reported that learners did not always recognize pragmatically 'good' test items. In a study of perception of pragmatic transferability, Takahashi (1996) found that the Japanese EFL learners could not identify the English requests that were functional equivalents of Japanese request strategies. For example, the functionally equivalent English request form for the Japanese *V-shite itadake-naideshoo-ka* in a highly imposing request situation is a biclausal form of *Would it be possible to VP*. However, the learners consistently identified its functional equivalent as the monoclausal English request form *Would/Could you (please) VP*, a formula with the same conventionalized form as the Japanese request, Given the observation that NSs of English embed the propositional content of requests in order to mitigate them in high imposition situations, Takahashi concludes that learners' L2 pragmatic competence regarding requests differs considerably from the pragmatic knowledge of NSs of English.

Bouton has conducted a series of studies on the interpretation of implicatures in English by NNSs (1988, 1990, 1992, 1994b). Bouton (1988) tested 436 international students arriving at the University of Illinois using a multiple-choice instrument with thirty-three items, finding that although NSs and NNSs interpreted the same implicature in the same context 75% of the time, that left a full 25% of the time in which different implications were drawn by the NNSs. Bouton (1992) retested thirty of the original subjects four-and-a-half years later and found that the NNSs had improved to the point where twenty items showed no significant difference in interpretation between them and the NSs, whereas only five of the items showed no difference in the previous study. Fifteen of the similarly interpreted items were related to Grice's (1975) maxim of relevance; five of the items involved understated criticism, related to the maxim of quantity. Bouton (1994b) reported on a second longitudinal study run on another group of university students which confirmed the findings of his earlier work – learners performed noticeably better on implicatures whose interpretation is idiosyncratically dependent on the meaning of the utterance in its particular context. Relevance-based implicatures are of this type.

In contrast, learners performed noticeably worse on implicatures based on a formula of some sort, whether structural, semantic, or pragmatic. One implicature of this type is the pope-question implicature, in which a speaker answers a question with a question whose answer is obvious. Pope-questions include examples such as *Does the sun rise in the east?* (for which the answer is 'yes'), the well-known *Is the pope Catholic?* for which the category is named (and for which the answer is also 'yes'), and *Does a frog have hair?* (for which the answer is 'no'). Bouton (1994b) gives the example of two students discussing the likelihood that a teacher will give an exam the day before a school vacation. The teacher has promised to give the exam and has said that no one would be excused from taking

Kathleen
Bardovi-
Harlig

it. When one student asks whether the teacher will actually give the exam, the second student responds with *Does the sun come up in the east these days?* (p. 96). Understanding the implicature generated by the pope-question requires that the learner know the answer to the second question (i.e., that the sun does in fact come up in the east), and must also assume that the answer to the first question is the same as the answer to the second question, and just as likely to be true. Without this formula, the learner cannot arrive at the implicature.

Pragmatic comprehension, the comprehension of speech acts and discourse functions, can also be inferred from conversational data, as Kasper (1984) showed. Conversational data from NS-NNS role-plays reveal that learners may understand phatic contributions as referential, and may also fail to identify the illocutionary force of indirect speech acts. In Example (20) the learner misses an indirect request in the first NS turn, but catches it in the second, after the NS restates the request more directly.

(20) NS: You're drinking a beer there.
      NNS: Yes.
      NS: Erm er will I might er if you were kind enough to offer me one I
             probably wouldn't say no.
      NNS: Of course of course yes (laughing).

Kasper suggests that learners may rely too heavily on bottom-up processing and have problems activating frames relevant in the given context.[2] Data from academic advising sessions can be interpreted similarly. Advisers often open the directive phase of the advising session (Agar, 1985) with questions such as those in Example (21).

(21) Okay . . . so you looked through the list of courses, so you pretty much
      know what you want to take?
      Do you have some idea of what you would want to take?
      Do you know what you want to do?
      (Bardovi-Harlig & Hartford, 1996)

The production data indicate that NS student participants interpret these questions as indirect requests for them to suggest a set of courses for the coming semester. In the case of at least some NNS students, the questions may instead be comprehended simply as direct questions to which they provide a literally correct answer, as in Example (22), but do not result in the perlocutionary effect desired by the adviser (Bardovi-Harlig & Hartford, 1990).

(22) A: Do you know what you want to do?
      S: More or less.
      A: Let's hear it.
           [Pause.]

---

[2] Other sources of difficulty in pragmatic comprehension may be that learners do not make use of illocutionary force indicating devices (IFIDs) and that they have too little flexibility for shifting the frame if an interlocutor's turn is not consistent with the current frame (Kasper, 1984).

Kathleen
Bardovi-
Harlig

A: You've done 530, 31, 43, so you probably want to do 542, I bet you . . .
S: Yes, that's phonological.
A: Yes, phonology.

From the student's response, it is clear that he has understood the literal mean-ing of the question, and in fact, later demonstrates that he is familiar with the courses. The student also misses the second prompting from the adviser (*Let's hear it*), perhaps because he may be unfamiliar with the expression, or reluctant to tell the adviser what his course selections are.

It is possible to discern what might be considered another type of compre-hension from production data, namely, recognition of the function of a speech act apart from its illocutionary force. Wolfson (1989a) argues that learners of English are often not aware that status-equal Americans use compliments as conversation openers. In Wolfson's compliment corpus, learners' responses to compliments show that they recognize their illocutionary force, but not their conversational function of opening a conversation, even in cases such as Example (23) in which the American makes a second attempt (Wolfson, 1989a, p. 230).

(23)   American female student to her Chinese female classmate:
     A: Your blouse is beautiful.
     B: Thank you.
     A: Did you bring it from China?
     B: Yeah.

A similar case may be made for the interpretation of what Boxer (1993) refers to as 'indirect complaints,' which, like compliments, are frequently used by NSs of English to build rapport. In conversational dyads, NSs favored commiserating responses to NNSs' indirect complaints (e.g., *Oh no*), whereas NNSs favored non-substantive responses (e.g., *uh hmn*). The nonsubstantive responses appear to be possible second-pair parts to indirect complaints, but ignore the function of the indirect complaint to achieve further interaction. Although there is no certain way of separating comprehension from production strategies in conversational data, these data do suggest that comprehension and pragmatic assessment may influence at least some of the learner productions discussed in the preceding section. It is fur-ther important to investigate perceptions of L2 speech acts addressed to learners. If we expect learners to use speech addressed to them as input, we need to invest-igate how learners perceive and understand such input.

Factors in determining L2 pragmatic competence
Several explanations for pragmatic differences between learners and NSs have been proposed: availability of input, influence of instruction, proficiency, length of expos-ure, and transfer. I will examine each of these.

Input
Of particular importance to a discussion of pedagogy and pragmatics is the avail-ability of relevant pragmatic input in academic encounters and in textbooks. Kasper (1997b) and Bardovi-Harlig and Hartford (1996) characterize academic talk (teacher–

Kathleen
Bardovi-
Harlig

student talk) as an unequal status encounter, where the speech of the higher-status speaker – the teacher – does not serve as a pragmatically appropriate model for the speech of the learners. Consider the case of the Spanish teacher who (appropriately) says to her students *Dígame* . . . (an imperative form meaning *Tell me* . . .) but who finds it quite impolite when her students say the same thing to her (Silvia Rodriguez, personal communication, 1997). Teacher-fronted talk can be supplemented by additional activities that broaden the range of speech acts and speakers, and that provide a broader range of models and opportunities for learners (Kasper, 1997b). If teacher talk is not intended as a pragmatic model for learners, textbooks with conversations are designed to be models for students, and yet they generally fall short of providing realistic input to learners.

In the title of his 1988 paper ('Language taught for meetings and language used in meetings: Is there anything in common?'), Williams captures the question investigated by a series of comparisons of textbook presentation and authentic language more generally (Scotton & Bernsten, 1988; Billmyer, Jakar, & Lee, 1989; Bardovi-Harlig, Hartford, Mahan-Taylor, Morgan, & Reynolds, 1991; Boxer & Pickering, 1995; Bouton, 1996). As an illustration, consider the results of a survey of textbooks on teaching closings (Bardovi-Harlig et al., 1991). The survey examined the presentation of closings by twenty contemporary ESL textbooks which contained dialogues, and found that only twelve included complete closings in at least one dialogue and that very few did so on a consistent basis. Only one text had several examples of complete closings. Textbooks typically represent conversations as getting only as far as shutting down a topic and occasionally as far as a preclosing. It is often the case that a particular speech act or language function is not represented at all. In other cases, speech acts are represented, but not realistically. For example, Bouton (1996) showed that 80% of the invitations in one ESL textbook used a form of invitation which appeared only 26% of the time in a published corpus on NS invitations. Scotton and Bernsten (1988) cited examples of direction-giving exchanges devoid of grounders and confirmation checks that characterize such exchanges. Boxer and Pickering (1995) found a general lack of so-called indirect complaints in textbooks, and no discussion of the function of the speech act as a social strategy. Boxer and Pickering also point to a lack of information about the interlocutors and the context of the textbook conversations. There are a few newer books which do try to present relevant information to learners (see Boxer & Pickering, 1995; Bardovi-Harlig, 1996), but it is important to recognize that, in general, textbooks cannot be counted on as a reliable source of pragmatic input for classroom language learners.[3]

Instruction

In addition to specific types of input available, other aspects of instruction may play a role in perpetuating some of the nontarget-like realization of speech acts.

---

[3]   For readers who are interested in improving the state of affairs described in this section, the pedagogy of pragmatics is discussed by Bardovi-Harlig (1992, 1996), Bardovi-Harlig et al. (1991), Billmyer (1990a, 1990b), Bouton (1990), Boxer and Pickering (1995), Cohen (1996), Holmes and Brown (1987), Kasper (1997b), and Rose (1994b, 1997), among others.

Kathleen
Bardovi-
Harlig

It should be clear that instruction may also increase a learner's movement toward the target-language norm. (See the review by Kasper, this volume, and the papers that follow. See also Bouton, 1994a; House, 1996; Kasper, 1997a.)

Instructional emphasis on L1–L2 correspondences may contribute to learners' inclination to use L1 strategies, but may not itself cause them (Takahashi, 1996). Instructional emphasis on one semantic formula over others, as in the case of *I'm sorry* in apologies (Mir, 1992), may encourage overuse of the formula. In fact, general course organization may contribute to lack of pragmatic focus or opportunities for communication (Cohen, 1997). We may also extend the curricular issue to the question of language assessment: For foreign language learners the success of learning is typically measured by being able to take some grammar-oriented language exam, whereas in second language contexts, even if there are tests to be taken, rewards are also provided by successful communication with NSs. As far as the consequences are concerned, the gap between grammar and pragmatics in EFL samples indicates that emphasis on microlevel grammatical accuracy in the foreign language classroom may be at the expense of macrolevel pragmatic appropriateness (Bardovi-Harlig & Dörnyei, 1998; but see Niezgoda & Röver, this volume). This may change somewhat as tests in pragmatics are developed (Hudson, Detmer, & Brown, 1995; see also the chapters by Brown, Hudson, and Norris, this volume).

Level of proficiency and length of stay

The influence of the level of L2 proficiency on pragmatic competence and performance has not been widely researched (Kasper & Schmidt, 1996). Nor have different stages of pragmatic development been investigated in any detail (but see Schmidt, 1983; Ellis, 1992; Bardovi-Harlig & Hartford, 1993). As Kasper points out, very little work in the acquisition of pragmatics has been done, and none of the published literature includes beginning language learners (Kasper, 1996; Kasper & Schmidt, 1996; Kasper & Rose, 1999).

It appears that proficiency may have little effect on the range of realization strategies that learners use: Both intermediate and advanced learners use the same range of realization strategies used by NSs (Kasper & Schmidt, 1996). Similarly, Takahashi (1996) did not find any proficiency effects on perception of L1 transferability to L2 pragmatics. Other areas are apparently more sensitive to level of proficiency. In a study of refusals made by Japanese ESL learners at two levels of proficiency, Takahashi and Beebe (1987) found that low and high proficiency learners differed in the order and frequency of semantic formulas they used. The lower proficiency learners were also more direct in their refusals than higher-level ESL learners. (Interestingly, proficiency did not make a difference in the EFL group that was studied, presumably because neither level of proficiency in the EFL situation receives enough input.) The use of external modifiers used in L2 Hebrew increases with linguistic proficiency, as does the number of words used (NNSs exceeded NSs of Hebrew on this measure; Blum-Kulka & Olshtain, 1986).

Proficiency may also influence transfer. Advanced learners were found to be better than intermediate learners at identifying contexts in which L1 apology strategies could and could not be used (Maeshiba, Yoshinaga, Kasper, & Ross, 1996).

Kathleen
Bardovi-
Harlig

The use of modality markers (downtoners, understaters, hedges, subjectivizers, intensifiers, commitment upgraders, and cajolers) also improves with proficiency (Trosborg, 1987; see House & Kasper, 1981a, for modality markers). Three groups of Danish learners of English (intermediate, lower advanced, and higher advanced) showed a noticeable increase in their usage at each level, more closely corresponding to NSs of English. Japanese learners of English as a second language showed a greater tendency to soften the directness of their refusals than did lower-level Japanese ESL learners, and they also showed a greater level of formality, both of which Takahashi and Beebe (1987) attributed to transfer from Japanese refusals. In a rare study which includes low-level learners, Scarcella (1979) found that when making requests, the low-level students invariably relied on imperatives, whereas higher-level learners showed sensitivity to status, using them only with equal familiars and subordinates. Koike (1996) also found a proficiency effect in the recognition of the intent of speech acts in a study of the perception of Spanish suggestions by English-speaking learners of Spanish. Third- and fourth-year students were significantly better at identifying the intended force of the suggestions than the first- and second-year students, although even the higher group identified the intent only little more than half of the time.

Length of stay is also a factor in pragmatic development. Olshtain and Blum-Kulka (1985) reported an increase in acceptance of positive request strategies and directness by NNSs of Hebrew as their length of stay increased from less than 2 years to more than 10 years. A 1-year longitudinal study of advising-session talk found that NNSs showed an increase in the use of speech acts favored by NSs in the academic context, and they showed a decrease in speech acts not used by NSs. In the same period, however, NNSs did not conform to NSs' use of mitigators and nonuse of aggravators (Bardovi-Harlig & Hartford, 1993). A study of awareness of deviations from the NS norm shows that tutored ESL learners are more sensitive than EFL learners to pragmatic infelicities; that is, learners in the host environment (with daily exposure to the L2, but who received no instruction in pragmatics) identified pragmatic problems more often and ranked them as more serious than did the EFL learners. Within the ESL group, learners at a high level of proficiency showed greater pragmatic awareness than learners at lower proficiency. Bouton (1992, 1994b) also found that ESL learners enrolled at an American university without specific training in pragmatics became increasingly target-like in their interpretation of implicature as length of stay increased up to 3 years. Even shorter lengths of stay might help learners become more target-like, particularly with respect to highly salient conversational functions such as greetings. American learners of Kiswahili who had been to Tanzania showed much more target-like use of multiple turns in lengthy Kiswahili greetings (Omar, 1991, 1992). American university students of French also adjusted their greetings to be more target-like during a semester in France, but theirs became shorter and less frequent (Hoffman-Hicks, 2000).

Grammatical competence may also limit the value of the input to the learner (Bardovi-Harlig, 1999a). For example, tense-mood-aspect morphology is often used in mitigation; both past tense and modals serve as play-downs (House & Kasper,

Kathleen
Bardovi-
Harlig

1981a; Færch & Kasper, 1989). A learner who has not achieved control over prototypical uses of tense-mood-aspect morphology may not be ready to extend the
use of those forms to politeness markers. As a case in point, an intermediate ESL
student was engaged in a pedagogical task derived from the video scenarios used
by Bardovi-Harlig and Dörnyei (1998). In one of the 'good' scenarios (no grammatical or pragmatic problems) a student responds to his teacher's invitation *Peter,
we need to talk about the class party soon* with *Yeah, if tomorrow is good for you, I could
come any time you say.* The learner identified the use of *could* as problematic, explaining that *could* was used for past, but that this sentence was talking about *tomorrow*
(Bardovi-Harlig, field notes, 1997). It is clear from earlier work that grammatical
competence does not guarantee pragmatic competence (Olshtain & Blum-Kulka,
1985; Bardovi-Harlig & Hartford, 1990), but it is not yet clear to what extent
the development of pragmatic competence depends on grammatical competence
(House, 1996; Bardovi-Harlig, 1999a).

First language, first culture

The most widely investigated influence on speech act realization is the first language and culture (e.g., Takahashi & Beebe, 1987; Mir, 1992; Bergman & Kasper,
1993; Maeshiba et al., 1996; Takahashi, 1996). The interest in L1 pragmatic influence
may reflect the strong link of interlanguage pragmatics research to crosscultural
pragmatics research. Pragmatic transfer – defined by Kasper (1997b, p. 119) as
'use of L1 pragmatic knowledge to understand or carry out linguistic action in
the L2' – may have positive and negative outcomes. Positive transfer results in
successful exchanges, whereas negative transfer, resulting from an assumption that
L1 and L2 are similar where, in fact, they are not, may result in nonnative use
(or avoidance) of speech acts, semantic formulas, or linguistic form. Examples of
L1 influence include the case of apology formulas used by Japanese learners of
English to express gratitude, and the use of proverbial expressions by Arabic learners in the same context (Bodman & Eisenstein, 1988). Form may also show L1
influence as in the use of *must* in directives by German-speaking learners of English
(House & Kasper, 1987). Takahashi (1996) identifies L1 as the primary cause of
the patterns identified, and instruction as a secondary influence.

Evaluating the empirical evidence

It is clear from this review of representative studies that the empirical evidence
shows that learners who have received no specific instruction in L2 pragmatics
have noticeably different L2 pragmatic systems than NSs of the L2. This is true
for both production and comprehension. This review is very much like a traditional error analysis. It has concentrated, as error analyses do, on apparent areas
of difficulty rather than on learner success, and on problematic areas rather than
on the acquisition process (in large measure because that is what is available in
the literature). Areas of difficulty have been traditionally interpreted as areas
in need of instruction (Ellis, 1994). It is also clear that learners are successful in
certain areas of pragmatics. Moreover, every study reviewed here (as well as
others) shows strong situational effect: Certain scenarios are harder to negotiate

than others. What we know with certainty is that there are differences between L1 and L2 pragmatics. Of the areas of divergence that have been identified, we do not yet know which will cause the most communicative difficulty, offense, humor, or even hurt feelings. Additional studies of conversation and ratings by target-language speakers may help to identify the potentially most disruptive differences (Kasper, 1997a).

Kathleen Bardovi-Harlig

Do differences in pragmatic production and interpretation actually warrant pedagogical intervention? Do we need to 'fix' every difference? Many of the pedagogical issues are beyond the scope of this chapter, but I would like to address my comments here specifically to the differences in underlying pragmatic systems and their potential causes.[4] What I will assume here is a group of language learners and their teachers who are desirous of improving L2 pragmatics. One of the easiest causes of non-target-like pragmatics to overcome pedagogically is incomplete or misleading input to learners in pedagogical materials. Although improving input to learners is undoubtedly more easily said than done, providing authentic, representative language to learners is a basic responsibility of classroom instruction (Williams, 1988; Scotton & Bernsten, 1989; Bardovi-Harlig et al., 1991; Rose, 1993, 1994b, 1997; Boxer & Pickering, 1995; Bouton, 1996; Kasper, 1997b). Providing opportunities beyond teacher-fronted status-unequal encounters is also indicated for its value in pragmatic input and practice (Kasper, 1997b), as well as for its more general pedagogical benefits.

Another clear area of pedagogical necessity is assisting learners with comprehension. Both comprehension and providing authentic input seems to fall under the heading of 'fair play: giving the learners a fighting chance.' Not only the comprehension of indirect speech acts and implicature fall under this heading, but also the social interpretations of certain speech acts. A learner may not want to offer compliments or 'indirect complaints' herself in a conversation with an NS, but she might want to be able to do her part to respond to attempts to initiate conversations which these speech acts often do (Wolfson, 1989a; Boxer, 1993). If a learner does not recognize the social function of such speech acts, then she cannot hold up her end of the conversation in response to such speech acts when other people use them. Going to the other extreme, the most difficult difference to tackle pedagogically may be the use or nonuse of certain speech acts as a result of cultural (or individual) preferences. (And, in fact, this may be one difference that we decide not to tackle.) Thomas (1983, p. 104) observed that

> correcting pragmatic failure stemming from sociopragmatic miscalculation is a far more delicate matter for the language teacher than correcting pragmalinguistic failure. Sociopragmatic decisions are social before they are linguistic, and while foreign learners are fairly amenable to corrections which they regard as linguistic, they are justifiably sensitive about having their social (or even political, religious, or moral) judgment called into question.

[4]   Clearly an important issue is the identity of the learner population and the learning context (Boxer & Pickering, 1995; Kasper, 1997b), both of which involve complex pedagogical issues that are not the focus of this chapter.

Kathleen
Bardovi-
Harlig

Thinking about this issue in the terms used in this chapter, consider the case of compliments in American English. In the English-speaking world, Americans are considered to be rather robust givers of compliments. Learners from other cultures who would feel uncomfortable or insincere giving as many compliments as Americans do may nonetheless want to give an occasional compliment. The role of instruction may be to help the learner encode her own values (which again may be culturally determined) into a clear, unambiguous message.[5] Using a commonly recognized compliment formula such as I *(really) like/love NP* or NP *is (really) ADJ* helps relay the message clearly without asking a learner to compromise her values and adopt those of the target culture. Similarly, instruction related to form may also be nonthreatening following Thomas's assessment, since language pedagogy is still generally geared to form.[6] Less clearly a matter of form, and therefore perhaps less 'linguistic' than 'cultural,' is the use of semantic formulas. Consider the case of direct complaints identified by Murphy and Neu (1996). Although most people I know would prefer not to have to lodge a direct complaint at all, especially to a teacher or a supervisor, it is occasionally necessary, as in the case of a student who thinks his paper may have been graded erroneously by his teacher (Murphy & Neu, 1996). Whatever the L1 preference for criticism as a semantic formula in complaints might be, faculty responses to student messages suggest that American faculty are somewhat put off by criticism and would respond better to a direct complaint (Hartford & Bardovi-Harlig, 1996). Learners could be aided by being pointed toward the (culturally) more successful semantic formula.

Taken as a whole, then, the research indicates that learners who receive no particular instruction in pragmatics show divergence in L2 pragmatics in several areas. I have argued that making contextualized, pragmatically appropriate input available to learners from early stages of acquisition onward is the very least that pedagogy should aim to do (see also Bardovi-Harlig et al., 1991; Bardovi-Harlig, 1996). Without input, acquisition cannot take place. I have also argued that we owe it to learners to help them interpret indirect speech acts as in the case of implicature, and the social use of speech acts, as in the case of compliments. Where instructors and researchers differ (not in opposition to each other, but as individuals) is in the determination of the most that pedagogy should aim to accomplish. The adoption of sociocultural rules as one's own in an L2 may have to be an individual decision. Providing the information so that a learner can make that choice is a pedagogical decision. The most appropriate and effective ways to deliver this information and the manner in which learners integrate such information into a developing interlanguage remain empirical questions.

[5]   By instruction I mean any action undertaken by a teacher to facilitate acquisition. This may be as subtle as engineering an input flood or bringing NSs into the classroom as interlocutors, or as direct as explicit instruction. The best means of facilitating the acquisition of pragmatics is another issue that remains to be resolved.

[6]   The ultimate success of any pedagogy would be subject to acquisitional constraints, as in other areas (Ellis, 1994; Bardovi-Harlig, 1997), and remains to be tested.

□ Bardovi-Harlig finds that native speakers (NSs) and non-native speakers (NNSs) can differ in the production of speech acts in four ways: choice of speech acts, semantic formulas, form and content. For each of these four, say what she means by the category, give an example from the article and then give an example that you have experienced yourself.

□ Set up a little experiment to look at the effect of learner perceptions and judgements of one of the following: conversational implicature, illocutionary force and conversation structure. Write five Discourse Completion Tasks (DCTs), each one with a brief scenario and four multiple choice answers for your subjects to choose the most appropriate comment or interpretation. Present your findings in public and discuss whether this is an effective way of finding learner perceptions and judgements.

□ Of all the factors that influence L2 pragmatic system development (input, instruction, level of proficiency, length of exposure, and L1 pragmatic transfer), which do you think influences it most and why? Are there other factors that influence it, that Bardovi-Harlig has not mentioned?

□ Choose one of the four factors that Bardovi-Harlig says influence L2 pragmatic system development, and test it out. This will mean finding two groups of learners (either studying the language in class or acquiring it by living in the target language country) that differ radically in terms of the factor that you have selected, e.g. one group has been exposed to the language for a month and the other for over three years. Choose one pragmatic feature, e.g. one speech act or one cooperative maxim. Collect your data any way you like: it could be by observation, by questionnaires or by interviews. Discuss your methodology with a tutor or other expert before you attempt this. The number of subjects that you include will depend on the time available, obviously.

□ Bardovi-Harlig concludes, 'The adoption of sociocultural rules as one's own in an L2 may have to be an individual decision. Providing the information so that a learner can make that choice is a pedagogical decision.' Do you agree?

BIBLIOGRAPHY

Adolphs, S. (2001) Linking speech acts and lexico-grammar: a corpus-based approach. Unpublished PhD thesis, University of Nottingham.

Adolphs, S. (2006) Modality clusters and politeness in spoken discourse, in P. Skandera (ed.), *Phraseology and Culture in English*, Berlin and New York: Mouton de Gruyter.

Adolphs, S., Atkins, S. and Harvey, K. (2006) Caught between professional requirements and interpersonal needs: vague language in health care contexts, in Cutting (2007).

Alba de Diego, V. (1995) La cortesía en la petición de permiso, *DICENDA Cuadernos de Filología Hispánica*, 13: 13–24.

Albert-Ludwigs University Freiburg workshop (2006) Corpora and Pragmatics: speech acts and context-bound interaction in the light of corpora and data-bases, http://www.corpora-romanica.net/2006/index_e.htm.

Auden, W. H. (1958) *A Selection by the Author*, Harmondsworth: Penguin.

Austen, J. (1962) *Pride and Prejudice*, London: The Zodiac Press.

Austin, J. L. (1962) *How To Do Thing with Words*, Cambridge, MA: Harvard University Press.

Bailey, B. (1997) Communication in respect of interethnic service encounters, *Language in Society*, 26: 327–56.

Baker, P., Hardie, A. and McEnery, T. (2006) *A Glossary of Corpus Linguistics*, Edinburgh: Edinburgh University Press.

Bardovi-Harlig, K. (2001) Evaluating the empirical evidence: grounds for instruction in pragmatics?, in Rose and Kasper (2001).

Bardovi-Harlig, K. and Hartford, B. (1993) Learning the rules of academic talk: a longitudinal study of pragmatic change, *Studies in Second Language Acquisition*, 17: 171–88.

Bardovi-Harlig, K. and Hartford, B. (eds) (2005) *Interlanguage Pragmatics: Exploring Institutional Talk*, New Jersey: Lawrence Erlbaum Associates.

Barker, P. (1991) *Regeneration*, Harmondsworth: Penguin.

Barnes, S. B. (2003) *Computer-Mediated Communication: Human-to-Human Communication across the Internet*, Boston, MA: Allyn and Bacon.

Barnlund, D. C. and Yoshioka, M. (1990) Apologies: Japanese and American styles, *International Journal of Intercultural Relations*, 14: 193–206.

Barron, A. (2002) *Acquisition in Interlanguage Pragmatics: Learning How to do Things with Words*, Amsterdam: John Benjamins.

BASE (2000) The 'British Academic Spoken English' corpus, developed at the Universities of Warwick and Reading, with funding from Universities of Warwick and Reading, BALEAP, EURALEX and the British Academy.

Baym, N. (1995) The emergence of community in computer-mediated communication, in S. Jones (ed.), *Cybersociety*, Thousand Oaks, CA: Sage.

Bayraktaroglu, A. and Sifianou, M. (eds) (2001) *Linguistic Politeness across Boundaries: The Case of Greek and Turkish*, Amsterdam: John Benjamins.

Beck, C. S., Ragan, S. L. and DuPré, A. (1997) *Partnership for Health: Building Relationships between Women and Health Caregivers*, Mahwah, NJ: Erlbaum.

Beebe, L., Takahashi, T. and Uliss-Weltz, R. (1990) Pragmatic transfer in ESL refusals, in R. Scarcella, E. Andersen and S. Krashen (eds), *Developing Communicative Competence in a Second Language*, New York: Newbury House.

Bellinger, D. and Gleason, J. B. (1982) Sex differences in parental directives to young children, *Sex Roles*, 8: 1123–39.

Belloc, H. (1896) *The Bad Child's Book of Beasts*, London: Duckworth.

Biber, D., Johansson, S., Leech, G., Conrad, S. and Finegan, E. (1999) *Grammar of Spoken and Written English*, Harlow: Longman Pearson.

Biber, D. and Reppen, C. (eds) (2000) *Corpus Linguistics: Investigating Language Structure and Use*, Cambridge: Cambridge University Press.

Blakemore, D. (1992) *Understanding Utterances*, Oxford: Blackwell.

Blum-Kulka, S., House, J. and Kasper, G (eds) (1989) *Cross-cultural Pragmatics: Requests and Apologies*, Norwood, NJ: Ablex.

Bouton, L. (1996) Pragmatics and language-learning, in L. Bouton (ed.), *Pragmatics and Language Learning*, monograph series vol. 7, Urbana-Champaign, IL: Division of English as an International Language, University of Illinois.

Bouton, L. F. (1994) Conversational implicature in the second language: learned slowly when not deliberately taught, *Journal of Pragmatics*, 22: 157–62.

Briz, A. (1998) *El Español Coloquial en la Conversación. Esbozo de pragmagramática*, Barcelona: Ariel.

Brodine, R. (1983) Referential cohesion in learner compositions, *Papers on Work in Progress*, 10: 13–20.

Brown, G. and Yule, G. (1983) *Discourse Analysis*, Cambridge: Cambridge University Press.

Brown, P. and Levinson, S. (1987) *Politeness*, Cambridge: Cambridge University Press.

Byram, M. and Grundy, P. (2003) *Context and Culture in Language Teaching and Learning*, Clevedon: Multilingual Matters.

Carbaugh, D. (2005) *Cultures in Conversation*, Mahwah, NJ: Lawrence Erlbaum Associates.

Carrell, P. (1981) Relative difficulty of request forms in L1/L2 comprehension, in M. Hines and W. Rutherford (eds), *TESOL '81*, Washington, DC: TESOL.

Carston, R. (2002) *Thoughts and Utterances: The Pragmatics of Explicit Communication*, Oxford: Blackwell.

Carter, R. (2004) *Language and Creativity*, London: Routledge.

Carter, R. (2006) Spoken grammars, written grammars, Edinburgh: NATECLA (National Association for Teaching English and Community Languages to Adults), Stevenson College, 22 April 2006.

Carter, R. and McCarthy, M. (2006) *Cambridge Grammar of English: a Comprehensive Guide to Spoken and Written Grammar and Usage*, Cambridge: Cambridge University Press.

Catterick, D. (2001) Mapping and managing cultural beliefs about language learning among Chinese EAP Learners. Unpublished paper, University of Dundee, BALEAP 2001.

Chase, M., Macfadyen, L., Reeder, K. and Roche, J. (2002) Intercultural challenges in networked learning: hard technologies meet soft skills. Paper presented at Networked Learning 2002 Conference, Berlin.

Cheepen, C. (2000) Small talk in service dialogues: the conversational aspects of transactional telephone talk, in Coupland (2000).

Chomsky, N. (1968) *Language and Mind*, New York: Harcourt Brace.

Coates, J. (2000) Small talk and subversion: female speakers backstage, in Coupland (2000).

Cohen, A. and Olshtain, E. (1993) The production of speech acts by EFL learners, *TESOL Quarterly*, 27: 33–56.

Conley, J. M., O'Barr, W. M. and Lind, E. A. (1979) The power of language: presentational style in the courtroom, *Duke Law Journal*, 1978: 1375–99.

Cook, G. (1989) *Discourse*, Oxford: Oxford University Press.

Cook, H. M. (2001) Why can't learners of JFL distinguish polite from impolite speech styles?, in Rose and Kasper (2001).

Corbett, J. (2003) *An Intercultural Approach to English Language Teaching*, Clevedon: Multilingual Matters.

Cotterill, J. (2007) 'I think he was kind of shouting or something': uses and abuses of vagueness in the British courtroom', in Cutting (2007).

Coulthard, M. (1985) *An Introduction to Discourse Analysis*, London: Longman.

Coulthard, M. (2004) Author Identification, Idiolect and Linguistic Uniqueness. *Applied Linguistics*, 25 (4): 431–47.

Coulthard, R. M. (2000) Whose text is it? On the linguistic investigation of authorship, in S. Sarangi and R. M. Coulthard (eds), *Discourse and Social Life*, London: Longman, 270–87.

Coupland, J. (2000) *Small Talk*, Harlow: Pearson Education Limited.

Cruse, A. (2000) *Meaning in Language: An Introduction to Semantics and Pragmatics*, Oxford: Oxford University Press.

Crystal, D. (1999) The future of Englishes, *English Today*, 15 (2): 10–20.

Crystal, D. (2001) *Language and the Internet*, Cambridge: Cambridge University Press.

Cummings, L. (2005) *Pragmatics: a Multidisciplinary Perspective*, Edinburgh: Edinburgh University Press.

Cutting, J. (1998) 'Opening lines from the floor', British Association of Applied Linguistics, *Language at Work*, 13: 123–6. Clevedon: Multilingual Matters.

Cutting, J. (1999) *Papers from Seminar of the British Association of Applied Linguistics 'The Grammar of Spoken English and its Application to English for Academic Purposes'*, Sunderland: Sunderland University Press.

Cutting, J. (2000) *Analysing the Language of Discourse Communities*, Oxford: Elsevier Science.

Cutting, J. (2007) *Vague Language Explored*, Basingstoke: Palgrave Macmillan.

Davies, A. (2005) *A Glossary of Applied Linguistics*, Edinburgh: Edinburgh University Press.

de Beaugrande, R. and Dressler, W. (1981) *Introduction to Text Linguistics*, London: Longman.

Drazdauskiene, M.-L. (1981) 'On stereotypes in conversation', in F. Coulmas (ed.), *Conversational Routine: Explorations in Standarisised Communiation Situations and Prepatterned Speech*, The Hague: Mouton.

DuFon, M. A. (1999) The acquisition of linguistic politeness in Indonesian as a second language by sojourners in a naturalistic context. Doctoral dissertation, University of Hawai'i, *Dissertation Abstracts International*, 60, 3985.

Eckert, P. and McConnell-Ginet, S. (2003) *Language and Gender*, New York: Cambridge University Press.

Eggins, S. and Slade, D. (1997) *Analysing Casual Conversation*, London: Cassell.

Enomoto, S. and Marriott, H. (1994) Investigating evaluative behaviour in Japanese tour guiding interaction, *Multilingua*, 13 (1–2): 131–61.

Evison, J., O'Keeffe, A. and McCarthy, M. (2007) Looking out for love and all the rest of it: vague category markers as shared social space, in Cutting (2007).

Fairclough, N. (1989) *Language and Power*, Harlow: Longman.

Fairclough, N. (2003) *Analyzing Discourse: Text Analysis for Social Research*, London: Routledge.

Farr, F. and O'Keeffe, A. (eds) (2004) *The Limerick Corpus of Irish English (LCIE)*, University of Limerick. http://www.ul.ie/~lcie/.

Ferrer, M. C. and Lanza, S. (2002) *Interacción Verbal. Los Actos de Habla*, Rosario: UNR Editora, Universidad Nacional de Rosario.

Fillmore, C. (1976) The need for a frame semantics in linguistics, in *Statistical Methods in Linguistics*, Stockholm: Skriptor.

Fouser, R. (1997) *Pragmatic Transfer in Highly Advanced Learners: Some Preliminary Findings*, CLCS Occasional Papers 50, Dublin: Centre for Language and Communication Studies, University of Dublin.

Garfinkel, H. (1967) *Studies in Ethnomethodology*, Engelwood Cliffs, NJ: Prentice-Hall.

Gass, S. and Houck, N. (1999) *Interlanguage Refusals: A Cross-cultural Study of Japanese-English*, Berlin: Mouton de Gruyter.

Geertz, C. (1976) *The Religion of Java*, Chicago: Chicago University Press.

Goffman, E. (1981) *Forms of Talk*, Philadelphia: University of Pennsylvania Press.

Golding, W. (1954) *Lord of the Flies*, London: Faber and Faber.

Graddol, D. (2006) *English Next: Why Global English May Mean the End of English as a Foreign Language*, British Council.

Greene, G. (1978) *The Human Factor*, London: Penguin.

Grice, H. P. (1957) 'Meaning', *Philosophical Review*, 66: 377–88.

Grice, H. P. (1975) 'Logic and Conversation', in P. Cole and J. Morgan (eds), *Pragmatics (Syntax and Semantics)*, vol. 9, New York: Academic Press.

Grundy, P. (2000) *Doing Pragmatics*, London: Edward Arnold.

Grundy, P. (2006) Salient meaning, intercultural communication and LAP teacher education. Paper presented in 12th IALS Symposium for Language Teacher Educators: Teacher Education in Teaching LAP, University of Edinburgh.

Gumperz, J. J. (1982) *Discourse Strategies*, Cambridge: Cambridge University Press.

Günthner, S. (2000) Argumentation and resulting problems in the negotiation of rapport in a German-Chinese conversation, in Spencer-Oatey (2000).

Halliday, M. A. K. and Hasan, R. (1976) *Cohesion in English*, Longman: London.

Halliday, M. A. K. and Hasan, R. (1989) *Language, Context, and Text: Aspects of Language in a Social-semiotic Perspective*, Oxford: Oxford University Press.

Hatch, E. (1992) *Discourse and Language Education*, Cambridge: Cambridge University Press.

Haufigkeitswörterbuch der deutschen Sprache, Steglitz: privately published.

Haverkate, H. (1979) *Impositive Sentences in Spanish: Theory and Description in Linguistic Pragmatics*, Amsterdam: North Holland.

Heller, J. (1962) *Catch 22*, London: Corgi.

Helm, J. (1967) *Essays on the Verbal and Visual Arts*, New York: Pergamon Press.

Herrero Moreno, G. (2002) Los actos disentivos, *Verba*, 29: 221–42.

Herring, S. C. (1993) Gender and democracy in computer-mediated communications, *Electronic Journal of Communication*, 3 (2).

Hill, T. (1997) The development of pragmatic competence in an EFL context. Doctoral dissertation, Temple University Japan, *Dissertation Abstracts International*, 58, 3905.

Hoey, M. (1991) *Patterns of Lexis in Text*, Oxford: Oxford University Press.

Holme, R. (2003) Carrying a baby in the back: teaching an awareness of the cultural construction of language, in Byram and Grundy (2003).

Holmes, J. (1992) *An Introduction to Sociolinguistics*, Longman: London.

Holmes, J. (2000) Doing collegiality and keeping control at work: small talk in government departments, in Coupland (2000).

House, J. (2000) Understanding misunderstanding: a pragmatic-discourse approach to analysing mismanaged rapport in talk across cultures, in Spencer-Oatey (2000).

Huang, Y. (2007) *Pragmatics*, Oxford: Oxford University Press.

Hunston, S. (2002) *Corpora in Applied Linguistics*, Cambridge: Cambridge University Press.

ICE-GB (1998) *International Corpus of English, Survey of English Usage*, London: University College London.

Jensen, J. (1990) *Redeeming Modernity*, Newbury Park, CA: Sage.

Johansson, S. (1991) Times change and so do corpora, in K. Aijmer and B. Altenburg (eds.), *English Corpus Linguistics: Studies in Honour of Jan Svartvik*, London: Longman.

Jones, S. (ed.) (1995) *Cybersociety: Computer Mediated Communication and Community*, Thousand Oaks, CA: Sage.

Kasper, G. and Rose, K. R. (2002) *Pragmatic Development in a Second Language*, Oxford: Blackwell Publishing.

Keenan, E. (1974) Norm-makers, norm-breakers: uses of speech by men and women in Malagasy community, in R. Bauman and J. Sherzer (eds.), *Explorations in the Ethnography of Speaking*, Cambridge: Cambridge University Press.

Kellerman, E. (1983) 'Now you see it, now you don't', in S. M. Gass and L. Selinker (eds), *Language Transfer in Language Learning*, Rowley, MA: Newbury House.

Kelly, T., Nesi, H. and Revell, R. (2000) *EASE Volume One: Listening to Lectures*, Warwick: CELTE, University of Warwick.

Kling, R. (1996) Social relationships in electronic forums: hangouts, salons, workplaces and communities, *CMC Magazine*, http://www.december.com/cmc/mag/1996/jul/kling.html.

Koester, A. (2006) *Investigating Workplace Discourse*, London: Routledge.

Komito, L. (2001) Electronic communities in an information society: paradise, mirage, or malaise?, *Journal of Documenation*, 57 (1): 115–29.

Kotthoff, H. (1989) So na und doch so fern. Deutsch-amerikanische pragmatische Unterschiede im universitären Milieu, *Info DaF*, 16 (4): 448–59.

Kramsch, C. (1998) *Language and Culture*, Oxford: Oxford University Press.

Kreckel, M. (1981) *Communicative Acts and Shared Knowledge in Natural Discourse*, London: Academic Press.

Kress, G. and van Leeuwen, T. (2001) *Multimodal Discourse*, London: Arnold.

Kuiper, K. and Flindall, M. (2000) Social rituals, formulaic speech and small talk at the supermarket checkout, in Coupland (2000).

Labov, W. and Waletsky, J. (1967) Narrative analysis: oral versions of personal experience, in Helm (1967).

Lakoff, R. (1975) *Language and Woman's Place*, New York: Harper and Row.

Larsen, S. (1983) Text processing and knowledge updating in memory for radio news, *Discourse Processes*, 6: 21–38.

Lave, J. and Wenger, E. (1991) *Situated Learning: Legitimate Peripheral Participation*, Cambridge: Cambridge University Press.

Lawrence, D. H. (1981) *Short Stories*, London: J. M. Dent and Sons.

Lederer, R. (1987) *More Anguished English*, London: Robson Books.

Leech, G. (1983) *Principles of Pragmatics*, Harlow: Longman.

Leech, G. (2005) Politeness: is there an East–West divide?, *Journal of Foreign Languages* (Shanghai), 6: 3–31.

Leonard, E. (1989) *Hombre*, London: Chivers Press.

Levinson, S. (2000) *Presumptive Meanings: The Theory of Generalized Implicature*, Cambridge, MA: MIT Press.

Levinson, S. C. (1983) *Pragmatics*, Cambridge: Cambridge University Press.

Li, W. (2002) 'What do you want me to say?' On the Conversation Analysis approach to bilingual interaction, *Language in Society*, 31: 159–180.

Liddicoat, A. J. (2006) *Introduction to Conversation Analysis*, London: Continuum.

Liddicoat, A. J. and Crozet, C. (2001) Acquiring French interactional norms through instruction, in Rose and Kasper (2001).

Macaulay, R. (1967) *Crewe Train*, London: Collins.

McCarthy, M. (2000) Mutually captive audiences: small talk and the genre of close-contact service encounters, in Coupland (2000).

McCarthy, M. and Carter, R. (1994) *Language as Discourse: Perspectives for Language Teaching*, London: Longman.

McCarthy, M. and Carter, R. (2004) 'There's millions of them': Hyperbole in everyday conversation, *Journal of Pragmatics*, 36: 149–84.

McCarthy, M., O'Keeffe, A. and Evison, J. (2007) 'Looking out for love and all the rest of it': vague category markers as shared social space, in Cutting (2007).

McEnery, T. and Wilson, A. (1997) *Corpus Linguistics*, Edinburgh: Edinburgh University Press.

Marx, K. (1844) *Contributions to the Critique of Hegel's Philosophy of Right*. Deutsch-Französische Jahrbücher.

Mey, J. (1993) *Pragmatics: An Introduction*, Oxford: Blackwell.

Mills, S. (2002) Rethinking politeness, impoliteness and gender identity, in L. Litosseliti and J. Sunderland (eds), *Gender Identity and Discourse*, Amsterdam: John Benjamins.

Mills, S. (2003) *Gender and Politeness*, Cambridge: Cambridge University Press.

Milne, A. A. (1994) *Winnie the Pooh. The Complete Collection of Stories*, London: Methuen Children's Books.

Mizutani, O. and Mituzani, N. (1987) *How to Be Polite in Japanese*, Tokyo: Japan Times.

Mountain, J. (1987) An investigation of some textual properties of discursive compositions written by native speakers and L2 (Italian) advanced learners. Unpublished MA project, University of Birmingham.

Myers, G. (1991) Pragmatics and corpora. Talk given at Corpus Linguistics Research Group, Lancaster University.

Nelson, G. L., Al-Batal, M. and Echols, E. (1996) Arabic and English compliment responses: potential for pragmatic failure, *Applied Linguistics*, 18 (3): 411–33.

Ochs, E., Schegloff, E. A. and Thompson, S. A. (1996) *Interaction and Grammar*, Cambridge: Cambridge University Press.

Ohta, A. (1995) Applying sociocultural theory to an analysis of learner discourse: Learner-learner collaborative interaction in the zone of proximal development, *Issues in Applied Linguistics*, 6: 93–121.

O'Keeffe, A. (2006) *Investigating Media Discourse*, London: Routledge.

O'Keeffe, A. and Adolphs, S. (2007) Using a corpus to look at variational pragmatics: listenership in British and Irish discourse, in A. Barron and K. Schneider (eds), *Variational Pragmatics*, Amsterdam: John Benjamins.

O'Rourke, P. J. (1984) *Modern Manners*, London: Panther.

Paretsky, S. (1995) *A Taste of Life*, London: Penguin.

Pavlidou, T.-S. (2000) Telephone conversations in Greek and German: attending to the relationship aspect of communication, in Spencer-Oatey (2000).

Pennycook, A. (1994) *The Cultural Politics of English as an International Language*, London: Longman.

Phillipson, R. (1992) *Linguistic Imperialism*, Oxford: Oxford University Press.

Quirk, R. (1960) Towards a description of English usage, in *Transactions of the Philological Society*.

Raga Gimeno, F. and Sánchez López, E. (1999) La problemática de la toma de turnos en la communicación intercultural, in J. Fernández Juncal, M. Marcos Sánchez, E. Prieto de los Mozos and L. Santos Río (eds), *Lingüística para el Siglo XXI, Vol. II*, Salamanca: Ediciones Universidad de Salamanca.

Ragan, S. (2000) Sociable talk in women's health care contexts: two forms of non-medical talk, in Coupland (2000).

Rankin, I. (1992) *Tooth and Nail*, London: Orion.

Rees, N. (1999) *The Cassell Dictionary of Anecdotes*, London: Cassell.

Reiter, R. M. and Placencia, M. E. (2005) *Spanish Pragmatics*, Basingstoke: Palgrave Macmillan.

Reynolds, M. (1962) *Little Boxes*, NewYork: Schroder Music Co.

Richards, K. and Seedhouse, P. (2004) *Applying Conversation Analysis*, Basingstoke: Palgrave Macmillan.

Rose, K. R. (2000) An exploratory cross-section study of interlanguage pragmatic development, *Studies in Second Language Acquisition*, 22: 27–67.

Rose, K. R. and Kasper, G. (eds) (2001) *Pragmatics in Language Teaching*, Cambridge: Cambridge University Press.

Rose, K. R. and Kwai-fun, C. N. Inductive and deductive teaching of compliments and compliment responses, in Rose and Kasper (2001).

Rosten, L. (2000) *The Education of Hyman Kaplan*, London: Prion Books.

Sacks, H. (1986) Some considerations of a story told in ordinary conversation. MS.

Sacks, H. (1992a) *Lectures on Conversation*, vol. 1, Oxford: Blackwell.

Sacks, H. (1992b) *Lectures on Conversation*, vol. 2, Oxford: Blackwell.

Sacks, H., Schegloff, E. A. and Jefferson, G. (1974) A simplest systematics for the organization of turn-taking for conversations, *Language*, 50: 696–735.

Sawyer, C. (1992) *BB King*, London: Quartet Books.

Schauer, G. A. and Adolphs, S. (2006) Expressions of gratitude in corpus and dct data: vocabulary, formulaic sequences, and pedagogy, *System*, 34 (1): 119–34.

Schiffrin, D. (1994) *Approaches to Discourse*, Oxford: Blackwell.

Schumann, J. H. (1986) Research on the Acculturation Model for second language acquisition, *Journal of Multilingual and Multicultural Development*, 7: 379–92.

Scollon, R. and Scollon, S. W. (1995) *Intercultural Communication: A Discourse Approach*, Oxford: Blackwell.

Scott, M. and Tribble, C. (2006) *Textual Patterns: Key Words and Corpus Analysis in Language Education*, Amsterdam: John Benjamins.

Scurfield, E. and Song, L. (1996) *Teach Yourself Beginner's Chinese*, London: Hodder and Stoughton.

Searle, J. R. (1969) *Speech Acts*, Cambridge: Cambridge University Press.

Seidlhofer, B. (2005) English as a lingua franca, *ELTJ Journal*, 59 (4): 339–41.

Shalom, C. (1997) That great supermarket of desire: attributes of the desired other in personal advertisements, in K. Harvey and C. Shalom (eds), *Language and Desire*, London: Routledge.

Sherrin, N. (1995) *The Oxford Dictionary of Humorous Quotations*, Oxford: Oxford University Press.

Siegal, M. (1994) Learning Japanese as a second language in Japan and the interaction of race, gender and social context. Doctoral dissertation, University of California-Berkeley. *Dissertation Abstracts International*, 56, 1692.

Siegal, M. (1996) The role of learner subjectivity in second language sociolinguistic competency: Western women learning Japanese, *Applied Linguistics*, 17: 356–82.

Sinclair, J. (1991) *Corpus, Concordance and Collocation*, Oxford: Oxford University Press.

Sinclair, J. and Coulthard, R. M. (1975) *Towards an Analysis of Discourse*, Oxford: Oxford University Press.

Skuja, R. (1983) An analysis of the organisation features of argumentative compositions written by teachers and pupils in Singapore. Unpublished MA project, University of Birmingham.

Smith, B. R. and Leinonen, E. (1992) *Clinical Pragmatics*, Oxford; Chapman and Hall.

Soerensen, K. (1985) Communicative Competence: some theoretical considerations and a study of text-based discussions in the Danish Gymnasium/HF classroom. Unpublished MA dissertation, University of Aarhus.

Spencer-Oatey, H. (ed.) (2000) *Culturally Speaking: Managing Rapport in Talk across Cultures*, London: Continuum.

Sperber, D. and Wilson, D. (1982) Mutual knowledge and relevance theories of comprehension, in N. Smith (ed.), *Mutual Knowledge*, London: Academic.

Sperber, D. and Wilson, D. (1987) Precis of relevance, *Behavioural Sciences and Brain Sciences*, 10: 697–754.

Sperber, D. and Wilson, D. (1995) *Relevance*, Oxford: Basil Blackwell.

Sproull, L. and Kiesler, S. (1991) *Connections: New Ways of Working in the Networked Organization*, Cambridge, MA: MIT Press.

Stenström, A.-B. (1984) Discourse items and pauses. Paper presented at the 5th ICAME Conference, Windermere. Abstract in *ICAME News*, 9 (1985): 11.

Stenström, A.-B. (1987) Carry-on signals in English conversation, in W. Meijs (ed.), *Corpus Linguistics and Beyond*, Amsterdam: Rodopi.

Stenström, A.-B. (1994) *An Introduction to Spoken Interaction*, London: Longman.

Stilwell Peccei, J. (1999) *Pragmatics*, Oxford: Routledge.

Stoppard, T. (1978) *Every Good Boy Deserves Favor and Professional Foul*, New York: Grove Press.

Stotsky, S. (1983) Types of lexical cohesion in expository writing: implications for developing the vocabulary of academic discourse, *College Composition and Communication*, 34 (4): 430–46.

Stubbs, M. (1983) *Discourse Analysis*, Oxford: Basil Blackwell.

Suzuki, T. (1986) Language and behaviour in Japan: the conceptualisation of personal relations in T. S. Lebra and W. P. Lebra (eds), *Japanese Culture and Behaviour: Selected Readings*, Honolulu: University Press of Hawai'i.

Svartvik, J. and Quirk, R. (eds) (1980) *A Corpus of English Conversation*, Lund Studies in English 56, Lund: Liber/Gleerups.

Swales, J. (1990) *Genre Analysis*, Cambridge: Cambridge University Press.

Swales, J. (2003) Is the university a community of practice?, in S. Sarangi and T. Van Leeuwen (eds), *Applied Linguistics and Communities of Practice*, London: British Association for Applied Linguistics and Continuum.

Takahashi, S. (2001) The role of input enhancement in developing pragmatic competence, in Rose and Kasper (2001).

Tannen, D. (1981) 'Indirectness in discourse: ethnicity as conversational style', *Discourse Processes* 4 (3): 221–38.

Tannen, D. (1984) *Conversational Style: Analyzing Talk among Friends*, Norwood, NJ: Ablex Publishing Corporation.

Tannen, D. (1986) *That's Not What I Meant!: How Conversational Style Makes or Breaks Your Relations with Others*, New York: William Morrow.

Tannen, D. (1994) *Gender and Discourse*, Oxford: Oxford University Press.

Tateyama, Y., Kasper, G., Mui, L., Tay, H. and Thananart, O. (1997) Explicit and implicit teaching of pragmatic routines, in L. Bouton (ed.), *Pragmatics and Language Learning*, monograph series vol. 7, Urbana-Champaign, IL: Division of English as an International Language, University of Illinois.

Thomas, J. (1983) Cross-cultural pragmatic failure, *Applied Linguistics*, 4: 91–112.

Thomas, J. (1995) *Meaning in Interaction*, London: Longman.

Thomas, J. (1996) *Using Corpora for Language Research*, London: Longman.

Thurber, J. (1963) *Vintage Thurber*, London: Hamilton.

Thurlow, C., Lengel, L. and Tomic, A. (2004) *Computer-Mediated Communication: Social Interaction and the Internet*, London: Sage.

Tognini-Bonelli, E. (2001) *Corpus Linguistics at* Work, Studies in Corpus Linguistics 6, Amsterdam and Philadelphia: John Benjamins.

Trask, R. L. (1999) *Key Concepts in Language and Linguistics*, London: Routledge.

Trosborg, A. (1995) *Interlanguage Pragmatics: Requests, Complaints and Apologies*, Berlin: Mouton de Gruyter.

Updike, J. (1970) *Bech: A Book*, Harmondsworth: Penguin Books.

van Dyk, T. A. (1993) *Elite Discourse and Racism*, London: Sage.

Verschueren, J. (1999) *Understanding Pragmatics*, London: Arnold.

Wajnryb, R. (2005) Shorten your convo to build bonds as easy as, *Collins Word Exchange*, http://www.collins.co.uk/wordexchange/Default.aspx?it=306&pg=97.

Walsh, S. (2006) *Investigating Classroom Discourse*, London: Routledge.

Wardhaugh, R. (1985) *How Conversation Works*, Oxford: Basil Blackwell.

Warren, C. (1953) *ABC des Reporters. Einführung in den praktischen Journalismus*, Munich: Fink.

Warren, M. (2007) { / [Oh] Not A < ^ Lot > }: discourse intonation and vague language, in Cutting (2007).

Websters New International Dictionary of the English Language (1920), London: G. Bells and Sons.

Wenger, E. (2000) *Communities of Practice*, New York: Cambridge University Press.

Wierzbicka, A. (1985) Different cultures, different languages, different speech acts: Polish vs. English, *Journal of Pragmatics*, 9 (2–3): 145–78.

Wierzbicka, A. (1991) *Cross-cultural Pragmatics*, Berlin: Mouton De Gruyter.

Williams, E. (1973) *George: An Early Autobiography*, London: Hamilton.

Wilson, D. and Murie, A. (1995) *Factors Affecting the Housing Satisfaction of Older People*, Birmingham: University of Birmingham.

Wodak, R. (1996) *Disorders of Discourse*, London: Longman.

Wodak, R. and Lutz, B. (1986) Ein Amerikaner in China. Nachrichten als Fortsetzungsroman, *Medien Journal*, 4: 202–7.

Wolfson, N. (1989) The social dynamics of native and non-native complimenting behaviour, in M. Eisenstein (ed.), *The Dynamic Interlanguage: Empirical Studies in Second Language Variation*, New York: Plenum Press.

Woolf, V. (1978) *Between the Acts*, London: Grafton.

Yule, G. (1996) *Pragmatics*, Oxford: Oxford University Press.

Žegarac, V. and Pennington, M. C. (2000) Pragmatic transfer in intercultural communication, in Spencer-Oatey (2000).

INDEX